"Scott Morton has produced one of the most practical and needful books for self-supported foreign missionaries that I have ever seen. This is a 'must-read' book for an itinerating missionary. I use it in my classes at Regent University School of Divinity and highly recommend it."

Dr. Howard Foltz
Professor of Global Evangelization at Regent University

"This is one book you have got to read! Very little has been written about personal support raising. And what has been written is anemic. *Funding Your Ministry* is not only extremely helpful, but fun to read. Scott Morton hits the bull's-eye on the issues that staff members and missionaries struggle with."

Ellis Goldstein
Director of Ministry Partner Development
Campus Crusade for Christ

"Whether seeking personal or institutional funding, principles like face-to-face solicitation or the importance of actually writing a plan are totally interchangeable. Morton has done all of us in resource development a favor by writing this book. Crafted in a light, airy way, it takes the mystery out of fundraising, without taking out the teeth. I intend to refer to it repeatedly in presentations. It has great cross-over appeal and application."

Chris Withers
Vice President for Development and University Relations
University of Richmond, Virginia

"This is more than a book on fundraising. It is a book on biblical thinking about money and ministry—filled with intensely practical guidelines on how to involve people in your ministry through giving and praying. I am impressed with this guide. It works—and has been tested in the fire of experience with hundreds of our Navigator staff. This is the best resource I have seen—a must for every organization and person who raises financial support."

Jerry E. White, Ph.D.
Former President, The Navigators

FUNDING YOUR MINISTRY

An In-depth, Biblical Guide for
Successfully Raising Personal Support

REVISED AND UPDATED

BY SCOTT MORTON

NAVPRESS

Discipleship Inside Out™

NavPress is the publishing ministry of The Navigators, an international Christian organization and leader in personal spiritual development. NavPress is committed to helping people grow spiritually and enjoy lives of meaning and hope through personal and group resources that are biblically rooted, culturally relevant, and highly practical.

For a free catalog go to www.NavPress.com
or call 1.800.366.7788 in the United States or 1.800.839.4769 in Canada.

Funding Your Ministry
An In-depth, Biblical Guide for Successfully Raising Personal Support
By Scott Morton

© 2007 by Scott Morton.

Editor: Leura Jones
Designer: Jamie Coraor

ISBN 978-0-97290-237-3

Unless otherwise identified, all Scripture quotations in this publication are taken from the *New American Standard Bible* (NASB), © The Lockman Foundation 1960, 1962, 1963, 1968, 1971, 1972, 1973, 1975, 1977.

Other versions used include:
Holy Bible: New International Version (NIV®), © 1973, 1978, 1984 by International Bible Society. Used by permission of Zondervan Publishing House. All rights reserved; *The Message* © Eugene H. Peterson 1993, 1994, 1995, 1996, 2000, 2001, 2002. Used by permission of NavPress Publishing Group; *Amplified New Testament*, © The Lockman Foundation 1954, 1958; and the *King James Version* (KJV).

Printed in the United States of America.

7 8 9 10 / 15 14

To Alma, my wife and partner in ministry,
who in our first year of ministry asked the question
that launched me into biblical fundraising:
"Are you going to support this family or not?"
Thank you. You've made me a better husband,
a better father, a better servant of God.

TABLE OF CONTENTS

ACKNOWLEDGMENTS

This book did not arise out of a vacuum. I'd like to thank especially the Navigator staff who had the courage to "try my stuff" in the early days, then passed it on to others.

And . . .

Rod Sargent (1927–1987), who encouraged me to put my seminar on video.

Ray Hoo, who suggested that if I was going to teach seminars on funding, I should be at least 100 percent of budget—not 92 percent.

Wayne Stayskal, who drew the cartoons that keep this book interesting.

Finally, I'd like to thank my parents, John and Mildred, who taught me the importance of saying thank you.

INTRODUCTION

If you look below the surface, you'll find a slow leak in the ministry of many missionaries, both overseas and stateside. It's not a sudden, devastating, rivet-popping calamity like an iceberg slamming a ship, but a small drain large enough to be noticed, though small enough to be pushed aside. This tiny leak contributes heavily to marital discord, personal stress, and ill-advised ministry strategy. But it rarely receives credit for the dreams it destroys. The culprit? Inadequate funding.

This book is written for you in Christian ministry who raise personal donor support, for your spouse, and for those who advise you—pastors, missions-committee members, and Christian leaders. This book is for anyone who longs to see missionaries and Christian organizations maximize their ministries and not be held back by the slow leak of underfunding.

Why a new edition? Because in the past eight years I've learned more that has helped me become more effective. And I think it will help you too. I've added some needed information for supervisors and mission leaders who frequently—albeit inadvertently—do more harm than good to their staff in fundraising.

I've also learned there's a lot more I don't know about fundraising. The new material in this book—such as fundraising among women and ethnic missionaries—describes areas we all need to learn more about. I hope my discoveries encourage you to keep learning too.

It is still my prayer that this book will bring you hope!

You may be:

- A new missionary, not knowing where to begin in fundraising
- A veteran missionary who is frustrated, discouraged, or bewildered by fundraising
- A missionary confident you know a lot about raising support but somehow not consistently funded
- A missionary's friend who winces when you see God's servants underfunded, ineffective, or worldly in their fundraising
- A pastor who is often asked for fundraising advice
- A member of a missions committee who wants to help missionaries do more than ask *you* for money
- A missionary spouse who feels trapped
- A mission-agency executive whose staff are underfunded

This book is for you if you've ever struggled with questions like:

- Is it right to ask for support?
- Why do I feel so worldly when I raise funds?
- Why can't I just "pray it in" like the famous missionary George Mueller?
- Where will we get the money to make our house a warm, loving home?
- Will I ever be able to save or invest? Own a home? Send our kids to college?

- What can I do—besides give—to help my missionary friends fully fund their ministries?
- What do I say when I'm asked for fundraising advice?

I welcome you to join me on this wonderful, scary journey. I promise you two things:

- The Scriptures will be our guide. I'm not going to advise you to use worldly tactics that abuse your conscience or your friends.
- Genuineness. I'll tell you "I don't know" when I don't know. And I'll admit my own fears and mistakes.

Let's get started!

Chapter One
THE MYTHS I BELIEVED

My fundraising adventure began the day I took my boss to lunch at Lum's Wiener Restaurant. I confidently told Carl I would soon quit my well-paying job at the newspaper to go into full-time Christian service. How I looked forward to it! No more hassles with the accounting department. No more criticism from money-grubbing shopkeepers. No more office politics.

Carl didn't seem impressed. "How are you going to support yourself?" he asked.

"Not to worry," I said. "The Lord will provide!"

Pause. Long pause. He smiled, looking me right in the eye. I smiled back, meeting his eyes. "A skeptic," I mused. "I'll show him." Nothing could deter me.

Two weeks later, the office gang sponsored a going-away party and presented me with a huge penny in the shape of a plaque. The inscription read, "In God we trust. All others strictly cash."

And so it began.

My first fundraising appointment was at the home of two elderly, blue-haired ladies from our former church. As I knocked on the door, I noticed the dilapidated front porch and won-dered if I had the right house. But they came to the door, glad to see me. After a few pleasantries, I asked if I could tell them about our min-istry. They eagerly rearranged the chairs so they could see the pictures in my presentation notebook. But as I turned the pages, I couldn't help noticing the worn furniture and the bare spots in the carpet. As I got closer to the financial appeal on the last page, I began to get a little edgy. I couldn't concentrate. I couldn't remember if I had clearly men-tioned finances when I had phoned to make the appointment.

I chickened out on my first few fundraising appointments. "These people are too poor!" I thought.

A voice inside me said: "Scott, you can't ask these ladies for money. Look at that carpet. Look at that sofa. Look at this house! You're better off than they are."

I retorted: "No, I've quit my job. I'm in God's work now. I've got to support my family. These ladies are glad I've come. Go ahead, *turn to the money page.*"

Back and forth the mind game raged as I flipped the pages and answered questions, smiling on the outside but sweating on the inside. Just as I arrived at the money page, a partially memorized verse of Scripture came to mind, the one in which Jesus said to the Pharisees, "You devourers of widows' houses." There was my answer! Scripture memory saved the day.

I quickly closed the book without mentioning financial support. I asked the ladies to pray for our ministry but did not mention giving. They asked me if I wanted some cookies. I drove home that day wondering if I should try to get back my job at the newspaper.

I repeated this "no-ask" scene several times. I wanted to make my financial need known, but I felt guilty doing it. Sometimes I would hint a little, but nobody seemed to catch on. Nevertheless, I had confidence that someday, somehow, people would mystically find out about my "calling" and start to give. A couple of friends volunteered support, perhaps out of sympathy, but that was it. The months were slipping by. The mailbox was empty.

Though normally courageous, missionaries often lose heart in face-to-face appeals.

During this time I got many suggestions. One missionary told me, "Money follows ministry." The people to whom we were ministering should support us. He quoted Galatians 6:6, "And let the one who is taught the word share all good things with him who teaches." But our ministry was mostly evangelism. I couldn't make financial appeals to a few new believers and nonbelievers.

Former ministries? Most of the people I knew were already supporting other missionaries. I felt guilty asking them.

A pastor in Cedar Rapids said, "Scott, don't ask people to give; just ask them to pray. They will sort of 'catch on.' " The osmosis method. That didn't work either.

Another adviser said, "Bible study materials. Sell materials to supplement your income."

Another suggested, "Christian businesspeople, that's the answer." Fine, except the businesspeople I knew from my newspaper days were not very "Christian." And I was scared to ask them to give anyway. Ralph, at Ralph's IGA, seemed interested but never gave. A business friend at church promised to give a portion of the profit from the sale of an apartment house, but it didn't sell.

Some people said they'd support us but never did. And sometimes large gifts came from strangers. But we were always well under budget. It made no sense.

In the back of my mind, I was counting on our mailing list. I sent a letter to 150 friends asking them to pray about our finances. Nothing came in. Not one response. Maybe they did pray—that's what I asked them to do!

Most of the time I felt secular trying to raise money. I criticized myself, wondering why I couldn't be like those great missionaries of the 1800s—George Mueller or Hudson Taylor—who saw money pour in by telling only God in prayer.

In the midst of this frustration, God was abundantly blessing our ministry. Nonbelievers were coming to Christ and growing in discipleship. Fundraising was definitely a sidelight, a necessary evil. Discipling was the "real" ministry, and I gladly gravitated toward it and away from money matters. Raising support was the Nyquil® medicine of ministry. Once a month, I decided to do something about it—usually the day we got our below-budget paycheck. But my motivation faded as I got busy with ministry.

I had told Carl, my boss at the newspaper, that the "Lord would provide." Did He? Yes, in a way. We didn't starve. We had a roof over our heads. We had food and clothing. But we were also in deficit to our mission agency with little hope of repaying it. I overdrew our ministry account a little each month, thinking, "Next month the money will come in . . . next month."

Not only that, but I also was financially irresponsible. My wife paid the bills and handled our finances. She was good at it, much better than I. But she also felt the pressure. I felt none. I'd abdicated.

Giving? We gave some, but not generously or consistently. In filing our income taxes one year, I noticed we had only seven receipts from a mission to which we pledged monthly. We should have had 12.

Looking for a solution, I started with Philippians 4. That day was the turning point.

I hoped to find a simple technique for funding, but God pointed out deeper issues—like my negative attitude. I hated it when bills came in the mail. When donors skipped a month, I inwardly criticized their spirituality.

I finally understood I was unbiblical in my attitude and in my whole view of money. The Word of God clearly pointed out my errors, and the Word of God enabled me to do something about it.

So, I come to you as a fellow traveler. I've made many mistakes, I've experienced frustration, and I'm still learning. But God has brought me from resenting fundraising to enjoying it. Oh sure, I still get butterflies when I pick up the phone to make an appointment. But I've come to see fundraising as a ministry and a privilege rather than a burden.

But before we can chart a new course for our adventure in fundraising, we must carefully identify some rocks in the stream—personal obstacles to raising support.

Chapter Two
OBSTACLES:
KNOW WHAT'S HOLDING YOU BACK

Many missionaries want a "quick fix" to meet their financial challenges. They are looking for the latest funding innovations from Wheaton or Colorado Springs with the hope that a catchy direct-mail phrase or software program will drive away low-income months.

But before you launch your latest fundraising efforts—stop! Answer this question: Assuming God has called you to vocational Christian ministry, what specific obstacles are keeping you from gaining 100 percent of your approved budget?

I'm not merely talking about obstacles to fundraising but rather obstacles to reaching 100 percent of your approved budget. There's a difference! Unless you identify your obstacles specifically, you'll short-change what Christ may want to do in your life, and you'll be in danger of developing a shallow financial plan.

I've struggled with several obstacles. At first, I thought I was the only missionary in the solar system who faced these issues, but I've since discovered missionaries of all backgrounds deal with these struggles.

To discover prospective donors, start with the people you know.

Solutions to these obstacles are addressed in the following chapters. For now, focus on identifying your obstacles to raising support. With which of the following do you most identify?

1. No Potential Givers

Some missionaries get discouraged, thinking, "I've run out of people to talk to" or "I've got a small mailing list." This is especially true for Christian workers who do not come from an evangelical background or for those who have purposely shrunk the size of their mailing lists.

In Chapter 6, you'll discover new ways of thinking to help overcome this roadblock, and you don't need the personality of a TV game-show host to do it.

2. Fear

I wonder if our "theological reasons" for not raising support are simply cover-ups for deep-down fears—perhaps the fear of rejection.

I once had a theological debate with a missionary over face-to-face fundraising. He argued vehemently that it put too much pressure on people, took too long, and wasn't biblically proper.

Finally, out of financial desperation, he made his first face-to-face appointment. He loved it! Then he visited 25 friends on a cross-country trip asking for support. He did not have one negative encounter. Half of those he visited made monthly pledges. His "theological" problems were suddenly silenced. Fear was the culprit.

Similarly, as a young believer in Christ, I had serious "theological" arguments against face-to-face evangelism—until I made my first Gospel presentation to a friend. It was fear of rejection that stopped me, not theology.

If you're fearful, call it that. Don't describe your hesitancy as a philosophical reservation.

3. Lack of Diligence

You may think there are more noble things you could do with your time, but don't forget that fundraising is ministry too.

I hesitate to mention a lack of diligence because most missionaries are hard workers—except in the area of money. Raising support is hard work. It takes energy, creativity, risk, and long hours. As I prepare to phone for appointments, I think of other things I would rather do—good things! Bible study. Planning. Counseling. Shuffling papers. Washing the car. Visiting the dentist. And no one would ever criticize me for doing those good things instead of fundraising.

But there's no other word for it—it's laziness! You know it, and God knows it.

4. "Get-By" Mentality

I once picked up a slightly inebriated hitchhiker at midnight on a county road in rural Wisconsin. I like to ask hitchhikers the question: "What is your major life goal?" My liquor-smelling seatmate announced resolutely, "My goal is to get by!"

He and I then launched into a lively discussion about setting a goal to know Christ rather than just "getting by." But in the weeks that followed, I thought about the hitchhiker's phrase "getting by." I confess that for years I had a financial "get-by" mentality. I never planned on raising 100 percent of budget. I drifted along month by month, year by year, hoping enough money would come in without my having to actively raise support. As long as we squeezed by each month, I was satisfied.

But after a few years, "getting by" wears thin, especially if you have a family. Missionaries who live day to day are tempted to overuse credit cards, and some are in serious debt because of it. I was surprised to discover how many Christian workers are hopelessly drowning in credit card debt—not just a few hundred dollars but thousands.

5. Fundraising Skills

It's easily demonstrated that Christians who have been trained with evangelism skills lead more people to Christ than those who have not been similarly equipped. The same is true in raising personal support. Some missionaries simply lack the skills.

I know of a missionary who did a great job asking for support face-to-face. He seemed to do everything right. Good fellowship. Clear statement of ministry. But he was getting only a 25 percent "yes" rate from his face-to-face appeals. That's too few.

After probing, I discovered he asked for three things: monthly support, a one-time gift, or prayer support. "They all seem to prefer the prayer option," he told me sadly.

His error? Too many easy options. A simple skills mistake. After learning to ask for one thing only, his response rate doubled!

Don't be naïve. Skills make a difference. Doesn't it make sense to honor the One who called you to His service by being as skillful as possible?

6. Time

We've heard all the excuses: "I just don't have time to raise funds. The 'ministry' takes all my time. I'm expected to evangelize, disciple, equip leaders, run conferences, write articles, go to staff meetings, counsel families, and raise 100 percent of my budget too. How can I add fundraising to the top of an already-too-busy schedule?"

What will you have to drop from your busy schedule to make time for fundraising?

Many missionaries fill their year with ministry activities, then try to do fundraising during vacation or on their days off. Sadly, they rob their families of much-needed interaction because they can't say no to other ministry activities.

We need to ask ourselves two questions:

1. Why do I not take more time to actively raise support?
2. What will I cut out of my to-do list to make time for raising support?

7. Target-Only Mentality (For missionaries on domestic assignment)

Some North American missionaries believe that their support should come primarily from those to whom they minister, such as Christian personnel at a military base, students on a college campus, or their Bible study groups. The Bible passage often used to promote this mentality is Galatians 6:6: "And let the one who is taught the word share all good things with him who teaches."

The people who receive my teaching should support me. That's true. But making this truth the prescription for missionary funding raises serious problems.

First, look at a pioneer ministry. Obviously, a missionary sent to an unbelieving people group is not likely to be supported by them. The unbelieving college students in my university ministry didn't seem to know Galatians 6:6.

Second, if the missionary's funding is primarily from his target group, will the missionary soften his teaching just to keep the money coming? For example, years ago I had to strongly exhort an erring brother in my ministry. I realized that I could lose his financial support by speaking to him like that. But I was able to confront him because most of my support came from outside. I wasn't dependent on him. It gave me more freedom.

Certainly, those in a ministry group should support their missionary-shepherd, but don't depend on this as your major source of income unless, of course, you are pastoring an established church.

Third, with 10 to 20 percent of Americans moving every year, it is not likely your target ministry will remain stable anyway. A support constituency outside your target is needed.

If you are looking to be fully funded by the people in your ministry, you'll be disappointed. You're also not following the example of the Scriptures. Paul took pride in offering the Gospel free of charge to the Thessalonians, a pioneering cross-cultural ministry. Galatians 6:6 is not the primary model for supporting a missionary.

8. Lack of Accountability

What will happen if you're not up to 100 percent of budget? Is your mission going to stop you from getting on an airplane? Will your supervisors confront you? They won't if they're not up to budget either!

Some mission organizations have a rule that you may not launch your ministry until you are 100 percent underwritten with pledges. That rule is easy to apply if you are going overseas—you simply can't leave until your budget is met. But it is easier to slide by when your assignment is stateside.

Although some mission agencies have a "100 percent" policy, it is seldom enforced.

I once taught a finance school for Illinois collegiate missionaries who were severely underfunded. Shortly before our lunch break, the Illinois director announced that no staff would be allowed to continue their campus ministries until they were fully funded—100 percent!

Up to that moment, the missionaries were jovial, talkative, enjoying the finance school. But now the mood changed. The air was thick with hostility. As the seminar leader, I tentatively cleared my throat and suggested we break for an early lunch.

During the break, pent-up emotions broke loose. "How can he do that?" the missionaries clamored. "Doesn't he know that our ministries will be devastated without our leadership?"

But the director stuck with his decision.

So nine Illinois missionaries had only four days to set their campus ministries in order before they pulled back to devote themselves to fundraising. To their surprise, within three months they were all fully funded and back on campus full-time.

Was the ministry devastated? As one of the missionaries said afterward, "Regrettably, no!" He considered himself so indispensable that he believed he could not leave even for a few days without the ministry falling apart. But his student leaders rose to the challenge. Besides getting fully funded, he learned something about humility.

Though sometimes hard to accept, accountability will help you succeed in your funding plan.

Contrast that scene with another school I taught in which the director did not insist on his missionaries leaving campus to begin full-time fundraising. The missionaries in his state tried to do both at once—raise support and minister on campus. After six months, they were nowhere near being fully funded.

I asked a missionary once, "Do you think your mission would ever tell you that you couldn't launch your ministry until you'd raised your full support?" He glanced around the room to make sure his leaders weren't around and then said, "Naw, I don't think they'd have the guts!"

Who will hold you accountable in your fundraising? If not your supervisor, who? A friend? A donor? Your pastor? Who?

9. Strategy

I suspect our yearly financial strategy is often 51 weeks of good intentions, followed by a fight with our spouse (if married) and one week of 18-hour days doing crisis fundraising. During this week, we send out desperate letters pleading for help.

Panic fundraising may produce results once or twice, but your donors will tire of it, and you'll be in danger of "crying wolf" once too often.

Build a long-range strategy and implement it month by month. You'll read more on that in Chapter 8.

10. Fuzzy Calling

If you're not sure of your ministry calling or if you no longer believe fervently in the importance of your ministry, you'll hesitate to invite others to support you.

Use these times of uncertainty to further clarify what God has called you to do. Perhaps it is time to move on or start a new ministry chapter in your life. Spending extended time alone with God, taking aptitude tests, counseling with your mission leaders, and asking your church and your friends will all help you refocus. Perhaps the Bible study on calling in the Appendix of this book will help.

Until you clarify your calling, you'll have difficulty raising money and communicating confidently to your constituency. Fuzzy vision is perhaps the biggest reason missionaries fall into one- and two-year lapses of failing to write their prayer and financial partners. They wonder, "What will I say?"

By the way, if you are not sure of your next step in ministry, you are in good company. Even the apostle Paul was fuzzy about his plans. In 1 Corinthians 16:6, Paul says, "And *perhaps* I shall stay with you, or even spend the winter, that you may send me on my way *wherever* I may go" (italics added).

Note the word "perhaps." Doesn't Paul know his itinerary? Note also his phrase "wherever I may go." Like Paul, you may not know the specific details of your ministry future. That's OK! Tell people what you *do* know, and ask them to help you accomplish that.

11. Long-Haul Pessimism

A missionary who had worked hard to get up to budget told me, "When I think of raising support the rest of my career, I get totally overwhelmed. I've been able to develop our funding for a few years, but how can I do it for the long haul?"

Likewise, many younger missionaries love the adventure of "living by faith" for a year or two, but as a career? No thanks.

Let me encourage you to put aside this overwhelming thought until you've finished the assignments in this book. You will then be able to view your funding challenge with less anxiety. Also, I find God gives me grace only for the present. It's hard to experience grace for the future. But it will be there when the future arrives.

Can you identify with these 11 obstacles? The first step in overcoming obstacles is to admit they are there. The famous educator Booker T. Washington said, "Success is not measured by the heights one attains, but by the obstacles one overcomes in the attainment" (*Saturday Review*, October 28, 1978).

Take a moment right now to identify two obstacles that keep you from raising 100 percent of your personal support. What is keeping you from full funding? Write it down in the space on the next page. Be specific.

For example, be honest enough to say to the Lord: "My main obstacle is that I'm scared. I'm particularly fearful of what my parents think." List names of people whose opinions you fear.

Then pray about your obstacles daily. In your devotional times over the next few days, discuss these obstacles with the Lord. If you're married, share them with your spouse. Quick fixes and easy answers won't resolve your obstacles. Identifying them specifically is the first step. But they are so deeply ingrained, we need the Holy Spirit and the Holy Scriptures to help.

Next, with your obstacles identified, you are ready to examine your attitude toward raising support. Ten biblical attitudes are crucial to becoming a biblical fundraiser—and these attitudes will help you deal with obstacles as well.

Obstacle #1

_____

_____

Obstacle #2

_____

_____

Initials _____ Date _____

Chapter Three
YOUR ATTITUDE MAKES A DIFFERENCE

You may know a few fundraising techniques or a couple of buzzwords—and they may even work. But that doesn't mean you're doing biblical fundraising. Just as effective evangelism is more than tricky questions and nifty illustrations, so is biblical fundraising more than clichés, like "Give until it hurts" or "I'm raising friends, not funds."

Over the years, I've met salespeople going into ministry who say, "Fundraising will be easy for me because I'm good at sales." But they have the same struggles as others. Sales and fundraising are *not* the same.

A young door-to-door salesman stopped at our home selling money-saving dry-cleaning coupons. He was extremely polished, but I found myself resisting him. He had the right techniques. He looked me directly in the eye. His presentation didn't sound memorized. He made his appeal politely and sincerely, then paused to wait for my answer just like the books say. When it was my turn to speak, I told him no, but I didn't know why.

He thanked me politely and left to go to our neighbor's house. Puzzled, I stared at the floor, trying to identify what bothered me about his presentation. After a few seconds I had it! He had talked down to me. He made me feel small. Suddenly, I raced out into the yard to catch him before he got to my neighbor's house.

Fundraising will reveal your core attitudes and values. And you may not like what you see!

I explained to my surprised "apprehendee" that the product he was selling was fine, but his *attitude* turned me off. I vowed not to be that way in my fundraising but to have biblical attitudes.

Before you step into one more living room or church meeting hall, check your attitudes. I've identified 10 absolutely crucial attitudes or values we must bring into our fundraising if we intend to be biblical. Check to see which ones are yours already and which you need to shore up.

1. God is the source—not our donors, not our plans, not our hard work.

The Levites understood that God was the source. Notice the pronoun "I" in Numbers 18:24: "For the tithe of the sons of Israel, which they offer as an offering to the LORD, I have given to the Levites."

The phrase "which *they offer as an offering to the Lord*" shows that the lamb or bundle of grain was not a *horizontal* gift—from Israelite to Levite. It was a *vertical* gift *to* God *from* the Israelites. The phrase, *"I have given to the Levites"* shows that the Levites received from God—not from their fellow Israelites. Giving and receiving are both vertical.

Paul understood this. In Philippians 4:18, he called the Philippians' gift a "fragrant aroma, an acceptable sacrifice, well-pleasing to God." From the Philippians to God to Paul. Vertical. When I place my gift in the offering plate at church, I like to imagine my envelope zipping to heaven and back before the ushers open it in the counting room, or wherever ushers do such things. I imagine an usher picking up my envelope with fresh burn marks on the edges (much like the reentry tiles on the space shuttle) and saying, "Whew! This envelope's warm!" Sure it is. It's been to heaven and back!

Biblical giving means donors give to God—vertically.

Because donors give to God, missionaries receive from God—vertically.

If you view people as your source of funding, you have a horizontal view. That's merely worldly charity. Furthermore, you alternately may feel deserving or undeserving of donor gifts.

For example, in my first year as a campus minister, one particular month I was lackadaisical. I skipped quiet times—on purpose! Instead of studying the Scriptures, I watched *Sesame Street* with my kids. I learned to count to 10 in Spanish! When I finally did go to campus, instead of talking with students, I watched daytime TV in the dormitory lounge.

The next month our donor income transfer arrived at our bank. It was the largest we'd ever received! I was humbled. People were investing money so I could watch *The Price Is Right*. Hoping for sympathy, I told my wife, Alma, "I don't know why *anyone* would ever want to give to a *sloth* like me." She surprised me by saying, "I don't either. I think they give to God."

Her comment helped. I thought donor income was something I earned. And I felt undeserving of it.

On another occasion, I felt deserving. Because I'd done extensive fundraising the month before, I was confident several new much-needed donors would show up on our donor printout.

After opening my income report on the first of the month, I quickly scanned it to find the total, the bottom line. My enthusiasm crashed to our beige linoleum floor. As I read the printout, disappointment turned to resentment toward those whose names were absent—people whom I felt ought to be giving. After all, they pledged! I'd worked hard to enlist their support.

My resentment showed that I was looking to people to supply my needs—not God.

Another example of trying to earn donor gifts is illustrated by a young missionary candidate who asked me for advice. "Scott, what am I gonna do? Our pastor has made some terrible mistakes, and I'm an elder. I've got to confront him."

"Go ahead, what's stopping you?" I asked.

He hesitated. "Well, you know the church is thinking about sponsoring me for $200 to $500 a month when I join the mission next year. If I confront the pastor, well . . . " My friend stopped to clear his throat. "Well, there's a chance I could lose that support," he said, staring at the ground.

A week later, he confessed that he had been looking at people as his financial source instead of God. He said, "I've been worried about minding my Ps and Qs around the church so I wouldn't offend them, so I would get a lot of money."

Let's look to God, not to people.

Besides looking to people, we sometimes look to ourselves as the source of funding—our own efforts, abilities, personalities, hard work, even our computers.

This may come as a shock to some, but having the latest software will not get you up to budget! Having a sharp presentation video will not get you up to budget. Being outgoing and friendly will not get you up to budget. Putting your picture on your pledge card will not get you up to budget. Even having a successful ministry will not get you up to budget. Sorry.

Is that what raising support is all about? Slick presentations? A talk-show personality? Computer-merged letters?

A few years ago, we sent a cash-project mailing asking for $8,000. We spent a lot of time on it and even included a cute cartoon that I was overly proud of. Convicted of my dependence on human effort, I finally told Alma, "You know, I think I'm forgetting the Lord. It's not the cartoon that will cause people to give; it's the Lord. We need to pray!"

Certainly we must communicate well. We must do our part. But let's depend on the Lord—not on our skills, not on our hard work. God is the source.

2. Prayer demonstrates our dependence on God as the source.

Of course, prayer ought to permeate all we do in ministry, but it's especially important in fundraising.

Nehemiah modeled this attitude. Only seconds before he asked King Artaxerxes for resources to rebuild the Jerusalem wall, he said, "So I prayed to the God of heaven" (Nehemiah 2:4).

In my second year as a campus minister, I was worrying and grumbling to a fellow Iowan, Duane Bundt, about our support. Duane had helped me when I was a young Christian, and I appreciated his down-to-earth practicality.

"Duane, what can we do?" I asked.

"Scott, do you pray about it? Do you pray about it every day?"

The more we see God as the source of our funding, the more we will depend on Him in prayer.

I said, "Well, I pray about it, but I don't pray about it every day."

"Well, I think you should pray about it—*every day.*"

So I prayed—every day—and our income went up without our doing anything differently. Jesus also modeled this practice. "Give us this day our daily bread" (Matthew 6:11).

May I ask you the question Duane asked me? Do you pray about your financial support *every day?* Do you ask the Lord specifically to supply your needs? Do you name people one by one before the Lord, asking Him to lay it on their hearts to join your support team?

I keep in my daily prayer journal the "next" 6 to 10 friends whom I hope will support us. Beside their names I include the amount I hope they will give. Then I pray regularly for each person and the specific amount.

Within a few weeks, I make an appointment with each one to invite them to join our support team. Frequently they will say, "It was interesting that you called when you did. We had been thinking about your ministry." I've heard that statement too many times for it to be coincidence. And sometimes these friends start supporting us before I even talk to them!

As you list people to pray for, you may not sense the freedom to appeal to some of them. That's OK. Keep praying. God may still honor your prayers without you asking the people directly.

Several years ago, Alma and I prayed specifically that four couples from our Bible study group would begin supporting us monthly for $50 each. (That was a sizable amount in those days.) We could have asked them to join our team, but we didn't

Pray and Ask

Name	Amount
_____	$ _____
_____	$ _____
_____	$ _____
_____	$ _____
_____	$ _____

By Prayer Alone

Name	Amount
_____	$ _____
_____	$ _____
_____	$ _____
_____	$ _____
_____	$ _____

feel right about it. We were in a discipling arrangement with them and didn't want a financial appeal to cloud our ministry. We weren't afraid; we just felt that God wanted us to ask Him in prayer alone. So I put their names down in my journal and began to pray daily. We also agreed not to hint to them about our financial needs.

A month later, one of the couples phoned to ask if they could give to our mission—specifical-ly for our ministry. The next month's report revealed their gift of $50, and it has continued every month since. The second fellow, an older man, stuck a check in my pocket one day and, rather embarrassed, said, "Send that in for us." That $50 gift continued monthly.

The third couple pledged at a conference. We were not the offering project. We did not make our needs known. They simply gave a $50 gift that turned out to continue monthly.

But the fourth couple didn't give. In my annual prayer review, which I hold every January 1 (instead of watching perky young soap stars host endless football parades), I remember congratulating the Lord that three out of four wasn't bad! But that next month, our income report revealed a gift from the fourth couple for $600. Divided by 12, that equals $50 per month!

God answers prayer!

May I suggest two action steps to take right now? As you've read the past couple pages, perhaps a few names of potential donors have come to mind. Jot their names down in the box on the previous page—or in your prayer journal or your finance strategy file. Can you think of three?

Second, start "by prayer alone" as a part of your strategy. Jot down names of people you want as do-nors, but you just don't feel led by God to ask them. (Make sure that fear doesn't influence your decision! If you're fearful, you probably *should* ask them.) Can you discover three names for your "by-prayer-alone" list? And three people to "pray and ask"? Take a mo-ment right now.

God's Job—Your Job

> Calling me to
> special ministry
>
> **God's job**

> Surrounding me
> providentially
> with friends and
> family and bringing
> "acquaintances"
> across my path
>
> **God's job**

> Inviting friends,
> family, and
> acquaintances to
> join me financially
> in ministry
>
> **My job**

> Providentially
> guiding friends,
> family, and
> acquaintances to
> make a stewardship
> decision to
> support me
>
> **God's job**

> Thanking, informing,
> and ministering to
> financial partners
> about ministry
> progress
>
> **My job**

3. Be clear on your job versus God's job.

Many missionaries feel trapped because they confuse their role and God's role in fundraising. They know ministry is God's work and they know they must not fundraise in the flesh, but they also know they have a lot of work to do themselves. If you're feeling pressure to raise money but don't know what action to take, it may be you're fuzzy on who does what.

God's "miraculous" provision comes when He does His part and you do yours.

When you try to do God's job in fundraising, you will be frustrated. Don't take His providential working as your responsibility. Just do your job—it's doable!

Of course, God could fund you without your lifting a finger—and that would be a miracle. But He will also do "miracles" when you do your job in fundraising. When God gives you the grace to get on the phone (your job) to set an appointment with someone who intimidates you—isn't that miraculous? Isn't it a miracle when God gives you the courage to invite a skeptical friend to give? Isn't it miraculous that you trust God to dive into ministry without a guaranteed W-2 every year?

And how good it feels when you do your job—getting on the phone, writing that difficult letter, sending a late-night thank you, e-mailing when you would rather go to bed—and then see God reward your "by faith" activity.

Look at the box on the previous page and find your jobs:

1. Inviting friends, family, and acquaintances to join you financially
2. Thanking, informing, and ministering to giving partners

You only have two jobs! God has three. Do yours with all the grace He gives. That's miraculous!

4. The Bible is the standard for fundraising tactics—not Madison Avenue or your own opinions.

Famous 1880's missionary George Mueller was once quoted as saying: "It is not enough to obtain means for the work of God . . . These means should be obtained in God's way."

Your task is not simply to raise your support but to do it in a biblical, God-honoring manner. The late Rod Sargent, former director of development for The Navigators and my mentor, said it best: "Just because a fundraising tactic works doesn't make it right."

Although it is not freely admitted, flagrant abuses of fundraising principles exist today among Christian ministries.

I received a letter from a television evangelist describing the Luke 17 story in which Jesus directs Peter to take a coin out of the fish's mouth to pay a tax. The fundraising letter similarly contained two coins—a big one for me to keep and a smaller one that I was to send back to the evangelist. He also instructed me to "wrap your largest bill around this smaller coin and send it to God's work."

Why couldn't he simply ask for a donation? What is all this two-coin hocus-pocus? It is simply a spiritualized version of a secular direct-mail tactic: "You keep this penny, but send the other one to me because it doesn't belong to you."

I also have a letter containing two packets of mustard seeds from the Mount of Olives, gathered by an evangelist's children. I am to keep one packet as my own, but I'm to return the other packet (which is his—not mine) along with a $33 love gift and prepare to receive a blessing.

The sad thing is—it works! The writers know they will get a better response if they include something that doesn't belong to the readers and ask them to send it back. We Americans are so conscientious that we will use a first-class postage stamp to return a penny simply because it is not ours.

I also received a thin "prayer sock" with instructions to wear it on my right foot overnight. Then, in the middle of the night when I wake up (probably because my right foot is too hot), I am to write down my "most special" prayer needs. In the morning, I'm to rush them back to the preacher, include a "seed gift" of $170, $100, $70, or $50, and wait for a miracle. I must also return the slightly used prayer sock.

The evangelist has the right to ask for a gift, but promises of wealth and health for sending a gift go too far.

Another manipulative practice is to use an envelope that looks nearly identical to a blue and white Federal Express overnight-delivery letter. The receiver is led to believe he's getting an overnight package—must be important! But if he looks closely, he will notice a third-class indicia in the upper right-hand corner. This "important" piece of literature has been in the mail up to three weeks.

Why isn't a regular envelope used? It doesn't "work" as well. Unfortunately, many gullible people respond to these tricks. And the ministry praises God for the good results it has seen from tricking Christian brothers and sisters into giving. It's abominable!

I'm not speaking merely as one who doesn't like his mailbox stuffed with Christian junk mail. Part of my job is to write national direct-mail appeal letters. It's tempting to use devices like these to increase response.

In 2 Corinthians 4:2, Paul used the phrase "not walking in craftiness" in winning a hearing with the Corinthians. Let's follow that example. We don't have to be "crafty" to receive support.

You may think you will never use manipulative tricks to raise money. You will probably never use a prayer sock, but don't think you are above being tempted to manipulate the truth to your own advantage—especially when funds are low. For example, the commonly used "P.S." in missionary letters—"Please pray for our financial support"—is often nothing more than a disguised appeal.

We also must not allow our own opinions to tempt us into unbiblical fundraising. I'm amazed at the number of missionaries who have never done a Bible study on money or fundraising yet have strong opinions about it. For me, that changed one sunny Saturday morning on the shores of Lake Mendota in Madison, Wisconsin, as I studied every passage in Proverbs dealing with money or possessions. Growing up in rural Iowa taught me some good, biblical guidelines about money, but I also developed some worldly views. Up until that day at Lake Mendota, I was a prisoner to my own opinions and "common sense."

Let's be biblical. Don't spout your personal opinions on money or fundraising until you've spent at least 20 hours in personal Bible study on these topics. If you've never studied what the Bible says about money or raising support, how do you know your opinions are biblical? You will bring to Christian service your parents' or your church's views or the amalgamation of all you've experienced in money matters. But is that biblical?

Start with the Bible study in the Appendix of this book.

5. Biblical fundraising is a spiritual ministry—not a worldly effort to be reluctantly or apologetically endured.

In America, Christians tend to separate life into the sacred and the secular. Sacred activities include discipleship, evangelism, Bible study, and prayer meetings. Money matters are usually viewed as nonspiritual.

By splitting life into "the secular" and "the sacred," missionaries relegate fundraising to "secular work."

A missionary once told me, "I could never choose money over the souls of men and women." Agreed. But does it have to be either/or? He saw fundraising as a plague, not a privilege. A curse, not a call. A menace, not a ministry.

But what does the Bible say?

In Exodus 25, God told Moses to "raise a contribution" for the Tabernacle. Did Moses consider it "secular"? Can you imagine him saying, "Lord, are You asking me to do fundraising? Filthy lucre? Anything but that! I'll lead the people. I'll get the Ten Commandments. I'll teach. I'll eat manna. I'll live in the desert for 40 years. But don't ask me to do fundraising! And especially not for a capital project! It's all going to burn anyway!"

Quite the opposite! Moses carefully received God's detailed instructions for the Tabernacle, then, in Exodus 35, he invited the people to give. And give they did! Everyone "whose heart stirred him" (verse 21) brought contributions, and the project was completed.

Neither did Paul abhor fundraising. Three times he called the collection for the saints in Jerusalem a "gracious work" (2 Corinthians 8:6–7, 19). He devoted a portion of his ministry to this financial project, even postponing his ministry trip to Spain until he had "put my seal on this fruit of theirs" by personally delivering it to Jerusalem (Romans 15:28). He didn't apologize for his financial work.

Similarly, today, when it's time to pass the collection plate, pastors in many churches say, "Let us *worship* God through the giving of our tithes and offerings." The pastor does not apologize and say, "I'm sorry, ladies and gentlemen, but we now come to that part of our service in which we must do something secular. I hate to do it, but the bills must be paid. Ushers, please come forward, and let's get this nasty business over with."

The late author Henri Nouwen originally considered fundraising "a necessary but unpleasant activity to support spiritual things." But he came to see it differently later in life: "Fund-raising is as spiritual as giving a sermon, entering a time of prayer, visiting the sick, or feeding the hungry."

He goes on to say, "Fund-raising is precisely the opposite of begging. When we seek to raise funds we are not saying, 'Please, could you help us out because it's been rather hard.' "[1]

Instead, Nouwen defines fundraising as "proclaiming what we believe in such a way that we offer other people an opportunity to participate with us in our vision and mission." Exactly! We are not asking people to give their hard-earned funds to our personal charity so we can put groceries on the table or buy socks, but rather we are asking them to join us in advancing the Kingdom. Nouwen concludes, "We must not let ourselves be tricked into thinking that fund-raising is only a secular activity."[2]

If giving is biblical, then can't the appeal for and collection of the gift also be biblical? It is worldly people who make fundraising worldly, just as worldly people can make evangelism worldly.

Furthermore, we don't *do* fundraising so we can do ministry. Biblical fundraising itself is a ministry. Why? It helps people lay up treasure in heaven. It helps them live Matthew 6:33, seeking first the Kingdom.

Philippians 4:10 gives a definition of fundraising: "You were *concerned* before, but you lacked *opportunity*" (italics added). People should have a *concern* for the Lord's work and an *opportunity* to show their concern. This simple equation from Philippians 4:10 helps me:

$$S = C + O$$

Support = Concern + Opportunity

---

1 Henri J.M. Nouwen, *The Spirituality of Fund-Raising* (Upper Room Ministries and the Henri Nouwen Society, 2004).
2 Ibid.

So-Called "Sacred" Ministry Activities

- Bible study
- Prayer
- Evangelism
- Discipleship groups
- Bible conferences
- Counseling
- Singing
- Worship services

So-Called "Secular" Ministry Activities

- Fundraising
- Budgeting
- Paying ministry bills
- Marketing
- Taking bids to pave the parking lot
- Newsletter production
- Paperwork
- Janitorial services at church

Most local churches utilize the $S = C + O$ formula every Sunday by passing the offering plate. The plate is simply an opportunity for parishioners to show their concern.

Your financial appeal gives your friends an opportunity to demonstrate their concern. If you raise their concern for your ministry but never give them an *appropriate* opportunity to give, you'll probably not fund your vision—no matter how great it is. If, on the other hand, you are constantly giving people opportunities but neglect to elevate their concern, you'll alienate your audience. They'll view you as money hungry.

Notice I said "appropriate" opportunity. A missionary told me he gave the 250 people on his mailing list an "opportunity" to support him monthly, but 249 said no. "How do you know they said no?" I asked. "They didn't respond to the letter!" he replied.

A letter asking for monthly support is too easy to turn down. It's like driving an ice cream truck through a neighborhood at 45 miles per hour. Just as a 45-mph ice cream truck doesn't meaningfully engage with customers, so a mass-mailed form letter asking for monthly support doesn't meaningfully engage potential donors. "High-altitude bombing" I call it.

Raising support also opens doors to further ministry. A personal appeal takes 20 minutes, but it gives me an entrance to other areas of my listeners' lives for an additional hour or more.

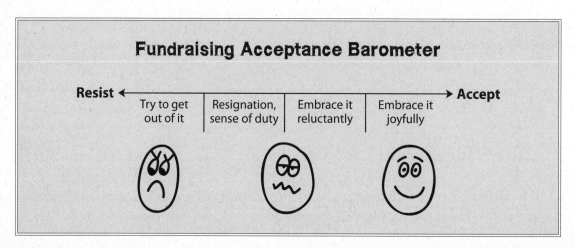

Fundraising Acceptance Barometer

Resist ← → Accept

| Try to get out of it | Resignation, sense of duty | Embrace it reluctantly | Embrace it joyfully |

As you look at the fundraising acceptance chart on the previous page, where would you place yourself today? What can you do to move toward "joyful acceptance"?

Let's change our minds about fundraising being the distasteful green medicine of Christian service. Biblical fundraising is a ministry, a privilege. Bring it over to the sacred side of life and enjoy it!

6. Receiving support is a biblical "right" but does not entitle you to be pushy or demanding.

Paul writes in 1 Corinthians 9:14, "So also the Lord directed those who proclaim the gospel to get their living from the gospel." He was paraphrasing Jesus in Matthew 10:10, who said, "For the worker is worthy of his support."

Clearly, we have a right to be supported by the Gospel. But Paul says earlier in verse 12, "We did not use this right . . . that we may cause no hindrance to the gospel."

When I was in the ninth grade, an evangelist came to our little country church. Several people came to Christ through his preaching. But the good the evangelist did was undermined by the fact that after the service, he joined the ushers in the basement to help count the money from the offering. I saw him in the basement as I left our little church that evening. Perhaps it was harmless, but it raised my suspicions.

Sure enough, a few days later a backlash sprang up against the evangelist. Because his doctrine could not be criticized, his handling of money became the focus, and his ministry was discounted.

It is possible to be demanding without realizing it. Christian workers are usually comfortable being in charge, leading, giving orders. In making financial appeals, missionaries often say, "I want you to pray about giving toward my ministry." Although not intended as a demand, the statement is a command—not an appeal. Let's be careful to make appeals for support rather than give commands for support.

A college alumnus who supported two missionaries returned to graduate school. He wrote both of them saying he was going to stop giving because he no longer had an income. One of the missionaries warmly responded with a letter of thanks for all this giver had done. He enclosed a small gift of appreciation and wished him well on his adventure in grad school. The second missionary, who had ministered to the young man when he was in college, also wrote back but asked him to keep giving (perhaps at a lower amount) because of all the benefit he had received as a student. The thought was, "Keep giving because of all we've done for you."

Now this young man is out of graduate school and has a really good job, but he supports only one of these two missionaries. Can you guess which one?

You do not have the right to be pushy or to use "leverage" to get people to give. Strong-arm tactics are not biblical.

I'm afraid some missionaries who attend fundraising seminars come away with the impression that they have the right to force pledge cards into the hands of reluctant listeners. Not true. You have the right to be supported, but you don't have the right to be discourteous—or pushy— thereby causing hindrances to the Gospel.

7. Expect to raise 100 percent of your approved budget.

Unfortunately, few Christians expect missionaries to be fully funded. Not their donors. Not their home churches. Sometimes not even their sending agencies, contrary to their official policy. And not even the missionaries themselves. We are so accustomed to missionaries being behind in funding that 100 percent support is not even their aim. After all, they're in God's work!

Why be so picky about missionaries being fully funded? Isn't 90 percent enough? I used to wonder this myself until I heard Margaret's story. Margaret was launching a new ministry at a state university, and it was tough going. Not many seemed interested in hearing about Christ.

But one skeptical student hesitatingly told Margaret she would like her to come by to talk about the Bible and Jesus. Margaret was ecstatic. Though the new girl was skittish, this might be a spiritual breakthrough. The appointment was set.

But the evening she was to go to campus, Margaret discovered she didn't have the two dollars necessary to buy her new friend a Coke while the two of them talked about the Lord. Sadly, Margaret called to postpone the meeting, not telling her the real

You may be able to "get by" on only 75 to 85 percent of your budget, but it won't feel so good in the long run.

reason. Because of a measly two dollars, the Gospel was lost that night. Could the appointment be reset? Maybe, maybe not. But Margaret did not share the Gospel that week because she was not fully funded.

Why do we excuse ourselves from full funding? It's not simply a private matter between you and God. The skeptical but hungry waiting world is at stake. It's a Gospel issue!

A few years ago, I was helping a missionary with his mission-agency budget and noticed he put $60,000 down on line 42, "Total Annual Budget." But he put only $48,000 for line 43, "Expected Annual Income." I asked why he wouldn't put $60,000 on line 43 as well as line 42. Why wouldn't he go for 100 percent of his budget?

"Well," he said, "we really don't need $60,000. We can get by on much less. And besides that, we'll never get it anyway."

"If you don't need $60,000, why did you put $60,000 as your annual budget?" I persisted. "And what do you mean you'll never get that much!?"

"Oh, I don't know. It's just paperwork. I've got more important things to do. And there's just no way we'll be fully funded," he said with a sigh.

Another missionary told me that her budget might as well be a million dollars, because she would never come close to it anyway.

I believe that most missionaries enter Christian service with the view that they will never have enough money. It's not a vow of poverty, but it's close! Sadly, many cultures support this mentality that missionaries are supposed to be poor—that's part of their calling. It's OK for Christian teachers, farmers, and businesspeople to have adequate funds, but missionaries must be poor. A missions administrator once referred to his staff's budgets as "wish lists."

I've heard mission leaders—godly men and women full of integrity—make unfunny jokes about their poor financial situation. Why do they do that?

On the other extreme, some Christian "professionals" have gotten rich from the sacrificial gifts of their flocks. The entire "name-it-and-claim-it" doctrine promotes the idea that if you are truly walking with God, you will be healthy and wealthy. All you need is a little more faith. Although this movement claims biblical support, I do not believe the Bible teaches that you have the *right* to be healthy and wealthy.

What I am suggesting is that there are enough resources in God's world to fully supply your "prayed-over annual budget" if God has truly called you.

Husbands, please understand the emotions your wives endure when finances are tight. A friend of mine in development was criticized by a missionary about the necessity of going for full funding. Although their conversation began over a pleasant lunch, the missionary vehemently sermonized that raising support was unbiblical and worldly. As he pontificated, his wife began to cry, but her husband didn't notice. My friend interrupted the missionary's lecture to inform him that his wife was weeping. Choking back tears, she wisely said, "It's great to live by faith, but I'm the one who has to buy the bread and cheese." Her husband had no idea she was under such pressure.

You can dream great dreams for God, but the rubber meets the road at the kitchen cupboard.

A lack of full funding is seen in a new way if your kids want to go to college. Recently, I reluctantly helped a missionary write a special letter to raise $14,000 for his daughter's first year of college.

I finally got him to confess that he disdained fundraising and that he tried to "get by" year after year below his approved budget. He confessed to ignoring saving for needs like college, old age, resettlement, and housing. Although his donors responded warmly to his appeal, he still had three years of college to pay for and admitted it would have been better to save month by month during his 20 years of overseas service.

But can't the money be raised by special projects? Sometimes, but donors get tired of constant personal emergencies. By the way, what would you say to a Christian businessman if he failed to save for his daughter's college? Should *he* write an emergency letter?

When you do not raise 100 percent of your approved budget, you can perhaps "get by" for the short term—until your car needs major repair, until you need to fly home for a parent's illness, or until your kids want to go to college.

Here's a new way of thinking for many in ministry. Ask yourself these questions:

- How would your ministry be different if you were at 100 percent of budget for the next 12 months?
- What would you do in ministry that you can't do now?
- What new initiatives could you start?
- If you are married, how would your marriage and family life be different if you were at 100 percent of budget for the next 12 months?
- What are some things you'd like to do as a family if you had enough money?
- What would you do for your spouse if the funds were available?
- How would you personally be different if you were at 100 percent of budget for the next 12 months?

I used to consider being at 100 percent of budget a luxury, not a necessity. Part of the problem was that Alma and I never seriously made a personal household budget. Nor did we do long-range financial planning. Oh, we talked about it, but we never prayed about it or put our financial goals down on paper.

I knew we needed more donor income, but I wasn't convicted by God to be a good steward. The only thing we knew about stewardship was giving. As a result, we had a "get-by" mentality.

In those days, I wrongly considered saving as a luxury. In fact, some days eating was a luxury. Shortsighted, I never saw the need to be at 100 percent. Sadly, I felt more *spiritual* being below budget, especially when others "accidentally" found out about it and gave me sympathy.

When I started taking fundraising seriously, I saw that I had to change my mind about stewardship before I could address fundraising.

Have you ever filled out a detailed personal household budget? This is just as important for singles as it is for married missionaries. If you don't have a personal household budget, you'll stop raising support at 70 to 85 percent because you can get your bills paid. But you'll have no margin, and you won't be able to save. You'll also end up asking your donors to fund your kids' college.

Starting from zero, write down what it will take to accomplish your ministry activities for the coming year. (This presupposes you've done serious ministry planning and scheduling!) Then add in your agency-approved salary (or personal allowance), benefits, and other charges.

Bring this total budget before the Lord, prayerfully evaluating each line item of your personal budget, ministry-expense budget, administrative budget, benefits costs, and other charges. (For a sample worksheet, check page 219 in the Appendix.)

Be sure to consider the ceilings or guidelines your mission agency follows for the budgeting process. Understand each line item carefully. If you don't believe every dollar of your approved budget must be there, you will not seriously try to raise it. But if you believe that every dollar on your budget is needed to accomplish your vision in the best way possible (including funding your personal needs, family needs, savings), you'll work to raise it all.

Husbands, don't "guesstimate" the budget line items. Look at last year's bills. Wives, you know what it costs to run a house. Be honest. Tell your "frugal" husband it might take more than $115 per month for groceries for a family of four! Get the facts, and be specific.

Single women, does your budget include money set aside for a vacation, a hobby, a new piece of furniture? Single guys, there are other foods besides macaroni!

Remember, you are a *steward* before you are a fund-raiser. Luke 16:11 warns us, "If you have not been faithful in the use of unrighteous mammon, who will entrust the true riches to you?" Let's take seriously our responsibility as stewards and then build upon that.

	Monthly	
Personal allowance/salary	$ _____	(include enough for modest savings)
Ministry costs	$ _____	
Administrative charges	$ _____	
Organization benefits	$ _____	(health insurance, auto, etc.)
Monthly total	$ _____	
x 12 =	$ _____	yearly need

8. Poor talk dishonors God.

What is poor talk? It's a mentality of wishing there were more money, usually expressed in complaining or hinting. Simply put, it's whining about the lack of money.

Most Christian workers have participated in a missionary pity party. Picture the scene. It's late at night at the missions conference. Two missionaries have been talking for an hour over coffee in Styrofoam cups. They have given their opinions on every problem in the mission, particularly the leadership structure. Now their talk turns to finances.

"How's your income doing?"

"Oh, pretty good. Picked up a new donor last month—$100."

"Hey, great! What did you say his address was? Ha ha, just kidding!"

"We lost our two biggest churches last summer—$1,400 per month. No way we'll make that up. And there's no good reason they stopped. I suppose Cindy could get a side job as a waitress or something. I feel bad for the kids. No toys for Christmas this year. We just can't find anybody who wants to give."

"That's not so bad. Do you know what our salary check was last month? Seventy-eight dollars! We're at 37 percent! I had to sell my memory-verse packet at a garage sale."

Poor talk can be very tempting, especially with other missionaries. Try to avoid it.

"That's nothing. Last month I didn't get a check at all. Headquarters sent me a bill! I owe them money!"

"This economy is just killing us Christian workers!"

"I tell you, these are the Last Days!"

Poor talk is extremely subtle. We don't even realize we do it.

Saturday Review magazine had this comment on poor talk: "Although poor talk is understandable, it is nevertheless debilitating. First, it makes us feel worse about our plight than is necessary. Second, poor talk focuses our attention on ourselves, thus blinding us to the needs of others."

Why do Christian workers talk poor? This is what missionaries confess to me:

- Public self-pity. Self-pity seeks to elicit a response from others, such as, "Oh, you poor thing. It must be so difficult to serve the Lord." Sniff. "Yes, it is."
- Poor talk is expected of missionaries. After all, don't poverty and spirituality go hand in hand? I've heard whining from missionaries who are extremely mature in other areas.
- Disguised financial appeal. "Maybe people will catch on to the fact that I need money." This is so common that missionaries do it subconsciously, but it's actually manipulation.
- Bad habit. Sometimes it is simply a bad habit inherited from parents or the missions environment.

What does poor talk communicate to our friends, particularly unbelievers? *Sympathy.* (Maybe!) Do they feel sorry for us? *Struggle.* If financial struggles continue year after year, our friends wonder if the hand of God is truly on us. Your donors don't like it when your finances are a constant struggle. They may begin to wonder if their investment in you is worthwhile.

I asked a missions-committee chairwoman of a large church, with a large missions budget, how she felt about missionary newsletters peppered with hints about finances. She knew exactly what I was talking about. She said, "It makes me feel bad, but I'm probably not going to do anything about it."

The apostle Paul had every opportunity to whine about money. Instead, he said, "Not that I speak from want; for I have learned to be content in whatever circumstances I am. I know how to get along with humble means, and I also know how to live in prosperity. . . . I can do all things through Him who strengthens me" (Philippians 4:11–13).

In our fourth year of marriage, Alma and I found ourselves in dire financial straits in Columbia, Missouri, where we were receiving missionary training. I didn't mind whining about it, hoping I would get a little sympathy. That's when Chuck Strittmatter, my supervisor, told me, "Scott, you may be poor, but don't talk like you're poor." What a helpful comment.

In the early days of The Navigators' ministry, whenever any of the staff missed a meal because of inadequate income, Navigator founder Dawson Trotman told them to "put a toothpick in your mouth anyway" in order not to draw attention to their low income.

In Luke 10:4, Jesus sent His disciples out two by two and told them not to take a "bag." The bag He had in mind was the knapsack commonly used by beggars. Anyone carrying such a bag would immediately be identified as a street beggar. Jesus clearly did not want His missionaries known as beggars. Furthermore, He told them not to move from "house to house" (Luke 4:7). Even today, beggars in Asia frequently have an itinerary, moving from house to house. But Jesus did not allow His laborers to think like beggars.

Alma and I have made four personal commitments regarding poor talk to ensure we don't impede the Gospel. First, we have decided we will not joke about money in such a way that it appears we want more. Even in low months, we don't "talk broke." In fact, we're not allowed to talk poor even to one another in the privacy of our own home.

Second, we do not hint about our financial needs. We don't ask for prayer for our finances. When we want people to give, we appeal to them face-to-face.

Third, we've stopped griping about high prices. Once, Alma came home from the grocery store, and we began going through the sacks, complaining about the high cost of string beans, soap, paper towels, and blueberry-muffin mix. We grumbled for 10 minutes about the U.S. economy and the President whom we blamed for the whole mess!

Finally, we caught ourselves. "What are we doing? We're whining in the presence of a sovereign God!"

Are prices too high? Probably. But that's not the issue. We will be frugal, we will not buy overpriced goods, and we will not whine.

Instead of drawing donors to us, poor talk scares them away.

Fourth, we have stopped comparing ourselves with others—including donors. Sometimes we become envious when we see the good fortune of "normal people." It's easy to think, "Wow! They sure have nice furniture. I wonder if we'll ever have a new sofa. Why can't we live like them?"

But it's even more subtle when we compare ourselves to other missionaries. Staff conferences used to be discouraging whenever I saw a fellow missionary with a new car or new clothes. But 2 Corinthians 10:12 helped me, "When they measure themselves by themselves . . . they are without understanding."

There is also another dimension to poor talk. Some missionaries think they must talk poor to keep their donors giving. They fear that donors will discover they're at 100 percent of budget and stop giving. No, they won't stop. They will be delighted! They'll also be surprised.

One of our donors once said, "Well, Scott, since you're up to budget, I guess we can quit giving, huh!"

I said, "Then we wouldn't be up to budget, would we?"

"Good point!" he said.

Because of the busyness of American donors, we may have to remind them to keep giving. No problem. And an honest answer to a question about our funding is appropriate. But when we hint instead of honestly appealing and when we whine instead of working, we are guilty of poor talk. Drop it!

9. Focus on the giver, not the money.

Paul set the standard for focusing on the giver in Philippians 4:17: "Not that I seek the gift itself, but I seek for the profit which increases to your account." Though grateful for their gift, Paul was not preoccupied with the Philippians' money but with the Philippians' spiritual progress.

If we view our donors as ATMs, we violate the example of Philippians 4. They have needs too. They must be treated with dignity and respect—not just so they will keep giving, but because they are worthy of it as fellow pilgrims.

A few months ago, I phoned Norman (not his real name), whom I hadn't seen since his college days. I had counseled with him half a dozen times in his junior and senior years regarding his career and spiritual journey. He and I had only seen each other once in 10 years, but he received our newsletters. Because I was passing through his town, I proposed we get together.

Norman seemed delighted with my call and agreed to meet. Then before I hung up, I asked if sometime during our get-together I could explain our financial situation and invite him to join our support team. Silence! What had I said? Finally, in a timid voice, he answered, "Sure." Cordial, but reserved. I couldn't get his hesitation out of my mind.

We met at one of those not-quite-so-fast-food places on a Sunday afternoon where you reload your own soft drinks. We had some wonderful fellowship and enjoyed catching up with one another.

After an hour, because our time was fleeting, I reminded him of my request on the phone to invite him to join our support team. But I added, "You hesitated on the phone, so I wonder how you're feeling about this."

Norman's eyes fell. He stared at his Coke in the red plastic cup. Then he looked up, "Sure, I'll pray about it, but . . ." He pursed his lips.

Awkwardly, I broke the silence. "Norman, this seems like a difficult issue for you; please tell me the background. And by the way, I'm not here to twist your arm."

"Yeah, I know. It's not you," he said, his eyes misty, his voice cracking.

Then Norman poured out his story about another missionary whom he felt had taken financial advantage of him 10 years earlier. "All he talked about was money. He was always hinting I should give more. I don't know; I guess it just left a bad taste in my mouth."

I'll spare you the details of our conversation, which switched from a fundraising appeal to a friend counseling a friend in great pain. Of course, there was more to the story than money.

As he thanked me for listening, I said, "Norman, I'm withdrawing my request for support. Obviously the time is not right. I'm more concerned with your spiritual progress and in helping you reconcile with this other missionary."

"Thank you," he said. "It's probably best."

As I drove away, I was grateful God enabled me to be more concerned for Norman's walk with Christ than my own need for support.

Another time, many years ago, I called an old friend to invite him to join our financial team. Tom was the first fruit of our ministry back in 1970. He had supported us for several years, then stopped, and we lost track of him.

As I dialed the phone, I prayed, asking for the Lord's leading to help me be sensitive and to minister to Tom in any way I could. Tom seemed overjoyed with the call. We laughed together as we remembered his coming to Christ "back in the day." Then we both recounted the major events in our lives since our last get-together. As I was about to launch the money question, I had the distinct impression from the Holy Spirit that I ought not appeal for support. Tom had no major problems in life. I was not afraid to ask. I just felt it was not the right time.

And so we enjoyed a pleasant, encouraging 30-minute visit. He repeatedly thanked me for taking the initiative to reestablish our friendship. But I hung up the phone without any new financial support and wondering if I'd just "chickened out."

Six months later, still needing support, I called again. This time I had freedom to ask, and Tom eagerly responded with a monthly pledge. To this day, I don't know why I sensed God's holding me back on the first call.

I'm glad I waited. But I didn't wait because of *fear*. I genuinely was more concerned about Tom's spiritual growth than I was with enlisting him as a donor.

But how do we keep our motivation clear? For example, a wealthy doctor comes into your circle of friends. You're tempted to pander to him, thinking that he might be in a position to help you financially. But you feel like a hypocrite putting a *Beginning with Christ* booklet in his front pocket while taking his wallet from his back pocket.

Our radar screens light up when we meet someone who is wealthy and generous. Missionaries who normally are low-key, shy, or introverted suddenly become warm, effusive extroverts with "big money" people—all because they need donors!

Proverbs 19:6 states a truth about human nature, "Many will entreat the favor of a generous man, and every man is a friend to him who gives gifts." This truth is not limited to missionaries, by the way!

Here's how I deal with the conflict between wanting a donor's financial support and wanting the best for him or her. First, I admit to myself that I want this person's money. I used to deny that money was even remotely motivating me to walk across the room to meet him and possibly become his best friend and spiritual mentor!

People give to accomplish a task—not because they feel sorry for you. And keep your feet off the furniture!

Now I admit it. "Lord, I want his financial support, and I want it bad!" Honesty reduces pressure.

Second, I decide to do what is right for that individual, whether I get any money or not. I pray, "Lord, I'd love for this person to support our ministry, but I want what's best for him even more. Please guide me."

I have a rhyme that helps me as I walk up to a prospective giver's house: "I put my hand upon their door, I quote Philippians 2:3 and 4." ("Let nothing be done through strife or vainglory; but in lowliness of mind let each esteem other better than themselves. Look not every man on his own things, but every man also on the things of others" in the King James version.)

Third, I determine not to hint. People pick up on money signals, and it repels them. It's not attractive.

If you are desperately behind in your funding, admit to yourself you want to meet with a prospective donor because of money. No harm there. At least you're authentic. Go ahead and set an appointment, but tell him exactly why you want to meet. Don't say it's for "fellowship" if you intend to roll the money grenade across the table. It's OK to invite a newcomer to support you, just don't trick him into it.

By the way, your motivation will never be 100 percent perfect in any issue of life. Jeremiah 17:9 (KJV) says, "The heart is deceitful above all things, and desperately wicked." It doesn't add, "except in the case of missionaries doing fundraising!"

If you're planning to wait until your motivation is 100 percent perfect before you ask for support, you'll not raise much support—nor share your faith, nor sing in the church choir.

10. Emphasize the greatness of your vision, not the greatness of your need.

In a Peanuts cartoon, Linus sits in a beanbag chair, staring at the TV. The announcer says, "This program needs your support." In the second frame, the announcer says, "We need your donations." Linus is still sitting there, staring. In the third frame, the announcer pleads, "If we don't hear from you, we'll have to go off the air." In the final frame, Linus finally speaks. "So long!" he says.

Too often, missionaries—like this TV announcer—view fundraising as the art of pleading for money more and more creatively. Let's change that distorted view of raising support by following Paul's model in Romans 15:

- Paul's dazzling vision (15:20)
- Paul's promise (15:21)
- Paul's appeal (15:24)
- Paul's relationships (15:24)

Paul writes in Romans 15:20: "And thus I aspired to preach the gospel, not where Christ was already named, that I might not build upon another man's foundation."

This is Paul's dazzling vision: "To preach where Christ is not named." That's an exciting ministry goal, isn't it? Not a bad motto for a church or Christian organization.

When I say "dazzling vision," I'm not talking about sensationalism or superficial hype. I'm referring to your genuine personal ministry dream. It is dazzling because you're deeply passionate about it. Too many missionaries forget this and present their need instead of their vision. Share your dazzling vision, the calling you have given your life to. Fundraising is inviting people to join you in this calling, not to buy your groceries.

As you describe your vision, avoid the tendency to engage in missiological talk—describing your specific methods. Sure, you need a little of that, but most of the time the only ones interested in discussing methodology are your own staff and the vice president of missions. Prospective donors want to know if you are changing lives. To quote my friend Chip Battle: "People don't invest in methodology. They invest in people."

Donors are not as enthralled with missiological strategy as you may be. Keep your presentations simple and interesting.

In Romans 15:21, Paul quotes the foundation behind his vision—a promise from God. Why does he strive to accomplish his vision? Because of an Old Testament passage that has obviously moved him deeply. "For what had not been told them they will see, and what they had not heard they will understand" (Isaiah 52:15).

A scriptural foundation or promise for your vision will give you confidence and keep you from veering off course. Reviewing my personal Scripture promises and motivating life verses keeps me focused. In fact, I've made it a habit that whenever I board an airplane, I spend the first 20 minutes of the flight praying over my life goals and promises.

Romans 15:24 says, "Whenever I go to Spain—for I hope to see you in passing, and to be helped on my way there by you."

This is Paul's appeal—"To be helped on my way there by you." Paul is not merely asking for warm, fuzzy encouragement. The Greek word used here is *propempo*, which means "practical assistance." Although the phrase "helped on my way" may appear indirect today, the Romans would have understood clearly. Paul tells them he is hoping they will outfit him for his mission to Spain, perhaps in the form of food, provisions, money, or even people to travel with him. The customs of the time dictated that you would never let a traveling rabbi pass through your town without significantly helping him on his journey.

But let's not forget the last phrase of Romans 15:24, "When I have first enjoyed your company for awhile." Paul's relationships! Paul wanted to hang around and visit, enjoying these people and not just hurrying off with their money!

To review, first, Paul names his dazzling vision, then he gives the underlying biblical promise, then he asks for the Romans' assistance. Finally, we see Paul's commitment to a relationship with his giving partners. Like Paul, we shouldn't merely explain our need. Go with (1) your dazzling vision, (2) a scriptural explanation that undergirds your burden for ministry, (3) an opportunity to join you, and (4) a commitment to relationship. Your vision—not your financial need—must be your flagship.

Most people want to give to a ministry that is going somewhere. It doesn't have to be spectacular or even humanly successful, but it does have to have God's fingerprints all over it. Invite people to give to God's most exciting work: your ministry!

Remember that just explaining your mission organization is not enough. Your mission agency is the background; you are center stage. Why? Because people want to give to people, not an impersonal organization. Tell them about your specific role.

Professional fundraising consultants are negative on this idea because they say it reduces giving to the organization. They argue that when a missionary leaves the organization, the donations supporting that individual missionary stop. They argue that if the missionary raises up contributors to the organization, those gifts will continue even after the missionary leaves.

There's truth to that argument, but it's flawed. First, there is no guarantee that the contributors will bond well with the organization. Second, no matter what perception they have of the organization, many donors are more loyal to their missionary friend than they are to the mission agency. People want to give to people. Baby boomers and post-moderns, in particular, want to know where their gifts are going.

For example, a missionary couple called on us a few years ago to explain their ministry in Africa and to ask for support. They described the ministry only in organizational terms without personalizing their presentation. They didn't even talk about their personal spiritual journeys. No personal war stories, no personal pictures, no personal illustrations. It was all institutional.

Had we "bonded" with this couple, we might have been tempted to give. But they missed a wonderful opportunity to elicit our personal friendship, and so we didn't pledge.

You can be personal and still bond your donors with your agency. It's not either/or. The more bonds a donor has with you and your agency, the better. Let's do both! But an organizational bond alone will not maximize long-term giving, friendship, or donor satisfaction.

Remember that your fundraising presentation is a framework upon which you hang your dazzling vision. Make it breathe by filling in war stories and pictures. You can never explain your ministry fully, but you can illustrate it! Illustrations help people see what you're trying to accomplish. And be sure to connect your vision to your agency so you are not perceived as a "lone ranger"!

One comment about enthusiasm. A missionary wondered out loud to me one day if his limited success in fundraising was because of his quiet nature. "Do I have a tendency to be a little too low-key?" he asked me, quietly and with no energy in his voice. Enough said.

Many dedicated, godly missionaries returning from overseas need to use more energy when talking to Americans. Being quiet and low-key is important in Asia or Africa. Unfortunately, in America, it is often interpreted as a lack of conviction.

I'm not talking about "hype." I'm not suggesting you buy a plaid sport coat and imitate obnoxious TV personalities. I'm talking about genuine zeal and enthusiasm for your personal vision. Don't change your personality; any personality type can show enthusiasm. To communicate your personal "dazzling vision," you must be genuinely zealous. Ralph Waldo Emerson said it well: "Nothing great was ever accomplished without enthusiasm."

Besides being enthusiastic, you must also be able to articulate your vision clearly.

I once joined a missionary for an in-home appeal to old friends of his. They had a great time of fellowship and getting reacquainted. This older couple really liked Bob, but they kept talking voluminously about their kids, their church, their retirement—all somewhat interesting, and we tried to listen attentively.

Finally, the wife leaned over, patted her husband on the knee, and said, "Now, dear! These young men have not come here tonight to hear us ramble on so."

"You're right," he said. Then he backed up in his chair, looked up at Bob, and said, "Enough about us. Tell me, what is it we need to know about your ministry?"

What an open door for Bob to explain his dazzling vision! "Here it comes," I thought, as both Bob and I straightened up in our overstuffed chairs. "Bob will mesmerize them with his dream!"

And so Bob began, "Well, uh, we are hoping to exegete the city and develop, uh, you know, uh, discipling units . . . uh . . . We're actually trying to facilitate an outreach to the E-3 segment . . . uh, in cooperation with . . ."

Bob fumbled the ball. He didn't have his first sentence prepared, nor did he give an interesting illustration. After a few minutes of his rambling, the couple started talking about themselves again. An opportunity squandered.

Ask yourself: (1) What is your "dazzling vision"? (2) Are you genuinely excited about it?

(3) Can you articulate it in an interesting way?

According to the *Chronicle of Philanthropy,* more than 1.5 million organizations are registered as 501(c)(3) charities in the United States. One million of these are religious charities. Don't be naïve. You have competition. Your giving prospects have a lot of options. How is your message unique? Why would a giver want to support you more than the other 999,999 other organizations? Remember, lead with your mission, not the money.

Adopting these 10 crucial attitudes will relieve fundraising pressure. Most missionaries who struggle emotionally with raising support do so not because of their people skills or technique, but because of unresolved issues of attitude. Review these attitudes now; check one or two about which you feel the Lord is speaking to you. Bring it to Him in your prayer time for the next few days.

Now, before we move on to developing a strategy, we must address 11 important issues of conscience to see how the Bible answers them.

Attitudes to Check

1. Do I consider God the source, or am I trying to "solicit" horizontally?

2. Do I pray specifically every day about my funding, or am I counting on my own efforts as revealed by my lack of prayer?

3. Am I clear and confident about doing "my job," or am I hoping God will do it for me?

4. Is the Bible my standard for fundraising behavior, or am I looking to "what works"?

5. Do I believe fundraising can be a spiritual ministry, or do I consider it a worldly activity I've got to do?

6. Do I believe I have a "right" to be supported, or do I abuse my right by being "pushy"?

7. Do I expect to raise 100 percent of my budget, or am I merely trying to "get by"?

8. Do I honestly explain my finances, or do I "talk poor" or whine about money?

9. Is my focus on the givers and their needs, or am I more interested in having my own needs met?

10. Do I radiate dazzling vision from God with a biblical promise underlying it, or am I just presenting my needs?

Chapter Four
QUESTIONS OF CONSCIENCE
Understanding the Biblical Basis for Raising Support

Everyone has opinions about "Christian fundraising"—especially about what's wrong with it! And there's plenty wrong with it. You have opinions too. But for now, I'm going to ask you to leave your opinions and emotions behind and come with me to the Bible to objectively discover what God's Word says about fundraising.

Missionaries often feel they must sear their consciences if they are to actively raise support. They are bothered by issues such as:

- Is it OK to *ask* for support? I feel more comfortable if the other person brings it up.
- Can I ask for my *own* support? I feel comfortable raising money for someone else but not for myself.
- What if the people I'm asking are poorer than I am? I feel guilty taking their money.
- Why doesn't the money come in miraculously like it did for legendary missionaries George Mueller or Hudson Taylor? Do I have enough faith?
- What about asking nonbelievers for support?
- What if someone already gives heavily to other ministries? I feel guilty asking for more.
- What about support from family members? Will I become my extended family's "charity case"?
- How can I ask people to support me when I have a large savings account?
- What about asking strangers for support? Shouldn't I minister to people before asking? Shouldn't money follow ministry?

Unanswered, these questions will nag at you like a disconnected muffler scraping along the highway—noisy, rattling, sending out sparks.

Unfortunately, most mission manuals are long on technique but give only a page or two on biblical answers to fundraising conscience issues. To free your conscience, you need more than a quick perusal of the missions manual. You'll need to study the Scriptures, struggling with your emotions and conscience. That way your convictions on fundraising will be biblically rooted. You no longer will be a prisoner of your own biases—or your parents' biases, your church's biases, or worse yet, society's biases.

Now it's time to put this book aside and do the Bible study in the Appendix. You see, I don't want you to simply adopt my beliefs—as profound as they may be! Start with the joy of discovering for yourself.

You may be tempted to bypass the Bible study and simply scan this book looking for quick answers. However, missionaries who grab fundraising conclusions without developing a biblical value system are in danger of becoming like a Valentine's box without the chocolates.

Think you don't have enough time? Here are two suggestions. Add this study to your daily devotions. Meditate on and pray over the verses. Second, think of this study as a professional development class. Set up a 50-minute period in your schedule and "go to class" each day for a week. You won't regret investing 6 to 10 hours in the Bible. It's more important than anything else I could tell you, and it will pay off with peace and new confidence.

So take some time now to do your own Bible study and pick up right back here!

Here are 11 conscience issues with insights from my study time. How do they compare with your understanding of the Scriptures?

1. What right do I have to be supported by others?

Unfortunately, many missionaries think of themselves as "charity cases," not earning an honest living. One father asked his missionary son, "When are you going to get a real job?" That hurts!

Some Christians equate fundraising with begging. One well-known Christian writer unknowingly feeds this false teaching by saying, "Lois and I almost did not come to the mission field. We couldn't bring ourselves to *beg* for support." Another dedicated African-American missionary said, "Our lifestyle was a peculiar mixture of prayer, faith, action, communication, and begging."

Fundraising is *not* begging!

An easy tip-off that a missionary doesn't feel legitimate is the apologetic nature of his or her appeals—written or in person. Apologetic backpedaling is the natural result of a shallow biblical understanding of fundraising and maybe even the missionary's sense of "call." Being apologetic has no place in Christian fundraising.

Many missionaries opt to support themselves through an outside job (tentmaking)—not because they prefer tentmaking, but because they can't stomach raising support.

A former missionary named Dorothy told one of our team members that she was glad she didn't have to raise personal support. She said she was raised on the premise that a workman is worthy of his support and "asking for money is like asking for a handout." She went on to say, "I don't think it's a matter of pride but of old-fashioned *inner feelings.*"

Inner feelings. Hmmm. Of course it is inner feelings. But who says my inner feelings are wise or biblical? My inner feelings last Saturday told me not to clean the garage. My inner feelings told me to take a second piece of chocolate cake at the office party. My inner feelings told me to indulge in an extremely R-rated HBO movie during my last hotel stay. When I was a new believer in Christ, my inner feelings told me I was unsaved every time I sinned.

We know our inner feelings should not lead us in other areas of our walks with Christ, so why do we let them dictate our behavior when it comes to fundraising and money? As with other areas of our lives, let's look to the Bible, not our inner feelings, to determine our values and behavior.

Insights from Scripture

The Bible shows that missionaries called to full-time service have the right to be supported because of:

- The example of the Levites
- The example of Jesus
- The teaching of Jesus
- The example of Paul
- The teaching of Paul

The Example of the Levites (Numbers 18:24)

"For the tithe of the sons of Israel, which they offer as an offering to the LORD, I have given to the Levites for an inheritance."

As one of Jacob's 12 sons, Levi, along with his 11 brothers, was entitled to receive an allotment of real estate in the Promised Land. But if you check the map in the back of your Bible, usually titled "Canaan as Divided Among the 12 Tribes," you'll not find Levi's name.

His allotment was given to one of Joseph's sons, and in place of land, he received a promise of the tithe. *Ma'aser,* the Hebrew word for tithe, means one-tenth.

Levi's offspring did not have a choice. They were born into this "calling." One tribe was selected to serve the other 11 tribes by administrating the sacrifices, recording and teaching the law, and attending to the duties of the Tabernacle.

Today, of course, the Levitical calling is not the same. As Christians, redeemed by Christ's once-

A salaried job can seem more legitimate than being on support, but the Scriptures say full-time ministry is a legitimate calling.

for-all sacrifice, we do not require a special family of Levi's descendants to administer sacrifices on our behalf. However, the model—one tribe not permitted to earn a "normal living" but to serve others full-time—is still a model today.

Paul thought so. In 1 Corinthians 9:13, he defends being supported by the Gospel: "Do you not know that those who perform sacred services eat the food of the temple, and those who attend regularly to the altar have their share with the altar?"

No land for Levi! Levi's allotment was the promise of a tithe.

Paul used the Levitical example to show that a missionary has the right to receive support. However, we must be careful not to take the Levitical example too far. They also were to retire at age 50!

Are you a modern-day Levite? In terms of New Testament theology, no. The sacrificial system is over. But if God has called you to full-time vocational ministry, then yes! Just as He did for the Levites, God will provide for you. In fact, I believe God already has provided for you. When God selected the Levites for special service, He already had the tithe in mind. Can you imagine God calling the Levites and then puzzling over how to provide for them? Similarly, your funding is there; you simply need to discover where and who and how!

The Example of Jesus (Luke 8:2–3)

"Mary who was called Magdalene, from whom seven demons had gone out, and Joanna the wife of Chuza, Herod's steward, and Susanna, and many others who were contributing to their support out of their private means."

Only three women are named here as supporting Jesus, but *"many others"* also contributed. And they didn't just contribute to Jesus but to the whole group. "Their support" means they supported the Twelve also.

If it were wrong to be supported by the personal gifts of others, Jesus Christ would not have allowed it in His own ministry. Jesus was not underwritten by a religious body, nor did He work an outside job once He began His ministry. He allowed Himself and His team to be supported by the gifts of a large group of followers. Some even gave sacrificially, traveling with Jesus' band from Galilee to Jerusalem, 60 miles from home (Mark 15:41).

Could not the One who turned water into wine have supported Himself? Could not the One who multiplied two fish and five loaves into enough food for 5,000 have supported Himself? If anyone could have been self-supporting, it was Jesus Christ. Yet He purposely chose to live by the gifts of "many others."

I spoke to a department manager at a mission-agency office about helping one of her workers raise personal support. "Oh, we don't do it that way!" she replied piously. No one in her department would ever "stoop" to receiving personal support. Too bad. Jesus did. Was He wrong?

For most people, it is humbling to be dependent on others. But if the One who truly didn't need to be dependent on others chose to freely, then you and I must be willing too. Besides, our dependence goes beyond others to God. He's the source.

The Teaching of Jesus (Matthew 10:9–10)

"Do not acquire gold, or silver, or copper for your money belts; or a bag for your journey, or even two tunics, or sandals, or a staff; for the worker is worthy of his support."

Jesus added validity to the concept of fundraising through His teaching. Jesus wanted the Twelve to be supported by others on this ministry trip.

If we had only this event of Jesus sending out the Twelve without the *teaching*—"the worker is worthy of his support"—it could be viewed as a one-time occurrence, not to be repeated. But Jesus repeats it again in Luke 10:7 when He sends out the 70. Paul paraphrases it in 1 Corinthians 9:14 and quotes it directly in 1 Timothy 5:18. "The worker is worthy of his support" is a timeless principle, reaffirmed throughout Scripture.

The Example of Paul (Acts 18:4–5)

"He [Paul] was reasoning in the synagogue every Sabbath and trying to persuade Jews and Greeks. But when Silas and Timothy came down from Macedonia, Paul began devoting himself completely to the word."

What does "completely to the word" mean? Did Paul suddenly become more dedicated? No, it's clear that he stopped making tents and started full-time preaching. It's possible Silas and Timothy brought living-expense money or worked themselves so Paul could preach.

Also, in Philippians 4:14, Paul compliments the Philippians for giving. He says, "You have done well to share with me." In verse 16, he affirms them for having given "more than once." If it were wrong to be supported, Paul would not have allowed others to help him. Instead, he warmly endorses their gifts.

The Teaching of Paul (1 Corinthians 9:1–18)

"Do we not have a right to eat and drink [at the expense of the churches]?" (1 Corinthians 9:4, Amplified).

Readers sometimes take this verse to mean simply "the right to eat and drink." But everyone can claim that right. Paul is asking, "Don't we missionaries have the right to eat and drink at the expense of the church?" In other words, "Who pays for the food and drink?"

In verse 6 (Amplified), Paul asks even more bluntly, "Or is it only Barnabas and I who have no right to refrain from doing manual labor for a livelihood [in order to go about the work of the ministry]?" Must Barnabas and I support *ourselves*? he asks. That's the issue. And it's the same issue we are addressing here. Aren't you glad Paul dealt with it first?

In verses 7–18, he gives the answer in five "Ls."

Logic—(Verse 7) Does a soldier serve at his own expense? Does a farmer plant a vineyard and not eat the fruit? Or tend a flock and not use the milk? Of course not! Common-sense logic teaches that.

Law—(Verses 8–10) Paul quotes Deuteronomy 25:4, "You shall not muzzle the ox while he is threshing." Even the ox benefits from his work, but Paul goes further by suggesting Deuteronomy 25:4 was given for our sake. "Yes, for our sake it was written" (1 Corinthians 9:10). The lesson is for us—not oxen. Or, as Martin Luther wryly commented, "Can oxen read?"

Leadership Spiritually—(Verse 11) Paul states a principle, "If we sowed spiritual things in you, is it too much if we should reap material things from you?" This idea is repeated in Galatians 6:6 and Romans 15:27, and it provides sound rationale for believers to support their spiritual leaders.

Paul's final two "Ls" are arguments we reviewed a few pages back.

Levites—(Verse 13) Those who attend the altar share the food of the altar.

Lord—(Verse 14) To cap his argument, Paul paraphrases Jesus' principle in Matthew 10 and Luke 10, "So also the Lord directed those who proclaim the gospel to get their living from the gospel."

Though forthright about asking, Paul wasn't pushy or manipulative about money. Don't trap donors!

But notice Paul's warning in verses 12 and 15–18. Paul reminds the Corinthians, "We do not demand this right over you in order not to hinder the gospel." Paul is not pushy about money. He is going to preach whether he receives support or not. He does not demand his "right," and neither should we.

It's reassuring to realize Paul faced the same issue we are tackling: Is it OK to receive support to minister the Gospel? First Corinthians 9:1–18 answers a resounding "Yes!" But it also gives a stern warning: "Don't demand your right or you may hinder the Gospel."

2. I feel worldly when I ask for support; I wish it would just "come in." Is it OK to ask?

One missionary told me, "I know I have a right to receive support; I just don't want to ask for it."

Asking, we think, puts us in the same camp as slick-haired TV evangelists or panhandlers at a busy intersection. We prefer to distance ourselves from these "askers."

One frustrated missionary told me her organization went part way with the guideline of "full disclosure but no appeal." She could tell donors how much she needed but could not "close"— ask for a decision. On the verge of tears, she described how she never knew how much to say.

OK, what does the Bible say about asking for support? First, what Scripture prohibits asking for support? None I know of. Some argue that because we have no record of Jesus asking for support, we shouldn't either. Of course, we also have no record of Jesus blowing His nose or piercing His ear.

Second, several Scriptures contain specific examples of appeals for oneself. But we may not notice them unless we understand the hospitality culture of the Middle East.

In the Middle East, when guests show up at a home, the hosts are obligated to take them in. In Jesus' day, custom dictated that a host take in a traveling rabbi for up to three days and supply him with what he needed for his journey. In the Middle East, a traveler showing up at your door is an indirect appeal for lodging, provision, and help. No words are necessary.

Knowing this hospitality culture helps us understand Matthew 10:11 where Jesus sent out the Twelve, saying, "Into whatever city or village you enter, inquire who is worthy in it; and abide there until you go away." Showing up at the door is tantamount to an appeal.

Notice this hospitality custom working also in Romans 15:24. After Paul has explained his dazzling vision of reaching Spain, he says, "I hope . . . to be helped on my way there by you." Remember from Chapter 3 that the Greek word is *propempo,* meaning "practical assistance." Vine, in his *Dictionary of New Testament Words,* concludes that the help Paul seeks is "in the sense of fitting him out with the requisites of his trip."

The Middle Eastern custom of accompanying the traveler a few miles down the road is also a possibility, but

Don't let your "theological feelings" excuse you from being a responsible provider.

Paul intends more than that. He makes the same comment in 2 Corinthians 1:16, "And by you to be helped [*propempo*] on my journey to Judea." *Propempo* is not merely encouragement. In that culture, it would be clearly understood as an appeal for practical assistance.

We see another example of solicitation when God tells Elijah to go to the widow to seek provision (1 Kings 17).

Obviously, the intent of these three examples is not to teach fundraising, but they establish a strong example that inviting others to support you is not a biblical no-no.

Third, you are not asking for yourself, but for the work of the Kingdom. I never ask people to give to me. That kind of giving is horizontal and makes me feel like a charity case. I raise support for the mission of God, of which I happen to be a part. Of course, their money eventually comes to me. But knowing donors give to God takes the emotion out of asking, and I'll sometimes remind donors that they are giving to God according to Philippians 4:18—"an acceptable sacrifice, well-pleasing to God."

Finally, mission agencies have no "every-Sunday collection device." Have you ever seen a highway sign saying, "Missionary collection station, one mile"? Have you ever Googled "missionary collection" hoping to find a missionary to support? In churches, the offering plate is passed Sunday morning, Sunday night, Wednesday night. People accept that as a legitimate appeal.

But mission agencies have no weekly collection device. So they develop their own in the form of mail appeals, fundraising banquets, telephone solicitations, and personal meetings. Some are effective; some are not. Some honor Christ, some do not. In themselves, these appeals are simply collection vehicles.

Which collection vehicle will you use? People need to know how they can support you. We are on firm biblical ground in making appeals, as long as we are not demanding or manipulative but are humble and looking to God.

But what about famous missionary George Mueller and his method of "telling only God"? That concept lives on today in statements like: "It feels better to me not to ask but only to pray."

A little history is helpful here. George Mueller lived in Bristol, England, in the late 1800s and raised thousands of dollars for his orphanage work—without making a single appeal. To use his words, he "relied on God alone." His life was filled with story after story of miraculous provision.

His method has been copied by others, and it was the intent of some parachurch founders to follow his "no-ask" example. For instance, in the early days of The Navigators, staff members were told to change the subject when people inquired about finances.

Why did Mueller hold this view? Before he was converted, Mueller was materialistic and manipulative. As a child in Germany, he stole money from his father's desk. His father had to lay an elaborate trap just to catch him. As a young man, Mueller checked into hotels wearing expensive clothes to give the impression he was well-off. Then he would duck out without paying. Later, miraculously, he became a believer in Christ and moved to England where he became a pastor.

As a pastor, he was dissatisfied with the custom of pew rents. The churches of his day were financed not by freewill giving but by renting or selling pews to parishioners, with the higher priced ones near the front. Mueller believed this violated the partiality teaching in James 2, and he requested a chest be placed at the rear of the church for freewill gifts.

This background helps us understand why Mueller developed his philosophy of telling financial needs to no one but God.

But there's another side to the story. Although Mueller never made appeals, he and his followers explained answers to financial prayers before hundreds of people in public speeches. He told the stories to give glory to God; however, people hearing these stories found out how *they* could give. The need was disclosed in the recounting. Mueller also sent official annual reports of the orphanage finances. Although Mueller made no "appeals," he did legitimately reveal needs.

Mueller's practice of informing but not appealing is only one method of fundraising. And it is not necessarily more spiritual than others. I suspect many missionaries are attracted to the "Mueller method" because it means they won't have to risk the embarrassment of rejection. Or maybe it helps them "feel more spiritual." But remember, the Bible's teaching on funding is broad—broader than one man's personal preference.

3. I find it easy to raise money for others but not for myself.

A veteran missionary was struggling to reestablish his donor base after years of being funded by the home office. His wife explained, "He has no problem raising money for the mission or other staff, but he feels funny asking for himself."

Most missionaries struggle with this, including me. Perhaps raising support for others makes us feel more in line with the biblical mandate to care for others rather than looking out for number one.

Recruiting support for others is certainly biblical. Paul raised support from the Corinthian and Macedonian churches on behalf of the saints at Jerusalem. John, the apostle, encouraged Gaius to send the traveling missionaries "on their way in a manner worthy of God" (3 John 6).

In 1889, Samuel Zwemer and James Cantine launched the American Arabian Mission. To raise money, Zwemer traversed 4,000 miles west of the Ohio River campaigning for Cantine, while Cantine traveled in the East campaigning for Zwemer. But why? Were they struggling with this same issue?

Perhaps you hesitate to raise money for your own ministry because you feel pressure to produce results, to meet donors' expectations. If you raise funds for the mission in general or for another missionary, you may not feel so "accountable." Or you might feel pressure to *deserve* your donor gifts. That's a signal you may be viewing fundraising horizontally. When Paul calls the Philippians' gift a "fragrant aroma, well-pleasing to God" (Philippians 4:18), we see that Christian giving is not horizontal but vertical. Step outside yourself and raise money for the Kingdom, in that part of the vineyard where you happen to serve!

Do you honestly believe your ministry is significant?

I remember hearing my colleagues at missionary retreats give glowing reports of dozens of conversions, booming Bible studies, and hundreds of seekers at meetings. By contrast, I would reflect on the meager attendance at my meetings in small dormitory rooms—with empty seats! It was depressing, and I wondered if my small ministry was worthy of support.

But ministries happen in growth stages. And each one is blessed differently by God. Your ministry is significant no matter what stage it's in. I don't care if it's a college Bible study in Platteville, Wisconsin, power lunch seminars in New York City, or as a behind-the-scenes missions secretary in Colorado Springs. Your ministry is significant, not because you're talented or successful, but because it is God's calling for you. There are no little people; there are no little places in God's vineyard.

We're reminded in 1 Corinthians 12:21, "The eye cannot say to the hand, 'I have no need of you.' "

Get excited about the important work God has called you to, and stop comparing yourself with others.

But what if you are questioning your calling?

When you are perplexed about your vision, raising support is an emotional battle. If that's your situation, stop raising support immediately and spend a couple of days alone with the Lord to review His leading. Also, discuss it with your spouse (if married) and a few trusted friends. Reexamine your life verses, your life goals, your reasons for entering Christian service in the first place.

But heed this warning: Don't let your fundraising dilemma negate your calling. As you ponder your life aims and vision for ministry, leave funding out of it. Funding the vision God has given you is a second question. Keep it separate from your calling struggle.

If you're confused about your future, you're in good company. Even the great apostle Paul could not definitively describe his future ministry plans. In 1 Corinthians 16:6, he says, "And *perhaps* I shall stay with you, or even spend the winter, that you may send me on my way [*propempo*] wherever I may go."

"Perhaps," Paul? Yet he asked the Corinthians to "send him on his way," even though he was uncertain about his ministry plans.

Tell people what part of your calling you *are* sure about. Then ask them to help, even though (like Paul) you don't know the specific future details.

To further examine your calling and ministry vision, work through the Bible study on calling in the Appendix of this book.

Back to asking for support for others. Let's look at it from the donor's perspective. By whom does the donor prefer to be asked?

Most Western donors prefer that you invite them directly, not through a third party. Their money ultimately is going to you—they need to hear the appeal from you, not your proxy. Furthermore, no one else will have a heart for your ministry as you do. No one can bring the passion like you. Donors need to see that.

When you send a third party, the bonding and friendship take place between the donor and the third party. Don't you want that bonding? The pledge will continue longer if they bond with you.

I once did some phoning to ask for monthly support on behalf of a missionary friend. It didn't go very well. One donor asked, "Why can't Joe come talk to me directly?"

"He's pretty busy," I stammered.

Silence.

Then it registered—too busy for the donor. Shameful.

Penny Thomas, a colleague of mine, was doing third-party phoning to ask for monthly support for a missionary named Bob.

A donor asked, "Why do you have to phone on Bob's behalf? Why won't Bob phone me directly?"

Penny responded without hesitation, "Cuz he's chicken."

"He is, isn't he!" said the donor. "Give me his phone number, Penny. I'm going to call him and talk about this issue right now!"

Penny told the truth. Are we sending third-party proxies because we're "chicken"?

There is one exception, however. In Asian cultures, third-party solicitations seem to be well accepted. My Asian missionary friends tell me that culturally many Asians are conditioned to say yes to any appeal in order to keep the asker from "losing face." A "no" would embarrass the asker and make the relationship potentially awkward. So Asian missionaries find third-party asks a better fit in their culture. I strongly affirm that.

In summary, although we see plenty of biblical evidence for sending a third-party emissary and it's the best scenario in certain cultures, don't do it just because you're chicken!

4. What about tentmaking? Isn't that the biblical model? Wouldn't it be simpler if missionaries worked part-time for income instead of raising funds?

In some countries, especially those that do not permit missionary visas, *authentic* tentmaking is the only avenue for ministry. And Paul modeled that for us—but only three times.

The first was in Thessalonica. Why there? Acts 17 tells us it was a young church hastily founded. Scholars say Paul was there only three to six months. Also, many Greeks were converted there, making it a cross-cultural ministry for Paul. Obviously, a Jew wouldn't ask new Gentile believers for support.

Later, the Thessalonian church became lazy, waiting around in excited idleness for the Lord to return. Paul chose to model physical labor for the good of the church. He says in 2 Thessalonians 3:8–9: "With labor and hardship we kept working night and day so that we might not be a burden to any of you; not because we do not have the right to this, but in order to offer ourselves as a model."

So Paul had good reasons for not accepting support at Thessalonica: It was a young, cross-cultural church with a tendency toward laziness.

Second, Paul took no money from the Corinthians. Why not? Look at the background. Even a casual reading of 1 and 2 Corinthians reveals a church with a party spirit, sexual controversy, divisions over what to eat, and a movement to discredit Paul, the church's founder! Corinth had too many problems! To receive money from Corinth would only add to the crusade to oust Paul.

But in 2 Corinthians 12:13, Paul says, "For in what respect were you treated as inferior to the rest of the churches, except that I myself did not become a burden to you?"

Although Paul may be speaking facetiously, it sounds as if he would have preferred support from Corinth but because of their many problems, he would not take it. By the way, because of this example, I do not appeal to extremely problematic or emotionally distraught people.

Often missionaries are tempted to seek "normal" employment instead of launching fundraising appointments.

The third place Paul made tents was Ephesus, which was neither a young church nor a problem church. Acts 20:33–34 reads, "I have coveted no one's silver or gold or clothes. . . . These hands ministered to my own needs and to the men who were with me." Why would he hesitate to receive money from Ephesus?

Prior to Paul, religion at Ephesus was centered on Diana of the Ephesians. Silversmiths and other craftsmen made a living selling idols of Diana. But as Ephesians converted to Christ, they stopped buying Diana idols. Could it be that the silversmiths felt Paul was trying to put them out of business? If Paul had received money, he might be accused of using the Gospel for profit—putting the silversmiths out of business and himself in business.

In summary, tentmaking was *not* Paul's main model of funding. He both made tents and received support, depending on how it would affect the progress of the Gospel.

And that's a position you and I can take. We must be willing to do either, depending on how it will affect the progress of the Gospel. I advise missionaries to ask themselves: "Is tentmaking the best way to gain access to this culture, or can I get access anyway?" As ministries grow, the need for a few focused, full-time laborers increases.

5. Is it OK to appeal to nonbelievers?

Professional fund-raisers advocate asking everyone. But giving is a touchy issue among nonbelievers—that's often their excuse for staying away from church. Furthermore, even if nonbelievers are willing, should they be invited to support the work of God?

First, this question presupposes we can distinguish between Christians and non-Christians. In my early days as a missionary, I was an "expert" at that! But over the years, I've noticed that some who were pillars in the faith 20 years ago have cooled down. And friends who years ago struggled now have a strong Christian testimony. Only the Lord knows for sure whose are His, and He doesn't tell me.

If only "true" Christians may be appealed to, then we have the impossible role of inquisitor—making sure our prospective givers are believers.

For example, if you currently have donors, do you know for sure they're all believers? How do you know? What about nondonors on your mailing list? Because you are not the Judge of the universe, it is likely that you could unknowingly appeal to nonbelievers, particularly in a mass mailing.

If it is wrong to appeal to nonbelievers, you must make a judgment call on every person on your mailing list. Furthermore, churches would have to pass the plate only to believers, forcing the ushers to whisper, "Excuse me, could you skip the gentleman with the Harley tattoo? He looks unsaved." And the implications for a Christian agency with 500,000-piece mailings are staggering.

Appealing to nonbelievers is impossible to avoid. Wheat and weeds look alike until harvest.

Second, the Scriptures give examples of nonbelievers receiving appeals from God's servants. The widow in 1 Kings 17:9 was a

Don't assume your funding candidate will be "hard." Be yourself! Assume people *like* you!

non-Jew living in Sidon, an area where pagan deities were worshiped. In verse 18, after her son became deathly ill, she accused Elijah the prophet of coming "to bring my iniquity to remembrance." Yet it was to this "pagan" widow that Elijah appealed for water and food—her last meal (verse 12).

Similarly, Nehemiah appealed to a pagan Persian king, Artaxerxes Longimanus, for timber to rebuild the gates of Jerusalem.

These examples show that two godly leaders appealed to nonbelievers in order to further God's purposes.

What about the Israelites asking the Egyptians for spoil the night they left Egypt? Although some Christian leaders consider that a proof for the validity of asking nonbelievers, I cannot. Under the circumstances, the Egyptians could hardly have said no—unless they wanted plague number 11!

Third, prohibiting a nonbeliever from giving might inhibit his or her pursuit of God. In Acts 10:4, Cornelius, a seeker of truth, gave alms that "ascended as a memorial before God." Perhaps alms were his way of demonstrating his search for God. Perhaps giving helped draw him nearer to God.

As nonbelievers seek God, many will include their pocketbooks in their search. Some seekers may give to try to buy God's favor, but a sensitive receiver of the nonbeliever's funds can use the gift as an opportunity to explain the Gospel. In fact, I believe it is incumbent upon us to do so.

But finally, look at the most specific passage on this topic, 3 John 7–8: "For they went out for the sake of the Name, accepting nothing from the Gentiles. Therefore we ought to support such men. . . . "

These traveling laborers were not depending on Gentile financing. Therefore, we believers "ought to support such men, that we may be fellow-workers with the truth."

We are not to *depend* on unbelievers to fund the missionary work of believers. Although there may be exceptions, I recommend that we not appeal to *known* non-Christians unless their giving will help them (even a little) in their search for Christ. And that is certainly possible. Matthew 6:21 says, "Where your treasure is, there will your heart be also." Giving can draw hearts heavenward. Help them understand that their money will not get them to heaven, but do explain the "secret" of getting to heaven. Gifts from non-Christians should be springboards for evangelism.

William Booth, founder of The Salvation Army, was once asked if he would accept gifts from nonbelievers—"tainted money" it was called. He responded, "Taint theirs and it taint mine!" (And 'tis God's!) Booth summed it up like this: "I will accept any kind of money—even the Devil's. I'll wash it in the blood of Christ and use it for the glory of God."

6. What about appeals to family members? I feel awkward asking for their help, yet they might be offended if I say nothing.

A missionary went overseas on a short-term assignment and mailed his cash-project letter to his entire family. Family members received the same "form" letter as everyone else on his mailing list, including a pledge card. Ten years later, he's still overcoming the offenses and barriers that one letter erected. Even though his letter was tactful, he erred by treating his relatives like everyone else.

Mark 6:4 says, "A prophet is not without honor except in his home town." You may be the prophet Elijah on Mount Carmel in your Christian ministry, but to Aunt Gladys back home, you'll always be the little kid who put her cat in the washing machine.

If your relatives seem to be believers and are warm to the things of God, certainly give them an opportunity to support you. But treat them differently. Don't just send them a mass-appeal letter with a pledge card. Call them ahead of time to let them know your money letter is coming, and then add a newsy personal note to their letter.

If your family members are not believers, you can still add them to your mailing list. They probably want to know what you're up to, and your well-written, jargon-free, interesting letters may be their only link with the Gospel. But hold back their envelopes when you send a financial appeal.

Before you appeal to your relatives, think through the implications. If you offend them, they will be slow to forget. It is your parents or those family members closest to you who must bear the gossip at family reunions.

By the way, having adequate finances will be a tremendous testimony to your relatives, especially if they are nonbelievers. Let's not communicate the limp-along attitude that they often expect from missionaries.

7. May I appeal to people to whom I have never ministered?

Recently, a missionary phoned me to lament the poor state of his donor income. He had 20 extremely faithful donors. With sincerity, he enumerated how God had used him deeply in the lives of each of his 20 donors. That was the kind of donor he preferred—someone he had influenced spiritually. And they enjoyed supporting him because of the close spiritual relationship.

"I guess I'll just have to work harder," he concluded, "to minister to more people, and that will bring my support up."

Don't expect your ministry audience to be your primary donor base.

Build a strong base that extends beyond those you're ministering to.

What a discouraging scenario. But do the Scriptures teach that you can appeal only to those to whom you've ministered in the past? Although I know of missionaries who are fully funded by only 20 donors (who all give huge gifts!), it is not a workable model for most.

The Scriptures show examples of both extremes—appealing to people whom we have influenced spiritually and appealing to strangers.

First, three Scriptures highlight the importance of giving to those who help you spiritually.

- "Let the one who is taught the word share all good things with him who teaches" (Galatians 6:6).
- "If we sowed spiritual things in you, is it too much if we should reap material things from you?" (1 Corinthians 9:11).
- "For if the Gentiles have shared in their spiritual things, they are indebted to minister to them also in material things" (Romans 15:27).

These Scriptures clearly show that believers should give to where they are getting help. Your church is helping you grow spiritually; support your church. If a Christian radio station also helps you learn the Word, support that station too. If a full-time Christian missionary is helping you grow, support that missionary. Give where you're getting help.

Unfortunately, some overly conscientious missionaries mistakenly assume they can only receive support from the receivers of their teaching. So they teach faithfully and hope their pupils will adhere to Galatians 6:6. They may even share this verse with their students and "appeal" in that way. "Money follows ministry," they intone.

But Galatians 6:6 is not meant to restrict missionaries' fundraising. What about the admonition to support the traveling missionaries in 3 John 5? "Beloved, you are acting faithfully in whatever you accomplish for the brethren, and especially when they are strangers."

Don't let your imagination scare you into avoiding appeals to people you don't know well.

These traveling teachers were strangers to their hosts! There was obviously no prior ministry. Furthermore, in Matthew 10, had the disciples previously ministered to the worthy men? No. Had Elijah previously ministered to the widow? No. Had Paul previously ministered to the Romans? A few, perhaps, but not all.

If giving is a privilege, why should I prohibit people—even strangers—from participating in my ministry just because I've never ministered to them? Maybe God wants them to participate. But I disqualify them by saying, "Sorry, folks, I've never ministered to you, and I'm not going to give you an opportunity to invest in this exciting ministry."

The Scriptures allow for both support from your "students" as well as from strangers. Don't take Galatians 6:6 too far.

Second, what about people with little ministry experience who are called to serve behind the scenes rather than in public ministry? Does this mean they may not raise support until they have ministered directly to someone? That's making out-front ministry more important than behind-the-scenes ministry.

God may call assistants, accountants, secretaries, and clerical people to fulfill nonpublic, mostly invisible, but highly important ministry niches. They are gifted for behind-the-scenes serving but not for highly visible teaching. If we limit receiving support to the form in Galatians 6:6 only, then are these people not to be supported because of the way God gifted them?

Hogwash! They are as worthy of support as any pastor or missionary. "The eye cannot say to the hand, 'I have no need of you' " (1 Corinthians 12:21).

Third, let's be honest. Most of us feel more comfortable appealing to someone who has already benefited from our ministries rather than to strangers or mere acquaintances. In the back of our minds, we may smugly assume they should support us financially because of all the spiritual benefit we've brought them. They "owe us."

And what about donors? Don't they want to support those who've ministered to them? Yes. It's generally true that people want to give where they have a relationship, but the relationship can be built after the giving begins.

My wife and I recently asked a couple we didn't know well for $100 to $200 a month. They didn't say, "Hey, wait a minute! You've never ministered to us!"

They pledged, and we're ministering to them now through newsletters, occasional visits, and prayer. Ministry can follow money.

In summary, you needn't have a long list of satisfied ministry pupils in order to raise support. I'm not advocating phone-book fundraising—cold calling is challenging and not as effective as appealing to friends. However, to get to 100 percent of budget, you'll have to leave your comfort zone of friends. This may be a stretching, taxing, fearful experience, but God may want to do something important in your life through these encounters.

8. May I appeal to those who already are giving heavily?

A few months ago, I was sitting at our kitchen table writing down names of prospective supporters. In the midst of making lists, I saw the name Joe Jones.

Joe and I had served together on the board of our former church before our family moved. As a doctor and leader in the church, Joe was an obvious target of many missionary appeals. I also suspected that he was a heavy contributor to the church. He was well-known for his enthusiasm for missions and his compassionate heart for people.

"What's the use?" I asked myself. "I'd have to stand in line behind 20 other missionaries just to get an appointment. Besides, he's probably giving all he can afford anyway."

But I phoned Joe and after a bit of casual talk told him I'd like to invite him to join our support team. "Could we get together?" I asked. "Sure, but I don't know if we can do anything," he replied.

The appointment was cordial, but Joe didn't tell me his decision. But two weeks after our meeting, his pledge card showed up in my mailbox with a generous monthly commitment.

Sound familiar? Many missionaries edit potential donors off their lists because they are "already giving." Let the donor decide.

Before I became a missionary, I worked for the *Ankeny Press Citizen* selling advertising to store owners. One bright Monday morning, I drove onto the cracked asphalt parking lot of Ralph's IGA—my biggest account—optimistically hoping for a warm response and a big sale from Ralph's growing business. But as I got out of the car, clipboard in hand, I heard a voice in my head saying,

"Ralph doesn't want to see you today. He doesn't want any advertising. You are bothering him. Let him do his work. You're just an interruption. He can't afford it anyway. In fact, Scott, Ralph doesn't even like you very much. Did you notice that he frowned the last time you were in?"

Then I went to the hardware store and found myself saying, *"Scott, the hardware man doesn't want to see you today. You are bothering him."*

What was happening? I was making the store managers' decisions for them. I wasn't even giving them a chance to say no!

We do the same thing in raising support. A voice inside says, *"I'd better not ask them. They are probably already giving. They probably can't afford it. They probably don't like me very much anyway."*

With thinking like this, we rob the giver of the privilege of deciding. As 2 Corinthians 9:7 tells us, it is the giver's decision to say yes or no: Every man as he has purposed in his heart. Not as Scott purposes for him!

Furthermore, how do we know people are already giving heavily? How do we know if they are giving at all? We often guess. We assume that because they serve on the board, or have a heart for missions, or are popular, they must be doing all they can.

But you're not their accountant! Don't make the decision for them. At least give them an "opportunity" to say yes or no. Remember Philippians 4:10. I'm glad I did with Joe!

It can seem discouraging that so many people are "fishing" from the same donor pool, but that's not a good reason to edit people off your list of potential donors.

Do you honestly believe God blesses those who give above and beyond their means? We read in 2 Corinthians 8:3 that the Macedonians gave "according to their ability, and beyond their ability." Paul praised them as a model of giving.

In Luke 21:1–4, Jesus commends the widow for sacrificial giving. If it is wrong to give sacrificially, why didn't Jesus stop her?

Sure, some of the people you appeal to already are giving heavily or even sacrificially. But that is no reason to withhold your appeal to them.

Actually, most of the believers to whom you will appeal do *not* qualify for the category of "sacrificial giving." Out of curiosity, I once asked my tax preparer what percent of income most Americans give to charity of any kind. He thought for a moment and then said 1 to 2 percent of gross income.

I was shocked. But IRS figures agree with his assessment; Americans give 1.6 to 2 percent of their income to charity of any kind. That range has been consistent for the past 30 years, even though personal income has risen dramatically. *Moody Monthly* estimates the giving of evangelicals at 6.4 percent, but most church boards would be ecstatic if their members gave 5 percent.

You are not robbing others with your appeal. Most Westerners do not come close to giving sacrificially.

Third, some people have the gift of giving. I was apologizing to one of our donors one day, realizing that he gave to many missions projects as well as to his church. I felt a little sheepish because, on top of that, he was supporting our ministry with $50 a month. He reminded me, "Scott, giving is one of my gifts." Now I invite him to give on every special project we have!

But suppose you find out that the person you are appealing to actually is the target of many missionary appeals. I've had people say, "Scott, you understand we get a lot of appeals. Every day in the mail we receive a stack of letters asking for money for missions. Plus, our church is raising money for a building program."

Be sensitive to donors who are bombarded with requests, but remember it is the heavy givers who most likely have discovered the joys of generosity.

This is called a "disclaimer." Is it now time to fold up your pledge cards and go home? That's what I used to do. But a disclaimer is not necessarily a "no."

I usually say something like, "Yes, there certainly are a lot of giving opportunities these days. Isn't it wonderful there's so much going on for God!" Then I ask, "How do you feel about receiving so many appeals?" Let them vent.

I acknowledge their disclaimer and empathize with it. I tell them I realize they are the target of many giving appeals and that it is impossible to give to every project that comes along. Donors appreciate the fact that you are aware of their dilemma. Then I add, "You know, I almost hesitated to invite you to join my support team for this very reason. I know you are bombarded by people asking you to do things for them."

Invariably, this makes me feel more at ease. And usually I'm the one who is most uncomfortable with the disclaimer.

Then I tell them I have felt led by the Lord to explain my financial situation to them. But I also explain that I'm not suggesting they cut back on other missions projects or their church giving in order to support me. I reassure them that no matter what their decision, our friendship is not on the line. They seem to appreciate that. And I always review 2 Corinthians 9:7 with them as I close.

So be sensitive to disclaimers, but remember it is the heavy givers who most likely have discovered the joy of generosity. And they most likely are more sensitive to the Lord. Don't shy away from people simply because they are giving already.

9. What if the person I'm asking is poorer than I am?

Dave, a missionary, confessed that he felt guilty appealing to Ken, who was going through tough times financially. Despite the fact that Ken and his new wife both had jobs, Dave worried that they barely got by month by month. But I encouraged him to ask Ken anyway. Later in the evening, as Dave invited Ken to join his monthly support team, Ken said he would gladly consider it. Three days later, after discussing it with his wife, he sacrificially pledged $35 monthly and was honored to do so.

I confess I've done the same thing. I scan my prospect's clothing, car, house, job, spouse's job, number of TVs, and so on. Then I make my judgment about whether they can afford to give based on these external things. Frequently, I've chickened out on my appeal if they "looked poor." But what does the Bible say?

Deuteronomy 16:17 says, "Every man shall give as he is able, according to the blessing of the LORD your God which He has given you."

Note the word "every." If a person has an income source, he or she also has the responsibility and privilege of giving. No exceptions. I like the way Navigator mission strategist Jim Petersen puts it: "People need to give much worse than I need to receive."

Of course, not everyone can give in the amounts we would like. Deuteronomy 16:17 also says, "as he is able." People are to give in proportion to how God has blessed them. Someone earning $30,000 per year won't be able to give as much as a person with a $100,000-per-year income—nor should they!

The following old story, from *Letters to Scattered Pilgrims* by Elizabeth O'Connor, shows how easy it is to misunderstand the Bible's instructions on giving proportionately:

> "I was the minister of a small Baptist congregation in a railroad town just outside of Lynchburg, Virginia. My deacon sent for me one day and told me that he wanted my help. 'We have in our congregation,' he said, 'a widow with six children. I have looked at the records and discovered that she is putting into the treasury of the church each month $4.00—a tithe of her income. Of course, she is unable to do this. We want you to go and talk to her and let her know that she needs to feel no obligation whatsoever, and free her from the responsibility.'
>
> "I am not wise now; I was less wise then. I went and told the widow of the concern of the deacons. I told her as graciously and as supportively as I knew that she was relieved of the responsibility of giving. As I talked, tears came into her eyes. 'I want to tell you,' she said, 'that you are taking away the last thing that gives my life dignity and meaning.' "

Like the deacons, we too tend to have a horizontal view of giving. We fail to see that giving vertically to God bestows honor and dignity—especially to someone with small means.

In Luke 21:1–4, Jesus could have stopped the widow from giving, but He chose not to. He applauded her giving and didn't deny her the honor.

Besides, how do you know people are not as well off as you? It is natural and wise to be observant; however, our quick conclusions based on our prospect's clothing or cars may be incorrect! Jesus said in John 7:24, "Do not judge according to appearance, but judge with righteous judgment." Let's avoid the worldly way of evaluating.

Although it is clear that you can appeal to people who are not as well off as you, keep in mind Jesus' warning in Matthew 23 to the Pharisees against "devouring widows' houses." It is not asking the widows to give that Jesus condemns, but rather the greediness of the Pharisees.

10. At what level should a Christian worker set his or her lifestyle? How "nice" is "too nice"? Should you live at the level of the people you minister to?

It's an unfortunate axiom that if you're in Christian work, you ought to be poor. In France, well-qualified, gifted disciple makers hesitate to enter full-time ministry because of the deeply ingrained rule of poverty modeled by the clergy for hundreds of years.

In the United States, a Child Evangelism Fellowship staff worker bought his wife a microwave oven. The pastor of their church noticed it in their home and recommended the church cut off their support.

A donor told a missionary he wouldn't support him because the missionary owned a nice leather coat.

Deacons at an Ohio church voted the new pastor's salary down by $2,000 to keep it below the annual earnings of the lowest-paid deacon. Just today I met with a pastor at a start-up church who had a parishioner call his $29,000 part-time salary "way too high." But the pastor's "part-time" work is 50 hours per week—about $11.50 an hour. Hmm.

Is it true that if you're in the ministry you ought to be poor? Several Scriptures contradict this poverty mentality.

The tithe in the Old Testament represented the *best* of the grain, the best of the flock. In Malachi 1:8, the people were upbraided for offering blind, sick, or lame lambs to the Lord and holding back the best for themselves. But the Lord commanded *the best* be given to the Levites.

Referring to traveling missionaries, 3 John 6 says, "Send them on their way in a manner worthy of God." How do you send people on their way in a manner worthy of God? It certainly implies you would do all you could for them.

In Luke 10:4, Jesus commanded the disciples not to take a bag—a "beggar's bag" is the literal word. Don't consider yourself a beggar.

We find in 1 Timothy 5:17 another passage that contradicts the mentality that missionaries must be poor: "Let the elders who rule well be considered worthy of double honor, especially those who work hard at preaching and teaching." What is this double honor referring to? The

Greek word is *timao,* and it literally means "the sale price or to fix a value upon."

Most of us have read that passage, but we don't take it seriously. Pay our leaders double if they rule well? Ridiculous! So we modify "double honor" to mean a nice plaque or a gift certificate presented at the Christmas Eve service. But before we dismiss it too casually, consider how *timao* is used in Matthew 27:6, where Judas returned the 30 pieces of silver—"the price [*timao*] of blood."

Also, the context backs up the financial implication. In the verse that follows, 1 Timothy 5:18, we read, " 'You shall not muzzle the ox while he is threshing' and 'The laborer is worthy of his wages.' " We don't know if Timothy paid them double, but Paul thought they were worth it.

I'm not advocating exorbitant salaries; I dwell on this verse because of how resistant we are to pay our pastors and missionaries generously. Paul had no such hang-up.

Despite what some may believe, living at the poverty level does not necessarily make one more spiritual.

On the other hand, there are devastating abuses spawned by the health-and-wealth emphasis. Ministry leaders or preachers who live extravagantly, making excessive profits through the Gospel, usually fall. You'll read about them in your newspaper.

So at what level should missionaries live? I'm not suggesting they live extravagantly, but let's drop the deeply ingrained idea that they deserve only a meager living. I find Proverbs 30:8–9 helpful: "Give me neither poverty nor riches; feed me with the food that is my portion, lest I be full and deny Thee and say, 'Who is the Lord?' Or lest I be in want and steal, and profane the name of my God."

You can expect criticism. Matthew 11:18–19 says, "For John came neither eating nor drinking, and they say, 'He has a demon!' The Son of Man came eating and drinking, and they say, 'Behold, a gluttonous man and a drunkard, a friend of tax-gatherers and sinners!' "

John lived meagerly—unless you consider bugs and wild honey gourmet food. He lived a subsistence lifestyle in the desert. Critics said, "He's got a demon." Jesus, on the other hand, circulated among tax-gatherers and sinners. And He was criticized as a glutton and a wine-bibber.

No matter how you live, someone will criticize your lifestyle. Be prepared for that. You can't please everybody. What some may consider a reasonable standard may appear to others as luxury.

Third, asceticism is not the answer. An ascetic would say, "Cut back. Do without. Cut back some more."

A guest preacher came to our church when Alma and I were young Christians and said, "I have but one suit." He told how he lived meagerly to save the Lord money. We were impressed by that, especially me. I admired his practical frugality.

A few years later, we were in tough times financially as missionaries. Alma and I were discussing how we could save money. She said, "You know, Scott, you don't need two suits." Bingo!

She went on. "You only need one suit, and actually, you only need one shirt. And really, Scott, you only need one pair of shoes. Furthermore, we don't need a refrigerator. In the summertime, we could go to the meat market daily. In the wintertime, we could hang meat in the garage."

There was no stopping the woman now!

"We don't need a sofa. We can sit on the floor. We don't need city water; we can collect rainwater." By the time she was finished, we were pretty meager. And I didn't have anything to wear on campus.

Alma knew where I was coming from. Growing up on a farm, I took my parents' value of frugality and expanded it to ultra-frugality. "Tightwad" was Alma's term. But I was slow to admit it until one quiet evening at home a few years ago.

I was relaxing and reading the Scriptures, when I came to the story in John 12:3 of Mary pouring precious oil—worth 11 months' wages—on Jesus. I stopped reading, lifted my head, and reflected, "They could have sold that perfume and used the money for the poor." Continuing, I read verse 5 where Judas said, "Why wasn't this perfume sold and the money given to the poor?" (NIV). Judas and I agreed! I identified more with frugal Judas than with Jesus, who commended Mary's generosity.

Certainly we must be frugal. That's good biblical stewardship, like Jesus collecting the leftover fragments of bread (John 6:12). But extreme asceticism hinders effective ministry, even though it might save money. There is nothing innately spiritual about living in poverty. I've found the same temptations toward greed when I had nothing as when we were fully funded.

In 1 Timothy 6:17, Paul wrote, "[God] richly supplies us with all things to enjoy." To enjoy! There is nothing wrong with owning possessions. The question is, do the possessions own us?

What about simply living the same kind of lifestyle as the people you're ministering to? That has merit and recalls famed missionary Hudson Taylor's model in China more than 100 years ago. But I'm afraid it is an oversimplified solution. Though we must identify with our people, they usually don't expect us to live exactly like they do. But may I add that you are wiser to "move down" economically to reach people than to build a nicer house or buy a luxury car—especially overseas.

Fourth, make sure your lifestyle does not hinder the Gospel. In 1 Corinthians 9:14, Paul affirms the right of Christian workers to "get their living from the gospel." But in 9:18, he commits to "offer the gospel without charge." Nothing is allowed to hinder the Gospel.

Paul hints at this in 1 Corinthians 8 regarding Christian liberties, particularly on whether to eat food previously offered to idols. Paul concludes it is an area of individual choice, a "liberty." But he continues in 8:9: "But take care lest this liberty of yours somehow become a stumbling block to the weak."

Yes, you may freely live in a nice home. You may freely drive a nice car. You may freely own nice things. But make sure this liberty you have is not a stumbling block to the Gospel.

Howard Hendricks of Dallas Theological Seminary tells of a missionary who prided himself on frugality. The missionary's newsletter described how he spent three days paddling upriver in a canoe, one day preaching, and three days paddling back in a canoe. He reported to his donors: "Six days in a canoe, one day preaching."

Hendricks suggested this: Why not hire Mission Aviation Fellowship to fly him into the jungle in one hour so he could preach six days and then fly back in one hour? It would cost more money, but he would get more ministry done. Is the goal to save money or to effectively advance the Gospel?

Similarly, a student once confided to me, "I am ashamed to bring people to the campus missionary's home. It's sloppy, and he dresses sloppy too. It hinders some of the young Christians around here."

I started to defend the missionary but held back. I discovered the missionary also was receiving food stamps.

Was this an unfair criticism? Perhaps. Nonetheless, the campus missionary couple were godly people and thought they were doing right. But their decision not to fundraise hindered the Gospel.

I suggest this guideline: Order your lifestyle such that you are at maximum fruitfulness in life, ministry, and marriage (if you're married). What kind of lifestyle will help you be most effective for the Lord? Don't live so frugally that you have to bum Coca-Colas off new Christians. And don't live so extravagantly that people whisper about your nice things. The balance is in 2 Corinthians 8:21, "We have regard for what is honorable, not only in the sight of the Lord, but also in the sight of men." Don't let your liberty become a stumbling block for someone else.

A note to husbands: Don't be so tight that your wife is under pressure to scratch out a meal when you invite a group over for supper. Your wife needs money to provide a warm, friendly home—that's a ministry! She feels the pressure of low income more than you.

And wives, be honest with your husbands. It's not a sign of "weak faith" to desire more money in the grocery account or to ask for reimbursement to the family grocery fund when you've spent much of it on ministry entertaining.

In summary, I'm not suggesting you ought to be rich. What I am suggesting is that you figure out what income will help you minister most effectively. Believe God for that. And through prayer and hard work, trust Christ to help you do your part. He'll do the rest.

11. How can I ask others for support when I have a significant savings account?

A missionary was preparing to serve in Russia but hesitated to ask for support. I couldn't put my finger on the reason. Finally, he confessed that he had built up a sizable personal savings account by frugally setting aside money each month. His savings could pay his entire missions expense.

Furthermore, he was so deeply committed to Christ that he was willing to use it all. Yet he didn't know if that was wise.

Some Christians believe that savings and investments should be cashed out—because it's all going to burn anyway—and used for the sake of the Kingdom. But what about Proverbs 13:22, an overlooked passage? "A good man leaves an inheritance to his children's children."

To leave an inheritance—and from the context, it is clear it is a financial inheritance—would require some type of wealth accumulation. It needn't be liquid; it could be land or possessions. I don't think this passage is telling us we must accumulate to leave a legacy, but it certainly implies there is nothing wrong with accumulation.

Proverbs 21:20 tells us, "There is precious treasure and oil in the dwelling of the wise, but a foolish man swallows it up." Again, accumulation. There is value in storing up valuable commodities at certain times, rather than spending it all immediately.

In Proverbs 6:6–11 we read, "Go to the ant, O sluggard, observe her ways and be wise, which, having no chief, officer or ruler, prepares her food in the summer, and gathers her provision in the harvest." Ants have a "cash-flow" problem. In the winter, they have no means of getting food, so they store it up ahead of time. There is a purpose in their storing up. It is not merely for the sake of accumulating excess but to provide food for when they are not able to "harvest."

Similarly, Joseph in Egypt followed the wisdom of the ants by saving up during good years for seven years of famine (Genesis 41:47–49).

Though the Scriptures advocate the wisdom of saving for the future, many Christians have not identified godly purposes for their savings or investments. If you don't know *why* you are saving, you may be guilty of hoarding. Identify your godly purposes for your savings and investments. Without a purpose approved by heaven, why indeed are you saving?

That helps solve the problem for missionaries. Once my young friend going to Russia figured out that his real purpose for the savings was to continue his education once he returned, he felt comfortable keeping his savings and asking for support.

What are godly purposes for savings accounts or investments? Some obvious ones are provisions for education, old age, children's education, to start a God-ordained business, transportation—almost anything that God has led you to do in the future that will require start-up capital. Of course, every dime a believer has accumulated must be available for the Lord to use as He directs. But you need not feel guilty keeping your savings intact so you can accomplish a future purpose in which the Lord has also led.

If you use all your savings and return from the field penniless to launch the next chapter of life, does that honor God? I don't think so. And you may have to quit missions service.

Furthermore, if you totally fund yourself, you are robbed of prayer partners. Sure, some friends will pray anyway, but not as fervently as when they give. "For where your treasure is, there will your heart be also" (Matthew 6:21). Also, you rob people of the privilege of giving—some sacrificially—toward your support. Each missionary has a unique web of relationships. No one else knows these people quite the way you do. They have the opportunity to learn to give through you—they might not consider giving to any other cause but yours. You are helping them experience the joys of giving.

Furthermore, you rob your donors of participating in world vision. One young missionary was complaining to her mother about having to raise one year's support for a Russia venture. Dreading the finance-training school, she desperately wanted to use up her savings and not bother inviting donors to participate. Her mother exploded, "Don't you ever talk like that again! *You* are the only way *I'll* ever get to Russia!"

Certainly nothing prohibits you from "sending yourself" to the mission field. But you might limit your future options, eliminate your prayer team, and rob your potential supporters who don't get an opportunity to give. Finally, you will rob yourself of the wonderful, stretching, faith-deepening experience of raising support.

Now it's time to ask yourself which of these questions of conscience has attracted your attention. You needn't have them 100 percent answered before you dive into the strategy of fundraising, but at least you must start. Let the Lord speak to you about any question of conscience still unresolved.

Will you surrender that issue in prayer before you begin the next chapter?

Chapter Five
FIVE MYTHS ABOUT RAISING PERSONAL SUPPORT

Now that you've addressed the issues of conscience and attitude, you are ready to put your funding plan on paper. But first, you need to identify and avoid five fundraising myths. These hover around missionaries like raccoons at the back door of a campground kitchen.

Myth #1: There's no money out there.

A missionary who had just returned to the United States for a new ministry assignment was anxious about funding. He asked a well-known Christian businessman for advice and was told, "Don't stay in full-time ministry; there's no money out there."

On the contrary, there's plenty of money "out there" for doing God's will, no matter what your culture. Especially in America. Each year, Americans give more than $200 billion to charity, with the greatest share going to churches and religious causes. And the amount increases each year, often exceeding inflation. Yet, as I mentioned in the previous chapter, the IRS says that Americans give only 1 to 2 percent of their gross income.

In the evangelical community, some believers are "maxed out" on their giving, but most are not. Pastors and denominational leaders lament that if their members gave even 5 percent, they would have plenty for their own programs and much more to give to other needs.

It is true that in some regions or countries, the economic conditions are so poor that survival is the daily goal. Nevertheless,

Why do we assume people won't give when we haven't even asked them?

regardless of the economy, each believer has the responsibility and privilege of giving according to his or her ability (Deuteronomy 16:17). Even the poor people of Burma gave a handful of rice to their pastors in times of great poverty.

I don't want to oversimplify economic problems and the genuine difficulties many countries face in supporting missionaries, but if God has truly called you for Christian service, He will provide—even in a bad economy.

You may face problems with potential donors in your culture not understanding how to support missionaries. Be creative. Educate them. The money is there.

Myth #2: Meetings raise money.

When most missionaries think of a fundraising strategy, they visualize a meeting where many people (usually strangers) come to see their pictures, eat apple pie, and hear their dazzling vision. Magically, after five or six of these meetings, the missionaries leave for their ministry assignment fully funded. But this is not reality.

A study was done of 100 Navigator staff actively fundraising during a 26-month period. They made appeals through meetings, face-to-face appointments, letters, and phone calls. Of the 736 people appealed to (mostly Anglos) at group meetings, only 9 percent pledged monthly. And this included follow-up after the meetings. With African Americans and Asian Americans, meeting results are better (see Chapter 21 for guidelines for ethnic-ministry funding).

Is it the "Let-George-Do-It" syndrome that elicits a low response? It works something like this: "Hmmm, a pledge card. Monthly support, huh? I'll bet ol' George sitting beside me or the nicely dressed woman across the room will pick up a good share of the support. She looks pretty well-off and seems to know the couple better than I do. I'll give a small one-time gift to show that I'm behind this missionary in spirit and let it go at that. Wonder what kind of pie we're having?"

Group meetings are a good way to say thank you to your donors, create enthusiasm for your vision, or recruit newcomers to meet you with a view to future giving. With Anglos, however, they are *not* an effective way to raise support, especially monthly support. You'll do much better going face-to-face.

Myth #3: Churches are your best prospects.

Where is it written that missionaries must make fundraising visits to 52 churches in 52 weeks and then leave for the field exhausted? Yes, you should have a home church solidly behind you, picking up 10 to 50 percent of your support from its missions budget. But you will be sadly disappointed if you are counting on recruiting more than a few churches.

Think about it. Why would a church want to support a stranger? Just coming once or twice to a missions festival or meeting with the missions committee (if you can even get an appointment) will not enamor them to you for a significant monthly or annual commitment. Furthermore, some churches are extremely sophisticated in deciding whom they support. Gone are the days when an Anglo church would welcome you with open arms just because you were a missionary. Most churches have a bias toward supporting those from their own congregations, and many have narrow priorities for ministries or countries they want to support. Even if your kids sing at the Sunday service and the congregation applauds wildly, all you're likely to get is a small honorarium with the words, "Hope this helps."

I don't mean to be negative, but it's time to think soberly about how you spend your valuable deputation time.

The exception might be if your ministry assignment takes you to a part of the world the church is already keen on—like a country in the news because of disaster or where a country's doors open miraculously as Russia's did in 1992. And sometimes the church wants to support a local ministry just because of proximity.

In general, however, you are wiser to spend your time recruiting individuals rather than churches. (More on churches in Chapter 12.)

Myth #4: Mr. Wonderful will raise it for me.

A missionary friend excitedly told me that a Christian businessman had agreed to raise his remaining support goal of $2,000 per month. The businessman told him: "Why should you have to do this money stuff rather than ministry? You're good at ministry; I'm good at money. I'll recruit a team for you!" Two years later, the missionary lamented, "I have yet to see one dime!"

"Mr. Wonderful" sounds good, but don't hold your breath. Even though Mr. Wonderfuls have genuine, concerned hearts, they usually don't know what to do, and they don't have time to do it. Because they have succeeded in business doesn't mean they can raise support. In fact, they often go through the same conscience struggles you do.

It's not wise to count on one "sugar daddy" to shower you with money. Even if he's good with money himself, he may not understand biblical fundraising.

To enable others to help you, you must train them in biblical fundraising. It can work, and it's a strategy more missionaries should adopt, especially those with few natural prospects. But it will not save you time, nor is it a panacea.

Myth #5: Raising support is like taking cough syrup.

Many missionaries view fundraising with the same enthusiasm as slurping down a delicious tablespoon of green syrupy cough medicine.

A few years ago, the director of an international sending agency wrote in a *Christianity Today* article that raising personal support is a "demeaning method." This nationally known leader is feeding the bias of American Christians who think fundraising is shameful. Let's read our Bibles more carefully! The Bible doesn't hint that fundraising for the Kingdom is a shame or even a hassle. It's actually an honor.

One missionary returned from a year in Russia describing the wonderful ways God had used him and changed his character. Not naturally outgoing, he was apprehensive about whether he would be able to initiate friendships with the Russian people. But he did.

When he returned two years later, he told me the Russia adventure had changed his life. "Was it the culture that changed you?" I asked. "No," he replied, "it was the fundraising!" He concluded: "My biggest step of faith and the biggest way God changed my character was not Russia, but when I stepped out in faith to raise support right here in the United States."

I shouldn't have been surprised. My life also has changed significantly because of stepping out in faith to raise personal support. Taking a risk in fundraising has allowed me to experience a bigger and more loving God than I knew before. Because of raising support, my faith is stronger and I experience more confidence that His hand is on my life.

Furthermore, far from being the despicable cough syrup of ministry, I have found raising support to be enjoyable—once I get the phone appointment made! I've had wonderful, life-changing times of ministry to donors in their homes. Let's begin to see fundraising in a different light.

Now it is time to learn how to avoid six simple mistakes as you develop your fundraising plan.

Chapter Six
SIX MISTAKES TO AVOID

Before you launch into developing your fundraising plan, you need to be aware of six pitfalls to avoid. Learn from the mistakes that I—and others—have made. I'm afraid many missionaries give up simply because they didn't know how to form an effective funding strategy.

Here are six common strategy failures you should avoid.

1. Failure to go face-to-face.

Do not rely on mailings for monthly support. A veteran East Coast missionary sent an appeal letter to 300 people on his mailing list. These 300 knew him personally and knew his excellent track record in ministry. His outreach was successful and exciting, and his financial need was real. But with a fallen countenance he told me, "Out of 300 people, only three sent a card back pledging monthly—and one was my father-in-law!"

If you hear of "tremendous responses" to mass mailings from missionary friends, ask if it was for monthly support. Well-written mass appeals for one-time gifts work fine, but for monthly

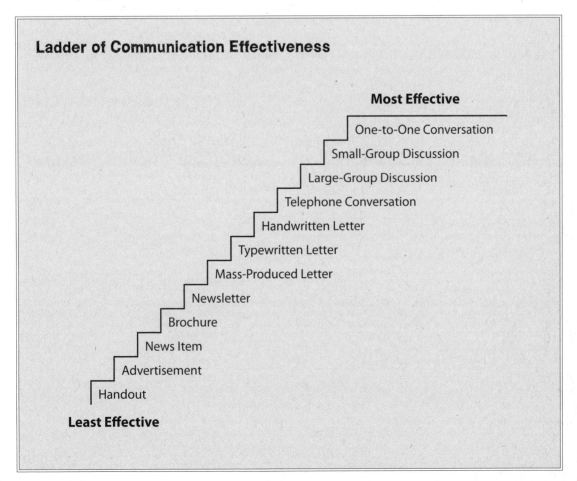

Ladder of Communication Effectiveness

Most Effective

- One-to-One Conversation
- Small-Group Discussion
- Large-Group Discussion
- Telephone Conversation
- Handwritten Letter
- Typewritten Letter
- Mass-Produced Letter
- Newsletter
- Brochure
- News Item
- Advertisement
- Handout

Least Effective

support, you'll do much better going face-to-face.

Study the diagram on the previous page, from *Harvard Business Review*.[1]

According to this study, one-to-one conversations are the most effective way to communicate. Mass-produced mail is in seventh place, yet that's a common strategy missionaries use. Also, a mail appeal quickly *uses up* all your prospective givers. If they don't respond to your letter, will you feel free to go back to them in person? Mass-mailing appeals for monthly support are a quick way to get disappointing results.

Don't rely on mailings for monthly support. You'll probably be disappointed by the response you get.

But face-to-face appeals take so much time! Yes, but fundraising is part of your ministry—not a distraction from it. Furthermore, the bonding you establish while sitting in a person's home, trying to enjoy their cat and letting their kids spill Kool-Aid on you, lasts a long time.

Sometimes missionaries send an unsuccessful mailing and say, "I've done all I can to raise my support. The Lord just didn't supply. Maybe I'm not called to full-time work."

Wait a minute! Maybe they did all they could using poor methods. Now try using good methods, like face-to-face appeals! Don't be too quick to conclude God is not calling you.

A study of 7,401 appeals from 100 Navigator staff produced the results shown below. This study is more than 15 years old so the amounts are lower than today's. The good news is that our more recent statistics show a slightly higher "yes" rate.

Results from Study of 7,401 Appeals from 100 Navigator Staff

# Appealed To	Appeal Method	Yes, Monthly	Avg. Pledge	Yes, Annual	Avg. Amt.	Yes, Cash	Avg. Amt.	Undecided	No
3,263	Face-to-face	1,486 (46%)	$38	126 (4%)	$522	339 (10%)	$293	419 (13%)	891 (27%)
1,882	Telephone/Letter	488 (27%)	$36	65 (4%)	$410	244 (14%)	$328	276 (15%)	730 (39%)
839	Personal Letter	113 (14%)	$32	13 (2%)	$932	131 (16%)	$215	99 (12%)	491 (56%)
736	Group Meeting	68 (9%)	$39	14 (2%)	$305	67 (9%)	$171	31 (4%)	557 (76%)

---

1 *Harvard Business Review*, March–April 1985, p. 24.

Study this chart! It shows you where to spend your deputation time. Note that 46 percent of the face-to-face appeals resulted in a monthly pledge, plus an annual gift was given 4 percent of the time. That's 50 percent who responded positively. Compare that with 27 percent for phone/letter appeals or 14 percent for letter appeals. Note the amount pledged is larger too. Furthermore, notice there was 10 percent from cash responses. That's 60 percent "yes" for face-to-face appeals. Work smarter!

A similar chart for African-American and Asian-American missionaries appears in Chapter 21. The results are similar, but you'll find some surprises too.

2. Failure to cultivate donors.

Some missionaries may have the good fortune to have a few wealthy close friends who totally underwrite them. They may not need a large donor base. Great, but that is the exception, not the rule.

Here's a way to never run out of prospective givers! Anticipate your future funding by building friendships, creating interest, genuinely making acquaintances with as many people as you can, and adding them to your mailing list. As they begin to get a feel for your vision, they will gladly hear an appeal for support.

My wife and I added a couple to our mailing list that we did not know well—they were practically strangers. For three years we wrote them a personal letter once or twice a year and stopped by for a casual visit once. Then we called to set an appeal appointment, but they were on vacation. So I called and made the appeal over the phone. They were delighted to give, even on the phone. They promptly pledged $60 a month. I wouldn't have been able to make an appeal if I hadn't added them to our mailing list and cultivated their friendship.

The easiest way to cultivate donors is through your mailing list. Well-written newsletters are an excellent way to stimulate interest in your vision. Many missionaries cut their mailing lists down to save money. I say expand them! As you keep telling your story to a broader and broader audience, you are developing the interest of more and more people who later may be glad to join your financial team. Even if they never give, you have had a ministry to them through your well-written newsletters.

Just this week, my friends at Mission Aviation Fellowship told me of a study they concluded this year showing that those missionaries with the largest mailing lists are its best funded. We can learn from them!

A second reason for having a large mailing list is that you never know whom God has appointed to share in your support. I've heard dozens of missionaries say, "Wow! We never dreamed so-and-so would support us." Because it is impossible to predict who will take an interest in you, let as many as possible be aware of your ministry.

We're instructed in Hebrews 13:2, "Do not neglect to show hospitality to strangers, for by this some have entertained angels without knowing it." Show hospitality to strangers through your newsletters. You'll be surprised to discover "angels" who develop a heart for you.

Jesus limited the number of His close-in disciples but not His financial benefactors. Luke 8:1–3 lists the names of three women who supported Jesus and the Twelve: Mary, Joanna, and Susanna. Then notice it says: "and *many others* who were contributing to their support" (italics added) out of their private means. *Many others!* Luke didn't write this to encourage large mailing lists, but isn't it interesting that Jesus had many financial partners?

Obviously, you can have *intensive* ministry with only a few, but you must also have *extensive* ministry when it comes to your support team. The first step is to add "many others" to your newsletter mailing list.

I can hear you saying, "But I'm full up on relationships now! How can I *add* more friends?" True, but remember, you are not going to have "intensive" ministry to 98 percent of the people on your mailing list. Through writing good letters and developing a simple communication plan, you can expand your capacity. More on this in Chapter 14.

So how do you add people to your mailing list? Try these ideas:

- Have a sign-up list at conferences or seminars.
- Make friends outside your mission agency.
- Ask casual acquaintances if you could have the privilege of adding them.
- After church, have an acquaintance over for lunch.

This is how I ask acquaintances for permission to send them my newsletter: "I've enjoyed our visit. Could we stay in touch? We have an interesting newsletter we send out four times a year. It tells about God's work in our ministry and our personal lives. I think you might enjoy it. I wonder if I could send it to you? It comes in a brown paper bag. No salesman will call."

Adding a bit of humor keeps it upbeat. My new friend smiles and says, "Sure."

To give yourself permission to expand your ministry list, ask yourself, "Would this person glance at my newsletter four times a year?" Don't ask, "Would this person give?" Wrong question!

Missionaries often ask how to purge a mailing list—condense it down to a smaller size. Why would you want to? Some missionaries unwisely purge their mailing lists by sending out a reply card to see if people still want their letter. We did that once, and our donors didn't even send back the card. I kept them on my mailing list anyway.

I don't recommend it, but if you must condense your mailing list, remove people one by one. Ask them personally if they want to stay on your list. If they say yes, also ask them if they'd be willing to have you come by sometime to explain your ministry more fully. Don't drop them in droves!

3. Failure to ask.

A veteran missionary told me, "In my first assignment, we just did the work of the ministry, and we were fully funded. We didn't have to beat the bushes to scare up support. It just came in."

Now they're in a different assignment, and their support is *not* coming in. They're wondering what's wrong.

We tend to idealize those ministries in which the money is supplied without asking. We say God did it. But when we take the risk to make appeals and the money comes in that way, is that any less God's working? Many veteran missionaries are silently waiting for those dozens they've led to Christ, those dozens who have attended their Bible studies, those dozens with whom they've served on church committees to start giving. But the giving won't start until the missionaries ask in a meaningful way.

Henry Ford once purchased a huge life-insurance policy from a man he hardly knew. Ford's close friend, a life-insurance agent, stormed into Ford's office and demanded, "Henry, why didn't you buy that policy from me? We've been friends for years!"

"You never asked me," was Ford's reply. Just because you have good friends "who will surely support you" doesn't mean they will. They still have to be invited.

To quote Chuck Singletary, a friend from Atlanta, "Ye have not because ye phone not."

Missionaries are headed for disappointment if they live on the assumption that success in ministry guarantees full funding. Money doesn't always follow ministry. I've found that money follows asking!

Don't ask for prayer when money is what you're hoping for. The donor can't read your mind. Be honest.

During his furlough, a missionary visited in the home of a couple from our Sunday school class. Our friends had known this missionary before he went overseas and received his newsletters during his term in Africa. They were good friends. They told us he stayed overnight in their home, had great fellowship, and presented to them an outstanding picture-book presentation of his ministry. They liked it so much they even showed it to us.

So I inquired, "Does your missionary friend have a financial need?"

"Oh, we're quite sure he does. He's returning overseas for a new assignment."

"Are you supporting him?" I pressed.

"No, we're not."

"So you knew he had a need, but you're not supporting him?" I asked.

"No, we're not."

"Why not?"

My friends looked at one another, smiled awkwardly, and said, "Because he didn't ask."

"Osmosis" doesn't work. People can't read your mind. Nor do they easily make giving decisions; they tend to avoid or postpone money decisions. If you want people to make a giving decision, you must ask them to make a giving decision—even friends!

Here's a classic, often repeated story about "asking for the order." A 13-year-old New York girl named Markita Andrews found that out. In 1984, she sold 25,000 boxes of Girl Scout cookies. Hearing of her incredible success, Walt Disney Productions featured her in a sales training film, and IBM flew her around the country to address its sales force.

Here's what this eighth grader said is the key: "You can't just chat; you have to ask for an order!"

I'm not suggesting raising support is like selling Girl Scout cookies, but the principle of asking for a decision instead of just chatting certainly applies.

4. Failure to limit options.

A missionary returned to the United States for a year and launched a support-raising campaign for his new ministry assignment. He had a list of friendly, prospective givers who had been on his mailing list during his overseas term. He made 113 phone calls to this group and

was able to get 63 personal appointments. But of 63 meetings with people who had once supported him, only 12 pledged monthly—not nearly enough. Disappointed, he didn't know where to go next.

He and I tried to figure out why less than 20 percent of his former donors pledged. He presented himself well. They knew he was coming for finances. It was a mystery. I finally asked him, "What do you say when you make your appeal?"

Too many choices diminish financial results. If you ask someone to pray or give, what are they more likely to choose?

"Well," he said, "I give them three choices: monthly support, a cash gift, or prayer. Most of them choose prayer!"

Bingo! Too many choices. Ask for *one thing*.

We've already learned this lesson in evangelism. There comes a time to ask a seeker for a decision, and we give only one choice: "Will you receive Jesus Christ?" We don't also ask, "And will you join my church? And will you stop smoking? Take your pick." One choice.

5. Failure to use a response vehicle/pledge card.

Years ago, a young missionary told me of his success in raising monthly support to be an administrative assistant at a mission headquarters. He had contacted 30 of his friends, and 29 of them agreed to give starting August 1. He was ecstatic! But I noticed he hadn't used a pledge card. So I quizzed him.

"They all know my mission's address. They are experienced at giving. They're my friends—they know what to do," he reasoned.

August 1 arrived. No money. September 1. Still no money. Then he sent out pledge cards to his 29 pledgers, and the money came in the next month.

Why do you need a response vehicle? Because even well-meaning friends need a reminder, a vehicle to express their intentions.

Even Paul used a response vehicle of sorts. In 2 Corinthians 9:5, he says, "So I thought it necessary to urge the brethren that they would go on ahead . . . and arrange beforehand your previously promised bountiful gift." Paul himself is coming to get the gift, and he even sends some brethren on ahead to get the gift ready. He was his own response vehicle.

In 1 Corinthians 16:2, he encourages the church to set aside its giving on the first day of each week "that no collections be made when I come." Paul was coming personally to pick up the money.

Similarly, the local church today has response devices. They're called offering plates or weekly envelopes. People need a vehicle through which they express their interest.

Once I gave a presentation on behalf of a missionary on his way to Indonesia. He invited 20 friends to his home, and I gave the talk of the century on why these 20 people should support Neil and Sue. The guests responded enthusiastically. "A good evening for the Kingdom," I thought. On the way out the door that evening, Neil thrust a pledge card in my face, looked me in the eye, and said, "Scott, I'd like to ask you and Alma to join our finance team!"

A pledge card is your silent representative, reminding people of your need and instructing them how to give.

At first I was startled. Then I laughed, "Good joke, Neil! I'm the speaker, not the giver!"

But he insisted, "No, Scott! We're serious. Would you pray about joining our team?"

I shrugged, reluctantly took the pledge card and an envelope, and grumbled to Alma (who didn't grumble) all the way home. "Neil's wasting his time with me; we're already supporting everyone we can," I reasoned. But I had agreed to pray about it.

I put the card on my desk the next day, and we prayed about it day by day. Then I noticed my attitude changing. After 10 days, we sent the card back to Neil saying we'd be delighted to pledge monthly toward his ministry! Because of that card, I couldn't get Neil and Sue out of my mind. A pledge card is your silent representative. Don't overlook its value.

By the way, make sure your mission account number is on the card so your headquarters' receipting department doesn't wonder where to put the gift. And, of course, the check is payable to the mission—not to you.

Be sure to remind your new giving partners *not* to write your name in the memo section or anywhere on the check. The IRS frowns on that.

What if your prospective giver doesn't send back the card? Give a deadline when you're making the presentation: "Would you be able to let me know of your decision in a week, say by July 15?" If you haven't received the card by that date, call and ask, "Have you come to a decision about joining our finance support team?" (Be sure to thank them for the visit and ask about the kids, etc., before you blurt this out!)

If you sent the appeal by mail and haven't heard back by the deadline, call them, but ask a different first question: "Did you get my letter?" It's possible they haven't replied because they never received or *never read* your letter. Be prepared to give a brief appeal on the phone, then send a second letter with a pledge card.

6. Failure to appeal in specifics.

Years ago, a short-term missionary doing deputation was gun-shy about personal appeals, but she stepped out in faith to make face-to-face visits.

"Scott, out of my top 25 prospective givers, 24 decided to give!" she said.

"Wonderful!"

"But there's a problem. Their commitments total only $960 monthly, and my budget is $2,900/month."

"Did you ask them to give a certain amount?" I asked.

"No, I'm just glad they are giving!" she blurted out.

She now had to raise an additional $1,940 from people she didn't know as well. By appealing specifically for $100 to $250 per month, she likely could have raised more than $2,000.

Never ask people just to give. Ask them to give an amount or within a range. This is called proportionate giving. Remember, people often give what you suggest. If you ask for $100, you'll likely get $100. Prospective givers need to know your plan. They may be overwhelmed by your total need, but they want to provide a meaningful share. Give them an idea of what would really help.

A donor friend of mine from Wisconsin receives many missionary appeals. She once told me, "Scott, tell the missionaries to ask for a specific amount. When we are asked simply to 'give,' with no amount suggested, we don't know what to do. What is it that would really help? Quick cash, $100 monthly, $5,000 annually? Most donors don't want to be a "sugar daddy" and give the whole amount needed. Nor do they want to give such a low amount it will keep the missionary on deputation the rest of her life. They want missionaries to be specific in their appeals."

But you may wonder if suggesting a specific amount isn't too pushy.

Years ago, I was calling on an Iowa farmer. We sat at his Formica-top kitchen table and went through my presentation book. Blue silos loomed outside the window, advertising years of successful crops. We got to the last page, which contained a diagram asking for $50 givers and $150 givers. I looked him in the eye and said, "If 10 people gave $150 per month and 10 people gave $50 per month, this need would be met."

With a twinkle in his eye, he said, "I suppose all the $50 ones are taken!" He wasn't offended, nor have I ever heard of anyone being offended by a missionary suggesting an amount in a face-to-face visit. He faithfully supported us for 27 years.

There's an important principle here, and I believe it's the same one that guided Moses to ask for specific articles in the construction of the first Tabernacle in Exodus 25:1–7. The Lord told Moses to raise a contribution "from every man whose heart moves him." In verses 3–7, the Lord lists specifically the kinds of articles needed for the Tabernacle—gold, silver, bronze, scarlet material, fine linen, goat hair, rams skins dyed red, porpoise skins, acacia wood, and so on.

By listing the specific items needed, the people could more easily participate. If you didn't have silver or gold but happened to have a porpoise skin brought from Egypt, you could still give.

In your appeals, let the donors know specifically what is needed, just as Moses did. Vague appeals communicate uncertainty, confuse the donor, and obstruct God's work. What if they can't give as much as you've suggested? They'll tell you. But they may be inwardly flattered you thought they could give that much.

I'm specific with my appeals, but I always close with 2 Corinthians 9:7 and encourage people to do as they "purpose in their heart." I tell them the amount is between them and the Lord—a spiritual decision!—and ask them to do as the Lord leads. I assure them I'm confident they will make the right decision and that decision may be "no."

Your time is too valuable to waste doing unwise fundraising. By avoiding these common mistakes, you'll become more effective in using your precious time.

Chapter Seven

BEFORE YOU BEGIN:
EIGHT MONEY MANAGEMENT MUSTS

Raising personal support is only half a missionary's financial battle. What's the point of fundraising if we don't wisely handle our new income?

Unfortunately, people in ministry do not have good financial reputations. I discovered that one August afternoon as I traveled from Chicago to Minneapolis after a tiring ministry event. I decided to take the River Road along the Mississippi to enjoy a tranquil drive amid the maple trees and quaint little towns.

I was halfway through Wisconsin, enjoying the lush, deciduous forests, when I pulled into a gas station that looked unchanged since the '50s. A neat place!

Trying to sound like Andy Griffith, I said, "Fill 'er up!" to the wizened old attendant in blue bib overalls coming slowly from the back where he was working on a pickup. Then it struck me—I had no cash except for a few coins in my pocket. My heart sank.

"Can you take a credit card?" I wistfully inquired.

"Nope," he said as he pulled out the gas hose and twisted off the gas cap.

"How about a company check from a Colorado bank?"

Without even glancing up, he twisted the cap back on and replaced the hose.

"But it's a corporate check—look! You can see the balance!" I argued, waving the checkbook in his direction. He started walking away. Desperate, I called out, "This check is good. I'm a Christian minister."

He stopped immediately. Then he turned around slowly and faced me. "Young feller, that's all the more reason I'm not going to take that check. Our pastor just ran off with the church money awhile ago."

I was stunned. But I was young. My Wisconsin gas station instructor introduced me to an unpleasant reality.

It gets worse. A friend in Omaha was a salesman for a major office-equipment company. As a believer, he got all the church accounts. "Because you know all the pastors?" I asked.

Too often missionaries have plenty of money for ministry expenses but neglect home expenses.

"No, the other salesmen won't take them. Our church and ministry customers don't pay their bills on time without a hassle. And when we charge a late fee, they subtract that from the total and pay only the original amount, even though we've carried them 60, 90, or 120 days. It's a horrible testimony to the sales guys I'm trying to win to Christ."

You may know of other sad stories. And we haven't even touched on the Christian TV personalities and their financial foibles.

I don't know where it will end, but I know where it starts—with me. As I look back on my financial management as a Christian worker, I confess I have not always done right. I regularly ordered stuff we couldn't afford and then postponed paying the bills. I pushed the doctor, dentist, newspaper, and other bills to the bottom of the pile because we didn't have the money. "They can wait," I reasoned. "The Lord will bring in more next month."

I once asked NavPress, The Navigators' publishing ministry, to identify its toughest customers to collect from. The immediate reply? "Missionaries." Sadly, I was one of their overdue "accounts receivable."

If fundraising is not built on a strong foundation of good financial management, you'll never have enough money. Not even if you bring in 120 percent of budget. I know missionaries with generous budgets who are fully funded, yet they are always short of cash for groceries and paying the rent. The problem is stewardship! Let's examine eight biblical financial management "musts" for missionaries.

1. Save from every paycheck. (It's not a sin.)

I have spoken with dozens of missionaries who think they should build up a savings account, but feel guilty doing it. It's not wrong for their donors to save, they believe, but it's different for them. It might show they are not fully trusting God to miraculously get them through hospital bills, car tires, kids' college, and old age. It is a sign of "going down to Egypt," trusting man instead of God.

ANTS DO IT !

FARMERS DO IT !

GOOD DRIVERS DO IT !

MISSIONARIES DO IT ?

Although you don't want to be guilty of "hoarding," saving for anticipated needs or emergencies is a biblical concept.

I can appreciate that. I came into Christian ministry with the uneasy view that insurance, savings accounts, investments, and even extra clothes were not needed if I would only trust God. I determined I was not going to be one of those Christians who hoarded.

My theory lasted until I got married. Alma saw the value of planning for the future, of anticipating financial issues. I also noticed in Proverbs a couple of passages that didn't fit my philosophy. One was

Proverbs 30:25: "The ants are not a strong folk, but they prepare their food in the summer."

Ants don't have very big brains, but they may be smarter than I am because they plan ahead by preparing food in the summer.

Proverbs 6:6–8 is even more clear on the wisdom of preparing for the lean times: "Go to the ant, O sluggard, observe her ways and be wise, which, having no chief, officer or ruler, prepares her food in the summer, and gathers her provision in the harvest."

And I was puzzled by Matthew 6:33, a favorite verse in my early days as a believer: "But seek first His kingdom and His righteousness; and all these things shall be added to you."

As a college student and six-week-old believer, I remember sitting down to lunch in Friley Hall with the guys from Bible study. One of the seniors had been approached to buy insurance, but he refused, saying, "I'll never have a savings account or an insurance policy because it is contrary to Scripture." Then he quoted Matthew 6:33. His simplistic application seemed suspect, but who was I to disagree?

A few years later, I picked up the hobby of bird watching. I observed that birds spend most of their waking hours—some researchers say 60 percent—searching for food. When birds walk around your lawn or flutter in your trees, they aren't just killing time—they are in a life-or-death search for something to eat!

Matthew 6:26 says: "Look at the birds of the air, that they do not sow, neither do they reap, nor gather into barns, and yet your heavenly Father feeds them. Are you not worth much more than they?"

Yes, God provides for birds, but they must do their part. The food is available if they will seek and find it.

That simple bird-watching lesson helped me understand Matthew 6:33. He will take care of us too, but He expects us to do our part—just like the birds. After all, the manna from heaven did not fall into the Israelites' mouths—they had to go pick it up! And it stopped when they crossed into the Promised Land.

Proverbs 21:20 was another verse that contradicted my "don't prepare" theory: "There is precious treasure and oil in the dwelling of the wise, but a foolish man swallows it up." In other words, a wise man accumulates treasure and oil rather than immediately "swallowing it up." Perhaps accumulation is not always a sin.

I have concluded that it is possible to accumulate without hoarding, even though some believers wrongly use this as an excuse to make accumulating wealth their life mission.

Having cleared this theological hurdle, Alma and I determined to save by putting whatever was left at the end of the month into a savings account. After several months, we still had no savings, but we learned a valuable lesson: We switched from "save what is left" to the old adage, "pay yourself first."

In those days, I worked at the newspaper and got paid every Friday. But our paycheck didn't last—we were broke by the following Monday at noon! Then we'd hold our breath until Friday's paycheck.

To break that cycle, I took our paycheck directly to the bank on Friday and deposited it all, except for $25 dollars. (That was big money in those days.) I took the $25 cash, walked across the street to the Savings and Loan, and deposited it in a savings account. We were still broke by Monday noon, but we had cash in a savings account. My self-esteem soared!

After a year of this weekly walk across the street, we had saved enough to pay for our move to Iowa to join the staff of The Navigators. "Pay yourself first" worked!

You can do this! Instead of depositing your entire paycheck, hold onto perhaps 5 to 10 percent and immediately deposit it in a savings account. These days, instead of walking across the street with cash, you'll probably do it online, but pay yourself first!

Alma and I learned to segment our savings into categories and keep them separate. Otherwise, the purposes get fuzzy—not to mention how easy it is to rob from one to pay for another short-term need. Study the diagram below to see how easy it is to organize your savings. (A blank **Savings Account Categories** worksheet is in the Appendix. You can easily do this with household budgeting software too.)

Savings Account Categories

Directions: Don't think of savings as one lump sum. Break it into categories related to your goals. Build up each category to a predetermined amount; transfer long-term categories to less accessible investment methods. Money shouldn't be "borrowed" from one category by another.

Balance	Date/Explanation	Deposit	Withdrawal	Emergency	Interest	Auto Replace	Christmas	Vacation	Old Age	College
$300.00	Monthly Savings Goal			$25.00	$	$30.00	$35.00	$75.00	$60.00	$75.00
9,600.00	Balance Carried Forward			650.00	40.00	1,750.00	100.00	300.00	4,510.00	2,250.00
9,900.00	2/1 Salary Save	300.00		675.00	40.00	1,780.00	135.00	375.00	4,570.00	2,325.00
10,200.00	3/1 Salary Save	300.00		700.00	40.00	1,810.00	170.00	450.00	4,630.00	2,400.00
10,425.00	4/1 Salary Save	225.00		715.00	40.00	1,830.00	200.00	500.00	4,665.00	2,475.00
10,020.00	4/16 Roof Repair		405.00	310.00	40.00	1,830.00	200.00	500.00	4,665.00	2,475.00
10,104.20	4/30 Interest	84.20		310.00	124.20	1,830.00	200.00	500.00	4,665.00	2,475.00
10,404.20	5/1 Salary Save	300.00		335.00	124.20	1,860.00	235.00	575.00	4,725.00	2,550.00
10,729.20	6/1 Salary Save	325.00		385.00	124.20	1,890.00	270.00	650.00	4,785.00	2,625.00
10,129.20	6/20 Vacation		600.00	385.00	124.20	1,890.00	270.00	50.00	4,785.00	2,625.00

Record your savings deposit in this column, then distribute it among your savings categories on the right.

"The ants are not a strong folk, but they prepare their food in the summer." —Proverbs 30:25

(The categories listed are for illustration only.)

Sometimes missionaries don't save because they believe that it's "other people's money." Poor excuse! It's still God's money. You've received it vertically from Him, not horizontally from donors (check Chapter 3).

How much should you save? Depends on your godly purposes, but I'd recommend you start with one or two months' salary in an emergency savings account. Make sure it is easy to access.

2. Avoid debt.

Most people agree that staying out of debt is a good idea. But when put to a test, we think it's a good idea until Sears has a sale on table saws. I used to think that missionaries would not be tempted to borrow, and if they did, they would quickly pay it off. I was wrong. Missionaries are just as prone to accumulate debt as others. They may have the added temptation to borrow because "God will surely bring it in next month."

Before you read further, may I ask you to put your personal money opinions up for review? For some missionaries, borrowing through credit cards has become a way of life. One missionary had the courage to say what I suspect many believe: "My credit card is God's provision to get us through tough times." But months later, they were sinking deeper and deeper into debt.

The average American carries credit-card debt in the $10,000 to $12,000 range. Missionaries are not exempt from this dire situation, and many are $20,000 or more in debt. They have little hope of paying off the debt, and their ministry dreams are dashed.

What do the Scriptures say about debt? Not much, directly. Only three verses comment specifically on debt. Here they are:

Proverbs 22:7: "The rich rules over the poor, and the borrower becomes the lender's slave."

True, isn't it? If you owe someone money, he or she owns you. You are not free to do what you'd like as long as you owe that money.

The first time Alma and I borrowed money was to buy an air conditioner early in our marriage in humid Columbia, Missouri. It cost $240, but we couldn't afford it. So we waited. And it got hotter and hotter and more and more humid. By mid-July, we finally agreed to $80 down and two more $80 payments. Although we cooled off, we sweated more over those two $80 payments than we did from the Missouri heat. We felt in bondage to Columbia Appliance until we made those payments. Proverbs 22:7 is true.

The second verse on debt is Psalm 37:21: "The wicked borrows and does not pay back, but the righteous is gracious and gives."

Sadly, some people today do not feel a need to repay what they owe. Although it may not be a sin to borrow, it certainly is a sin to not pay back. Yet today in America, it is common to declare bankruptcy to avoid paying creditors and get a "fresh start." I have a friend who lost big in bad real estate deals, but he is slowly paying back all he owes rather than declare bankruptcy. I commend him.

Do you intend to pay that credit-card balance? When? It won't happen if you don't stop using the cards.

The third verse does not directly refer to financial debt, but the "debt" we all owe one another to love. Romans 13:8 says, "Owe nothing to anyone except to love one another; for he who loves his neighbor has fulfilled the law."

In summary, the Scriptures do not condemn debt as sin, but they warn against its danger. If you are in consumer debt, you need to ask yourself how this happened. What underlying values allowed you to buy something you could not afford? Difficult questions, but unless you answer them, you will likely be under financial bondage all your life. And be sure to look at materialism. That's a big reason for much debt today.

What about home mortgage debt? Because a home is usually an appreciating asset, you will not usually lose money in the long run. Still, you may be wise to eliminate the debt as soon as possible, because the tax advantage is not as great as having no mortgage at all. But your other debts—credit card, student loans, second mortgages, or loans from family—eliminate them!

How? Here are a few tips:

- Get rid of your credit cards immediately—keep only one. If you cannot control your use of them, you should not have them. Don't store them in a drawer—too tempting. Store them in the oven and turn it to 350 degrees. That will keep you from using them! The one credit card you keep should be used only for things like renting a car on a business trip. (Better yet, have your host pick you up!)
- Live on a budget, and make sure you pay down your debt every month.
- Have a sale and use the proceeds to pay down your debt. It is amazing (particularly in America) what people will buy at a garage sale.
- Ask the question, "Do I really need this thing I'm tempted to buy?" The answer depends in part on how you were raised. I've noticed that what used to be a luxury now seems a necessity.
- Avoid shopping malls and mail-order catalogs. Cut off the temptation before it begins!

Debt is a serious problem for the next generation of missionaries. In America, college students graduate with an average debt of $18,950. This is the first generation to fund their education primarily through loans (*Chicago Tribune,* January 5, 2005). When these young men and women join the mission force, they must add debt repayment to their list of expenses. I believe it's reducing the number of young people signing up for full-time ministry.

3. Live on a budget.

The "B" word—budgeting. Why is budgeting so unpopular? Perhaps it's because we don't want anyone or anything telling us how to spend our money.

Alma and I have lived on a budget for 29 years, and it is not always pleasant. I can't order a flannel shirt from Lands' End just because I like it. I must first check the clothing envelope, which, if empty, doesn't affirm my spur-of-the-moment catalog whims!

Budgeting enables you to live by priorities. Although I don't like the discipline a budget brings, I do like the results. We have stayed out of debt, have growing savings accounts that allow us to reach our life and ministry dreams, and we pay our bills each month on time and in full. And our kids made it through college debt free! We live in one of the most nonpressured, option-filled homes in America!

Be skeptical of people who tell you budgeting is easy. It's not, especially when you start. But find a system that works for you, and you will love the results. Now, let me correct a misunderstanding of what it means to budget.

A missionary friend constantly was having trouble paying household bills. He was at 70 percent of budget and short each month; he used his credit card to make up the difference. But after attending a fundraising seminar, Bob decided to make a change. So for a year he worked hard at his funding plan, and soon his income stood at 98 percent of his approved organizational allowance. A huge increase!

As his funding sponsor, I congratulated Bob on his progress, but he was not enthusiastic. Something was still wrong. Finally, he told me he was $250 short each month, even though he was "fully funded."

So we talked about budgeting. Had he been living on the budget that I had helped him set up? After he described the elaborate accounting system he and his wife had organized, he said, "Scott, I can tell you where our money goes down to the last dime—budgeting is not the problem."

As I listened, I knew that didn't sound right, but I didn't know what to say. Silence. Finally, it came to me. "Bob, is it possible you are mistaking budgeting for cost accounting?" Now it was his turn to be silent. "What do you mean?" he asked.

I explained that just knowing where your money goes is not budgeting. That's accounting. Budgeting requires "gates"—something that will tell you to stop spending. No gates, no budget.

"Hmmm," he said. I went on to wager a White Castle burger that a strict budget would give him an excess each month instead of the $250 deficit. "Hmmmm," he said again. I'd struck a chord.

So Bob and Ronda set up the old-fashioned envelope system of budgeting—one that Alma and I have used successfully. First, they deposited their salary check in the bank, putting in enough to pay their mortgage, utilities, and giving.

Then they took cash to their home—twenties, tens, and a few fives—enough, they hoped, to cover their household expenses for a month. They laid out eight blank envelopes on the dining

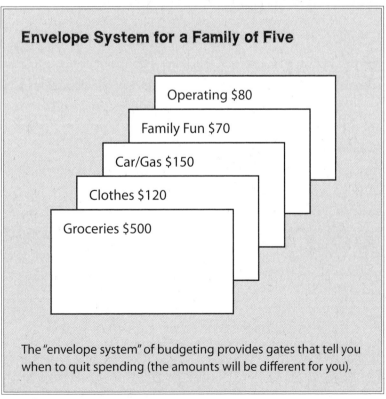

Envelope System for a Family of Five

Operating $80

Family Fun $70

Car/Gas $150

Clothes $120

Groceries $500

The "envelope system" of budgeting provides gates that tell you when to quit spending (the amounts will be different for you).

room table and labeled them as shown on the previous page. Then they distributed an appropriate amount of cash to each envelope.

Now here's the secret of the envelope system: When the envelope is empty, you stop spending in that category! For example, if the clothing envelope is empty by the 12th of the month, you stop buying clothes until next month. Even if Lands' End has a sale!

It will take a month or two to get the amounts right for each envelope, but you now have a budgeting system with "gates" to keep you from overspending. The other advantage of the envelope system is that you need not keep records.

Worried about having a lot of cash around the house? No problem—most of it is gone in 10 days anyway!

Any budgeting system will work if you don't blow past the gates. Some people keep their records on the computer. Others record their daily spending in a notebook. Fine. Use whatever works best for you—but you must have *gates*.

Some people argue that they are naturally frugal and not tempted to buy stuff. I know several missionaries who don't think they need a budget because they "spend as little as necessary" anyway. Right?

Wrong! A budget is still needed because it gives or denies "permission to spend." Living under constant pressure to "spend as little as possible" is *bondage*. I'm not advocating wild spending. I am advocating freedom to spend up to an agreed-upon limit. It reduces pressure. Wives tell me how freeing the envelope system is because they feel freedom to spend up to the limit instead of being under pressure to spend as little as possible.

Though it may seem awkward at first, try it. Years from now, as you watch your children graduate from college without debt, as you help your son or daughter start a small business, as you buy that special house, as you come back from overseas to visit your aging parents for no reason except that they are your parents, as you use emergency funds to replace your car engine, as you see your retirement funds grow to where money problems will not plague you in old age—then you'll be glad you budgeted.

But you won't have to wait for years before you experience the joy of budgeting. As you begin to pay bills on time, save each month, and live on financial margin, you will experience new freedom.

What about Bob and Ronda? Three months after my White Castle wager, instead of being $250 short each month, they had $150 extra. The problem was Bob's picking up "this and that" at the store when he ran errands. Often, the things he bought were helpful items for ministry, such as books to give away. The envelope "gates" brought Bob's good-hearted but undisciplined spending to a halt. And today they are succeeding in saving for their personal and ministry dreams.

4. Know well the condition of your flock.

Too many Christian workers are so spiritually minded they downplay the pragmatic matters of life—like paying bills or paying attention to insurance expiration dates. Though we are spiritual beings, we are also physical beings. To quote the singer Madonna, we live in a "material world." That is why we must heed the proverb to "know well the condition of your flocks, and pay attention to your herds; for riches are not forever" (Proverbs 27:23–24).

You may not own a flock of sheep, but you do have assets that need your close attention because "riches are not forever." By being inattentive, you could lose your "flock."

This verse reminds me of my dad back on the farm in Iowa. We raised hogs, farrowing 15 at a time. That means 15 sows had baby pigs within a 10-day period. It was my task to let the 15 sows out of their separate pens at evening chore time so they could eat and drink. No problem there. The sows were eager to get out of the pens after being cooped up with the piglets all day. The problem was getting them back into the same pen they came from. A 250-pound sow in the wrong pen with the wrong piglets creates aggressive snorting, broken gates, and a lot of shouting. Every farm kid knows you don't mess with angry, agitated sows with piglets.

But to me, all the sows looked alike. They were all white Landrace crossbreeds. No colors or spots. I couldn't tell one from the other. So I wrote a number on their backs as they left their pens in order to get them back in the right place.

Not Dad. He recognized each one. "Their faces are different," he'd say. And he noted other characteristics too. That took time. He'd watch them eat. He studied them. He "knew well the condition" of his hogs.

Similarly, you and I need to take the time necessary to "know well the condition" of our assets. Take time to study and understand where your money goes, what savings accounts you have, what your mutual funds are doing, the exact interest rate on your mortgage, how much insurance you have, what your spouse will receive if you were to die today, what you have budgeted for groceries, for clothes, for family fun.

Both husbands and wives should know "the state of their flock"—their financial assets.

Too many missionaries can't answer those simple questions. Many men say, "Ask my wife." They do not "know well the state" of their assets, and they will suffer financially for it.

Perhaps the reason we don't pay close attention to our assets is because we tend to divide life into the sacred and the secular. One is spiritual and worthy of our time; the other is worldly and deserves only a pittance of our valuable time. But this attitude is contrary not only to Proverbs but also to Luke 16:11: "If therefore you have not been faithful in the use of unrighteous mammon, who will entrust the true riches to you?"

Jesus did not explain "true riches." They likely include unseen spiritual matters, such as the souls of people, eternal truth, or the working of the Holy Spirit—things we cannot see. But He did explain that the prerequisite for getting these true riches is being faithful in the things we can see—unrighteous mammon. Jesus put a premium on looking after the material part of life.

All of life is spiritual. Every decision is spiritual. We err when we separate life into a sacred-spiritual dichotomy.

I used to feel guilty spending time on my budget, paying bills, or figuring out how much insurance we had. Or cleaning the garage.

One Saturday morning, I was feeling sorry for myself as I swept the garage. Alma noticed my lackadaisical attitude and confronted me. "You think this is beneath you, don't you? Stuff like cleaning the garage, paying bills, just living life. You'd rather be out doing ministry, wouldn't you?"

I gulped. "No," I lied. She saw through my fake spirituality. I felt I should be doing something more "spiritual" like studying the Bible or sharing my faith. After that day, I decided to read Luke 16:11 more closely.

A word to husbands: You are wise to delegate certain financial tasks to your wife, especially if she has a knack for it. Many wives

"Doing" your ministry is not more spiritual than funding your ministry.

see these issues more clearly than their husbands. However, do not delegate the responsibility of knowing the state of the flock. Too many wives feel 100 percent of the pressure of finances. Husbands, take Luke 16:11 more seriously.

5. Identify your financial goals.

In the back of your mind, you have financial dreams or at least half-formed thoughts, although they are probably not written down. Do you have the courage to put them down on paper so you can see which ones are valid and which came about because your parents wouldn't give you a bigger allowance? Don't feel guilty about your financial dreams. Write them down, study them, pray over them. God will help you separate those that are proper from those based on greed.

Financial goals are closely related to your life dreams and desires. In fact, financial goals are simply the price tags attached to your life goals. For example:

- To live on margin each month—bills paid on time, monthly savings for God-ordained purposes.
- To get your kids through college or job training without debt. That is one of the biggest acts of love you can do for your kids. Many college graduates enter the workforce with an $18,000 college loan that someone told them they could easily pay off. After buying a car

and a refrigerator and marrying someone who brings a dowry of another
$18,000 of debt, the couple is now two
years into marriage with a child on the
way and $36,000 in debt. Both partners
will have to work full-time, and they
may never be able to buy a house. And
it all started with a harmless low-inter-
est college loan. Don't do it!

- To have a liquid emergency fund equal
  to two months' salary. Most financial
  advisers suggest six months' salary, but
  let's be realistic. Also, most missionaries
  don't suddenly get fired.
- To never borrow for a vehicle but save
  for it instead.
- To not need to raise support after
  age 66. I'm not suggesting you retire,
  but give yourself the option to stop
  fundraising. Many retired missionaries thought that some magic was going
  to happen to fund them generously in
  retirement. It didn't, and it won't.
- To give $1,000,000 to missions in your
  lifetime.
- To visit 50 countries at your own expense to encourage missionary friends.
- To be able to put down 30 percent on a
  house for home assignment.

Priorities in Financial Management

The stairstep of financial priorities in establishing financial goals:

#4 Long-term saving
House down payment, college fund, old age, bonus, dreams

#3 Short-term saving
Auto, appliances, vacation

#2 Establish a liquid emergency fund
Two months' living expenses for unanticipated emergencies

#1 Get out of consumer debt and stop paying interest
Credit cards, auto loans, home equity loans, etc.

Tip: Focus on getting out of debt and establishing a liquid emergency fund first.

Do you get the idea? Your financial goals will be tied to your personal and ministry dreams. Get both down on paper. Pray over them. Ask the Lord if your ideas are from Him. Then work on a plan to make them reality. (And it will probably mean you will need to be at full support!)

I have adapted the diagram to the right from Ron Blue, a financial planner from Atlanta, to help me know where to begin and how to keep going without getting confused.

Where to start? Get on a budget and get out of debt. The next section describes information I learned that helped me understand the tremendous power of debt and savings.

6. Understand the power of debt and savings.

Americans are far too casual about the cost of going into debt. It is so common today that the terrible penalty is overlooked. However, the chart on the following page reveals the devastation.

Let's say you overspend by only $80 per month. Harmless enough, totaling only $960 in a year's time. But at a normal credit-card interest rate of 18 percent, the total owed after one year is $1,133. After five years, $4,800 (5 x $960) is actually spent, but $6,104 is the amount that must be paid back.

Now let's say that you want to correct the problem. To pay off the $6,104 in five years, you pay not $80 each month but $150.

The total interest paid for the privilege of overspending by $80 a month is $7,494. That is known as working for your money!

Now contrast the debt trap with the savings chart on page 90. Instead of overspending by $80 per month, let's say you save $83 per month ($1,000 per year), earning only 6 percent interest. After five years you'd have $5,975, but after 15 years, you would have accumulated $24,672!

Now suppose you wanted to withdraw not $1,000 per year, but $2,000. You could take out $2,000 per year for 20 years, and you'd still have $1,142 left over! That's making your money work for you!

Do you see the tremendous power of saving and the tremendous devastation of borrowing? And the difference is made in the small decisions regarding what to do with $80 per month. Those little decisions to deny spending and save make a huge difference years later.

7. Don't buy a dog. (Just kidding! Or not.)

8. Avoid simple mistakes.

Here are a few money-saving tips, especially for those living in America who are in debt and need to cut costs:

- Don't replace your vehicle every two years. According to Christian financial consultant Ron Blue, you will save money by keeping your car as long as it will run safely, even if it means frequent repairs.
- Eliminate options on your phone service, such as call waiting (a good way to make two people angry at the same time) or last-call return.
- You can do without magazine subscriptions and cable TV! Play Scrabble instead!
- Avoid using your credit card, even if you can pay it off. Studies show that Americans spend 19 percent less when they pay by cash or check.
- Having fun needn't cost money. Be creative on family fun nights. Our family favorite was "Paper Sword Jousting Night" using no more than rolled-up newspaper. Use your imagination!

The Debt Trap: An Illustration

Overspending

Here's what overspending your income by $80 a month will add to your debt total in five years at 18 percent annual interest.

Year	Debt Addition	Interest	Total Debt
1	$960	$173	$1,133
2	960	377	2,470
3	960	617	4,047
4	960	901	5,908
5	960	1,236	8,104

Debt Repayment

And here's what it will cost you to repay that debt in the next five years at $203.17 each month.

Year	Annual Payment	Debt Paydown	Total Debt
6	$2,438	$1,350	$6,912
7	2,438	1,142	5,616
8	2,438	894	4,072
9	2,438	582	2,216
10	2,438	222	—

Interest First 5 Years	$3,304
Interest Last 5 Years	4,190
Total Interest	$7,494

Savings: An Illustration

$1,000 saved annually at 6 percent interest compounded annually for 15 years:

Year	Addition	Interest Earned	Ending Balance
1	$1,000	$60	$1,060
2	1,000	123	2,183
3	1,000	191	3,374
4	1,000	262	4,636
5	1,000	383	5,975
6	1,000	418	7,393
7	1,000	503	8,897
8	1,000	593	10,491
9	1,000	689	12,180
10	1,000	790	13,971
11	1,000	898	15,869
12	1,000	1,012	17,882
13	1,000	1,132	20,015
14	1,000	1,260	22,276
15	1,000	1,396	24,672

At the end of 15 years, you could start to withdraw $2,000 annually:

Year	Addition	Interest Earned	Ending Balance
16	2,000	1,360	24,032
17	2,000	1,321	23,354
18	2,000	1,281	22,636
19	2,000	1,238	21,874
20	2,000	1,192	21,066
21	2,000	1,144	20,210
22	2,000	1,092	19,303
23	2,000	1,038	18,341
24	2,000	980	17,321
25	2,000	919	16,241
26	2,000	854	15,095

At the end of 11 years of $2,000 withdrawals, you still have more on deposit than you invested originally.

Year	Addition	Interest Earned	Ending Balance
27	2,000	785	13,881
28	2,000	712	12,594
29	2,000	635	11,230
30	2,000	553	9,783
31	2,000	467	8,250
32	2,000	375	6,625
33	2,000	277	4,903
34	2,000	174	3,077
35	2,000	64	1,142

You invested $15,000 of your money in 15 years. Because of interest, you withdrew at $2,000 per year during the next 20 years ($40,000) and you still had left $1,142.36.

That's known as having your money work for you!

The Magic of Compound Interest: An Illustration (12 percent return)

The chart below shows the incredible power of saving a little and saving it early. Study it and take savings steps immediately!

	Example A			Example B	
Age	Payment	Accumulation End of Year	Age	Payment	Accumulation End of Year
22	$2,000	$2,240	22	$ 0	$ 0
23	2,000	4,749	23	0	0
24	2,000	7,559	24	0	0
25	2,000	10,706	25	0	0
26	2,000	14,230	26	0	0
27	2,000	18,178	27	0	0
28	0	20,359	28	2,000	2,240
29	0	22,803	29	2,000	4,749
30	0	25,539	30	2,000	7,559
31	0	28,603	31	2,000	10,706
32	0	32,036	32	2,000	14,230
33	0	35,880	33	2,000	18,178
34	0	40,186	34	2,000	22,599
35	0	45,008	35	2,000	27,551
36	0	50,409	36	2,000	33,097
37	0	56,458	37	2,000	39,309
38	0	63,233	38	2,000	46,266
39	0	70,821	39	2,000	54,058
40	0	79,320	40	2,000	62,785
41	0	88,838	41	2,000	72,559
42	0	99,499	42	2,000	83,507
43	0	111,438	43	2,000	95,767
44	0	124,811	44	2,000	109,499
45	0	139,788	45	2,000	124,879
46	0	156,563	46	2,000	142,105
47	0	175,351	47	2,000	161,397
48	0	196,393	48	2,000	183,005
49	0	219,960	49	2,000	207,206
50	0	246,355	50	2,000	234,310
51	0	275,917	51	2,000	264,668
52	0	309,028	52	2,000	298,668
53	0	346,111	53	2,000	336,748
54	0	387,644	54	2,000	379,398
55	0	434,161	55	2,000	427,166
56	0	486,261	56	2,000	480,665
57	0	544,612	57	2,000	540,585
58	0	609,966	58	2,000	607,695
59	0	683,162	59	2,000	682,859
60	0	765,141	60	2,000	767,042
61	0	856,958	61	2,000	861,327
62	0	959,793	62	2,000	966,926
63	0	1,074,968	63	2,000	1,085,197
64	0	1,203,964	64	2,000	1,217,661
65	0	1,348,440	65	2,000	1,366,020

By waiting six years, the person in Example B needs to make an additional 31 payments of $2,000 to achieve the same retirement results as the person in Example A.

You might find yourself reacting negatively to some of the suggestions in this chapter. Let me ask you again to reevaluate your financial behaviors and values. Following your parents' example may be comfortable, but it may not be right. Following the advice of Christian friends may be more cultural than Christian. Difficult though it may be, make sure the Bible is your guide in financial matters. As Dick Towner says in his Good $ense Movement course (from the Willow Creek Association): "There's no such thing as being right with God and wrong with our money."

Chapter Eight
HOW TO SET A FUNDRAISING STRATEGY

At last! We've made it to the "meat and potatoes" of fundraising—setting a fundraising strategy. Sadly, this is where many missionaries go wrong in their fundraising. I once tried to help a missionary develop his funding strategy, but we weren't getting anywhere. He nodded in agreement to my suggestions, but mostly I was talking and he was staring blankly. I felt like I was talking to a Cadillac car dealer about trading in my Volkswagon van. Finally I said, "You haven't put much time or effort into this, have you?"

"No, I haven't," he confessed awkwardly. And though he didn't seem motivated to put in the effort, I sent him back to pray through his mailing list name by name and to think about when he could schedule his appeals. He finally decided to work hard on the assignment and returned brimming with confidence. He now had a workable plan!

In other aspects of ministry, we work hard to discover what tactics God wants us to take. But we often backstroke our approach to fundraising.

Don't just dive into fundraising flippantly. Think it through. How many donors do you need? How many personal appeals can you make? To whom will you make them? When will you do it? What will you say?

Just as David did not fit into Saul's armor, so you should not try to copy

A solid fundraising plan will keep you from getting distracted and off course.

someone else's fundraising plan. Get a strategy from the Lord. Then you'll be confident. Without a strategy, your fundraising will go from crisis to crisis. That takes the joy out of ministry. Following these six steps will help you develop a wise strategy.

1. Analyze your donor base and mailing list.

"Know well the condition of your flocks" (Proverbs 27:23) also applies to your mailing list. Before you can launch a wise funding strategy, you must "know the condition" of your financial flock. I'm amazed at the number of missionaries who don't know answers to simple questions like these:

- How many people are on your general mailing list?
- How many monthly donors?
- How many annual donors?
- What size is your average gift?
- How many give $100 or more per month? Less than $25 per month?
- What is your current donor-income average?
- What is your total budget? Your salary?
- How much (exactly) do you still need to raise?

Once you know the answers to these questions, you are ready to develop your plan. To analyze your current status, fill in the **Donor Base Analysis** worksheet on the next two pages. (If you are just starting out and have no previous donor income, skip this step.)

Please do not think of this as busy work. Knowing the state of your flock will give you *confidence* and will trigger *ideas.* For example, years ago, the night before Thanksgiving, I was discouraged about our income. I knew we were behind, but I didn't know how much. Lethargy had set in—I knew I should act, but it seemed overwhelming. I had postponed taking action for weeks. But that Wednesday night I forced myself to at least figure out exactly where we stood. What was the condition of our flock?

I stayed up late, sitting at the Ping-Pong table that would be used for Thanksgiving dinner in 12 hours. As I studied our records and prayed, I discovered we were $900 below budget monthly. In filling out the paperwork, I also noticed we had only six $75 to $100 monthly donors. So I considered inviting 10 additional people to give $90 a month. The idea seemed workable, and my sense of being overwhelmed disappeared as I began finding names of people who would be willing to hear my story by December 31.

Don't wait until Thanksgiving! Take a couple of hours now to fill out the **Donor Base Analysis** worksheet. Also, jot down ideas for action.

2. Determine your fundraising goal.

Determining a goal is not as easy as it sounds. Please don't dishonor Christ by merely picking a number out of the air: "Oh, we need about $3,500 ballpark."

How much do you need exactly? If you are fuzzy about your goal, you will not sound credible. I applaud those mission agencies that tell their missionaries exactly how much they must raise.

If your mission agency dictates your funding goal, filling out the worksheet on page 98 will be easy. If, on the other hand, your agency lets you determine your budget (with their approval, I hope), you'll need to take more time with this next worksheet, **Determining Your Fundraising Goal.**

Gather your financial forms and start now. You can probably finish in a few minutes.

The monthly amount you need to raise may seem overwhelming. But rather than lowering

Donor Base Analysis (Veteran missionaries only)

Previous 12 Months

Month	Total Donor Income*	Number of Donors	Average Gift Size	Church Amount	Average Gift Without Church	$100 or More	$50–$99	$25–$49	$25 or Less
	$		$	$	$				
	$		$	$	$				
	$		$	$	$				
	$		$	$	$				
	$		$	$	$				
	$		$	$	$				
	$		$	$	$				
	$		$	$	$				
	$		$	$	$				
	$		$	$	$				
	$		$	$	$				
Total	$		$	$	$				
Averages		Donor Base							

* Do not include income from other sources such as boarder's rent or material sales. List donor income only.

Donor Base Analysis

A. What is the size of your total general (all included) mailing list? _____

B. In the past 12 months, how many regular monthly donors have skipped three or more months without resuming? _____ (Check month-by-month donor summary.)

What will you do to restart them? _____

_____

C. How many financial appeals did you make during this time period? _____

Face-to-face _____ Telephone _____ Letter _____ Group _____

D. How many newsletters did you send during this time period? _____

E. Cash-project income/special income

Amount received $_____

Total number of donors _____

Number of first-time donors _____

Which of these first-time donors could be approached for regular monthly support?

_____

F. Other observations/comments _____

_____

_____

the amount to meet your comfort zone, let it sit for a few days. If your A–G analysis is honest, that's the amount you ought to aim for—that's your "holy number"!

If you're married, don't forget to check your holy number with your spouse (obviously) and your supervisor. Don't be alone in your goal.

3. Determine how many donors—monthly and annual—you'll need.

To determine how many donors you'll need, simply divide your fundraising goal (Line J) by your average gift, as shown on page 99.

For example, to raise $2,250 per month in new support (Line J), divide $2,250 by $50 (average monthly pledge from the **Donor Base Analysis**). That means you need 45 new donors.

If you feel your average gift will be higher, say $75 per month, you'll only need 30 new donors at $75 per month ($2,250 ÷ $75 = 30).

If you can secure some $100-per-month partners and a few annual commitments of $2,000 to $5,000—or a church to back you at $700 per month—then you will not need as many $50 donors.

Now, using the example above, how many fundraising appointments will be needed to recruit these 45 new monthly donors? Only 45 if all pledged, but we know they won't all pledge. Experience has shown that about half of those you'll ask face-to-face for a monthly or annual pledge will indeed give, assuming your skills are good and that God is calling you to the mission. Therefore, 90 face-to-face appointments are needed.

Please note that I'm not talking about start-up or "one-time project" donors. First, you must determine how many regular (monthly or annual) donors you'll need. Raising cash to launch a ministry or for a special one-time need is easy compared to generating a monthly donor base. Too many missionaries are deceived by an enthusias-

An undefined, fuzzy goal won't motivate you to fundraise, and it may cause you to lose credibility with potential donors.

tic response to a cash appeal, only to discover the harsh reality that they can't buy groceries by month three. Cash projects will be dealt with in Chapter 15. Concentrate on your monthly base first.

Note: If your goal is $5,000 or more, you must think in terms of "anchor donors" (another name for "major donors"). You will not reach your goal with $25 and $50 monthly commitments. Identify 10 "anchors" you could invite for $2,500 to $5,000 per year.

4. Identify your top prospective givers.

To follow through with the $2,250 example, 45 new donors at $50 per month are needed. Assuming 50 percent will pledge when seen face-to-face, 90 appointments are needed. So how do you find the 90?

Here's where missionaries often lose common sense. Instead of considering people they already know, they attempt to get appointments with complete strangers. Back when I lived on the farm, we saw the folly of young, ambitious farmers eager to rent new land but unable to keep up with harvesting land they already farmed.

Determining Your Fundraising Goal
(Doing your homework pays off when you make appeals!)

1. What is your total monthly budget as approved by your mission agency? (Do not include cash projects.)

	Original	Adjusted
A. Salary/Living Allowance	$ _____	$ _____
B. Ministry Expense	$ _____	$ _____
C. Benefits (Health, Life, Pension)	$ _____	$ _____
D. Administrative Charges	$ _____	$ _____
E. Other	$ _____	$ _____
F. Total	$ _____	$ _____

2. Are you allowed to adjust your budget? If so, adjust it here. You may want to change your salary portion from agency allowances for the following reasons:

   • You have an outside income and don't need the entire salary allotment.

   • You have an adequate outside insurance benefit.

   • You know your ministry expenses will be different from those allowed.

3. Enter your monthly "donor base" income from the Donor Base Analysis worksheet. If you have no current donor income, enter "0."

   G. Monthly "Donor Base" $ _____

4. Subtract Line G from Line F (adjusted).

   H. Monthly Gross Goal $ _____

5. Subtract income from other sources you will use to reduce your donor income need (i.e., materials sales, honoraria).

   I. Other Income Total $ _____

6. Subtract I from H

   J. Monthly Amount Needed to Raise ("Holy Number") $ _____

Note: Cash needs will be covered in another section, but you may want to list special "one-time" cash projects here.

Project Description	Amount Needed	Due By
_____	_____	_____
_____	_____	_____
_____	_____	_____

Donors and Appointments Needed

		Sample	Your Figures
Regular monthly amount needed to raise (From Line J)	1.	$2,250	$ _____
Size of your average gift without churches (From your **Donor Base Analysis** worksheet. Use $50 if you are skeptical of your figures or just starting out.)	2.	$50	$ _____
Divide Line 1 by Line 2 (New monthly donors needed)	3.	45	_____
Multiply Line 3 by Line 2 (Because about 50 percent of those you see face-to-face will make a pledge)	4.	x2	x2
Face-to-face appointments needed	5.	90	_____

Why look to strangers when your friends and acquaintances will gladly support you? Start with those you know. Go to strangers only after you've exhausted your own networks.

I've found the following technique works for me and many others. I pray through the 700 names on my mailing list, name by name, asking the Lord to impress upon me those people I ought to go see. Notice that I add almost everyone with whom I am acquainted to my mailing list.

I pray, "Father, is this person one who ought to hear my story?" Sure, it's subjective, but I'll mark a few names and continue to pray over them. As I pray, I'm asking the question, "Would this person be willing to hear my 'dazzling vision' of ministry?" I don't ask, "Would this person be willing to give?" Wrong question.

If you feel you have no one to go to, try the **Mailing List Chart** on page 100. Here's how it worked with Joe, a missionary friend who took me to lunch to ask about referrals because he'd "used up" his mailing list.

Here are the numbers we worked out over his Philly sandwich special. Does Joe have prospects? Yes, according to the chart—497! And they are well-cultivated too, because most had been on his mailing list for years.

Joe hadn't even finished his sandwich when he asked, "What's the next step? I'm ready to get going now that I know I've got prospective donors who already know me."

Try this exercise yourself. Jot in your own numbers beside Joe's. (If you're just starting out in missions, then nearly everyone on your mailing list is a candidate.)

This chart gives you the number of people—whom you know at least well enough to send a newsletter to—who have not had the privilege of hearing your story face-to-face in their own

Mailing List Chart

	Joe	You
Mailing List Total (number on your general or broadest mailing list)	647	_____
Minus current monthly donors	-45	_____
Minus annual or regular donors	-15	_____
Minus nonbelievers	-10	_____
Minus family members	-15	_____
Minus other missionaries	-45	_____
Minus people who don't like you!	-5	_____
Minus those you've appealed to face-to-face in the past two years	-15	_____
Subtotal	150	_____
Subtract Subtotal from Mailing List Total	497	_____

living rooms (at least in the past two years).

I like what a Canadian missionary said: "I want to give every person on my mailing list the privilege of saying no to my face." Of course, most said yes!

Now, write down the names of those friends and acquaintances to whom you hope to appeal. You can do this on a computer spreadsheet, but you'll save time and avoid frustration if you transfer all your prospects to the **5 Ws Financial Appeal Worksheet,** at the end of this chapter. Seeing all these names in *one place* will make the job seem more manageable.

Remember, as you think of potential donors, don't ask, "Who would be willing to support me?" When I ask that, I can't think of even one. But I come up with many when I ask, "Who would be willing to hear my story?"

5. Plot your top prospective donors on a map.

After you've written down each "who" on the 5 Ws sheet, the next step is to figure out "where" they are located. It is impossible to plan a fundraising strategy until you've identified where your top candidates live.

A cluster of three or four in one geographical area is certainly worth a trip. If only one pledges $50, that's $600 per year—$3,000 after five years of support, $6,000 after 10 years. That's a good ROI (return on investment) even if you bought a no-discount plane ticket.

Plot your top prospective givers on a map and begin planning your schedule, making as many personal visits as possible. Remember, you'll get at least twice the response to personal visits as you do to phone appeals.

6. Draft your action plan.

Now that you have clarified your "holy number" fundraising goal, discovered the number of donors you'll need, identified those you'd like to explain your dazzling

> **5 Ws**
>
> <u>Wh</u>om shall I invite?
> <u>Wh</u>ere do they live?
> <u>Wh</u>at is their phone number?
> <u>Wh</u>en will I appeal?
> <u>Wh</u>at will I ask?

vision to, and plotted them on a map, you are ready to draft your action plan. Use the worksheet at the end of this chapter (page 102).

When writing your action plan, your first draft needn't be perfect. Just get your main points down, then analyze your plan using these six checkpoints from this chapter. Then consult with your fundraising sponsor for feedback.

Note: If you are on a short-term assignment of one year or less, you may be able to raise half of your support through a cash-project letter. Many friends will give a "one-time" gift for your short-term mission, and you need not focus as much on monthly donors. But be sure to line up a few one-time major donors. See Chapter 15 for how to develop a successful cash-project letter.

Start with those closest to you rather than strangers.

Financial Appeal Action Plan
(Be specific!)

Amount Needed to Raise	$ _____ Monthly	Due By: _____
Phase 1: To Raise	$ _____ Monthly by _____ (date)
Phase 2: To Raise	$ _____ Monthly by _____ (date)
Phase 3: To Raise	$ _____ Monthly by _____ (date)

1. **Number on Mailing List:** _____ **Increase by** _____ **by** _____ **(date)**

   I will increase my mailing list through these actions:

   _____

   _____

2. **I will appeal to the following for major gifts (at least $200–$1,000 monthly or $2,500–$15,000 annually):**

Name	Amount	By (Date)	Name	Amount	By (Date)
_____	_____	_____	_____	_____	_____
_____	_____	_____	_____	_____	_____
_____	_____	_____	_____	_____	_____
_____	_____	_____	_____	_____	_____
_____	_____	_____	_____	_____	_____

3. **I will make _____ face-to-face appeals (names listed on attached 5 Ws).**

4. **I will make _____ letter/phone appeals (impossible to visit in person—names listed on attached 5 Ws).**

5. **I will invite _____ current donors to increase support (listed on attached 5 Ws).**

6. **I will network with _____, _____, _____, to appeal by referrals (if needed).**

7. **Other** _____

   _____

8. **I will trust the following to start giving through "prayer alone."**

   _____ _____ _____ _____

   I will e-mail a weekly report to my fundraising sponsor, who is

   _____ , e-mail address _____

   Signed _____ **Today's Date** _____

Financial Appeal Worksheet (5 Ws)
(Photocopy extra sheets for personal use as needed.)

List below the names of people who you think would be willing to hear about your ministry and vision. You don't know if they will give or not—that is between them and the Lord—but you would like to give them an opportunity. Thinking in sets of 10 makes it a little more "bite-sized." Under "Appeal," limit your answer to the five possibilities listed.

	Preparation					Appeal	Results			
	Whom Shall I Invite?	Where Do They Live?	What Is Their Phone Number?	When Will I Appeal?	What Will I Ask?	Type of Appeal*/ Date Made	Results (Monthly, Annual, Cash Gift, Undecided, No)	Sent Thank You	Money Received	Comment
	Jim Shoe	Los Angeles	210/520-0000	5/1–7/07	$50/month	F/May 5	$50/month	5/22	6/8	Moving to WA
1										
2										
3										
4										
5										
6										
7										
8										
9										
10										
11										
12										
13										
14										
15										

*F=Face-to-Face, L=Personal Letter, T=Telephone, G=Group Appeal, O=Other

PHONING FOR A FUNDRAISING APPOINTMENT

Now that you have identified a list of prospective donors and plotted them on a map, it's time to phone them to ask for appointments. This is the toughest part for most missionaries. Many say, "I'd enjoy fundraising if it weren't for phoning." Why is it so hard?

It's hard because that's when rejection is most likely. Once the appointment is set and the prospective giver knows why you're coming, rejection is less likely.

At the seminars I teach, I begin this section by getting on the phone in front of the entire group and asking for an appointment with one of my prospective donors. Unrehearsed. No checking ahead of time. Rejection is a definite possibility! Sweaty-palms time for sure, but I try not to let on. I do this to help the missionaries overcome fear and to demonstrate that it is not as big an obstacle as it seems.

Don't think of the phone as your enemy! It's the first step toward a positive fundraising experience.

I ask for silence so I can concentrate and so the person on the phone won't hear the laughing (or praying) in the background. At a seminar in Indianapolis, one missionary said, "I wish you would make that phone call shorter; I can't hold my breath that long!"

Sure, the phone is scary, but follow these suggestions, and you'll do fine.

1. Make an outline and pray before you start.

Don't "read a script," but don't rely on spur-of-the-moment wit and wisdom either. An outline allows you to relax, forget yourself, and concentrate on the needs of the listener. The more confident you are of what you're going to say, the better you can listen to your friend.

You also ought to rehearse your phone call a few times to the mirror, a friend, or, if you want really helpful suggestions, your spouse.

I can hear extrovert readers saying, "Nah! I can wing it; no point in wasting time writing an outline." Sure, you can wing it, but you'll be more effective with an outline. I learned long ago I'm not naturally articulate. Most of us aren't. Sorry!

At the end of this chapter, you'll find a sample phone outline and a blank one to fill in yourself. Keep your phone outline beside you when you call.

2. Make sure you have the listener's full attention.

Have you ever received a phone call just as you were headed out the door? Or in the middle of

Don't assume people are sitting idly by the phone, waiting for your call. Be sure to ask if this is a good time to talk.

putting the kids to bed? When your listener is preoccupied with being on time to Little League practice or trying to fix supper while caring for a cranky baby, you're not going to have her undivided attention. She will not seriously consider your request for an appointment. She has but one goal—to get off the phone.

After a brief greeting and perhaps a little small talk, I ask, "Do you have a minute to talk? Or shall I call back later?" Your listener will tell you if it's a bad time.

3. Mention money when you ask for an appointment.

If you do not mention money on the phone, you cannot mention it at the appointment. We must not lead our friends to believe we are coming to their home to fellowship when, in fact, we intend to make a financial appeal. And just praying that the subject will come up is naïve. It usually doesn't.

Furthermore, if you haven't explained that one purpose of your visit is to invite them to join your financial team, you will not be yourself. You'll be as nervous as a young pastor on Stewardship Sunday. Instead of relaxing and enjoying the fellowship, you'll be preoccupied with looking for a money opening, such as, "Speaking of high prices, let me tell you about our financial situation."

Instead of focusing on your friend's need, you'll focus on your need for a lead-in to talk about money—like a frazzled Christmas shopper frantically seeking an open parking space at the mall. Forget it. Tell them on the phone why you're coming, lest you be put into the same camp as the pyramid sales folk.

However, don't say so much on the phone about money that the listener thinks you are asking him to make a financial decision right then.

A missionary friend preparing to go to Indonesia was 0 for 7 in securing appointments from his best prospective givers. He was discouraged! He told me he was extremely "up-front" with these friends on the phone and explained in detail that he was seeking financial support. But no appointments.

I suggested that he tone down his financial talk because the listeners may have thought he wanted them to make a financial decision right there on the phone.

He changed tactics. He still mentioned money but was clear that he was not expecting a financial decision on the phone. His next five phone calls resulted in five appointments and eventually five pledges!

Remember, the goal of the phone call is to get an appointment.

I usually say something like this: "This month I am working on a special project—developing our financial support team. As I considered whom I'd like to have on the team, I thought of you."

If my friend hesitates to give me an appointment, I say, "There is no

If you plan to ask people to give during your presentation, let them know that when you phone for the appointment.

obligation. It would be an honor to tell you about my ministry whether you are able to give or not." I want people to feel free to say no without jeopardizing our relationship.

4. Confirm date, time, place, and directions.

Appointments are tough enough without going to the wrong house on the wrong night. Be discerning about your appointee's ability to give directions. Some people just can't do it: "Sort of angle to the left after you cross the tracks near where the old Shell station used to be." Use an online map or buy the old-fashioned kind, and allow plenty of time to find the place.

Also, if you plan to show a video, be sure they have the right player (or bring it yourself).

5. Be your *enthusiastic* self.

Please don't try to change your personality, but you must express enthusiasm about your mission. Your listener cannot see you, so you have only your voice to carry enthusiasm. Avoid the temptation to slip into a monotone or low-energy telephone voice.

6. Expect to get an appointment.

This concept of expecting God to act reminds me of the young preachers who sought counsel from the great British preacher Charles Spurgeon. They said they were not seeing many people come to Christ and wondered if Dr. Spurgeon had any counsel. He said, "Surely you don't expect someone to come to Christ every time you preach, do you?" "Of course not," the young preachers chorused. Slowly Dr. Spurgeon replied, "That is your problem."

Be sure you're clear on the date and time of your appointment.

On the phone, we either expect God to act or we don't.

A negative, apprehensive demeanor communicates a negative, apprehensive response from the listener. Of course, you won't get an appointment every time, but you'll get them more frequently if you plan on succeeding.

That's why prayer is so important before you begin. Review your calling. If you know God has called you to ministry, how dare you be nonexpectant? Picking up that phone is your act of obedience by faith, calling on God's grace.

7. Keep the door open.

If your friend says no (after you've explained "There is no obligation"), have a plan ready. Instead of breaking into tears or waiting out an awkward silence, affirm your friend. Perhaps he feels badly that he can't meet with you. I say something like, "Well, I sure understand, Bob. But may I keep you on our mailing list so we can keep you informed about our ministry and how to pray for us?"

"Fine."

"Thank you. Maybe I'll check back with you in the next year or two?"

8. Get started!

Does this scene sound familiar? A missionary is getting ready to phone for appointments. First, he postpones it as long as possible by playing with the kids and reading the paper. Then he finally goes downstairs to his study but has to come back for a cup of coffee.

"I'm ready now!" he declares. But he forgot sugar, so up he comes again. Then he clears off a space on his desk, rereading the day's mail and reorganizing a couple of files. Finally, he pulls out the 10 cards he was going to call and reads through them one by one, trying to decide who might be the "easiest" to call first.

Having decided on his first call, he now comes dashing up the stairs for more coffee. Back down again. But before picking up the phone, he searches for his phone outline.

The notebook is upstairs. On his way back down he detours through the kitchen. "Honey, do we still have any of those oatmeal cookies?" he asks his wife. She icily replies, "I thought you were phoning for appointments so we could afford to put oatmeal in the cookies."

He heads back downstairs and begins revising his phone outline. That finished, he tidies up the desk . . . prays . . . picks up the phone . . . dials six digits . . . hangs up.

The first card was not right. Goes to the second one. Picks up the phone. Dials the number.

Little beads of perspiration bubble on his forehead. His hands are so slippery he wipes them on his pants. It's ringing. Once. Twice. Still no answer. Three times. Four. Five.

In relief he hangs up the phone. "Praise the Lord! Nobody home. Time for another cup of coffee."

If you've ever experienced an evening like this, here are some suggestions to make your phoning time more productive:

You'll be more motivated to call if you have a start/stop time set in advance.

- Set aside a start/stop time, say from 7:30 to 8:30 on Tuesday night. Tell yourself you're stopping at 8:30. That will force you to not waste time, and the ending point is motivating.
- Get your cards, phone numbers, and details set up beforehand—including your coffee.
- Ask a friend or two to pray for you the entire time; even have the friend come to your house.
- Gather with another missionary or two to make calls together.
- Now, just get started!

Sample Phone Outline

- **Greeting**

  "Hello! Is this . . . May I speak to . . . ?"

  "This is (your name), from (your agency)."

- **Chat briefly, exchange pleasantries**

  "Jim, do you have a minute to talk? Is this a good time?"

- **If bad time**

  "Could I call you back . . . in a few minutes? In an hour? Tomorrow?"

- **If good time to talk**

  "As you know, I'm on the staff with (your agency) in the New York City metro area. We're in our tenth year of ministry and are excited about what the Lord is doing."

- **If on mailing list and relationship is casual to distant**

  "Have you been receiving our newsletters? Great! I hope you like them."

  "This month I'm working on a special project. I'm in the process of developing my financial support team. Part of my ministry is to develop a group of friends who will join us in prayer and finances."

  "As I thought about whom I'd enjoy having on my team, your name came to mind!" (Chance for humor here!)

  "I wonder if there would be a time within the next week or two that I could stop by for about 45 minutes? I have a ministry video and an update of our ministry I want to tell you about. Then, sometime during our time together, I'd like to personally invite you to join our financial support team." Or "I'd like to leave an invitation for you to join our finance team."

- **Or**

  "You have shown a significant interest in our ministry in the past through your gifts and prayers. And we are grateful."

  "I wonder if there would be a time within the next week or two that I could stop by for about 45 minutes to an hour? I have some information and pictures I'd like to show you, and I'd also like to update you on our financial goals for the coming year."

- **If they hesitate**

  "There is no obligation whatever. I would consider it an honor to tell you about our ministry and be able to catch up face-to-face."

  "Do you have a DVD player? I have a 7-minute video that is excellent, and I'd like to show it to you!"

- **Confirm appointment date, time, and directions to their home (or meeting location)**

- **If "no"**

  "I certainly appreciate your willingness to consider this, Jim. Maybe we could talk again in a year or two." (Pause)

  "In the meantime, I'll continue to send our newsletter for prayer. Our major prayer request is . . . When you think of us, that's the prayer need. Thank you!"

Your Phone Outline

Use the space below to create your own personal phone outline.

Greeting

_____
_____
_____
_____
_____
_____

Transition (why you are calling)

_____
_____
_____
_____
_____
_____

Ask (for an appointment to present your ministry and financial challenge)

_____
_____
_____
_____
_____
_____

Close (details clear, directions, date, time)

_____
_____
_____
_____
_____
_____

Photocopy extra sheets for personal use as needed.

Chapter Ten
HOW TO MAKE A FACE-TO-FACE APPEAL

You've survived the toughest part of raising support—the phone call to set up your face-to-face interview. Now you're ready to drive, fly, walk, bus, or taxi to meet your prospective team member! With you (and not sitting on your desk at home!) are the following:

- Directions to your friend's home or business and the phone number
- Presentation materials (video, photo book, or presentation folder)
- Pledge card and return envelope
- "Leave-behind" piece of literature
- Thank-you gift, such as a small booklet on Christian growth

How you look and communicate are important. In addition to your other presentation materials, it's not a bad idea to include some breath mints!

And you've prayed for the meeting. As you anticipate it, think of it in five segments, as depicted in the diagram on the following page.

1. Opening

Relax. Be yourself. Don't rush into your presentation. Get acquainted or reacquainted. Be observant. Notice your friends' interests by observing pictures on the walls or how the home is decorated. Ask your hosts questions. Be a learner. If you're relaxed, they will be relaxed.

Avoid running your mouth without engaging your brain—blithering disease, a friend of mine calls it. Missionaries who are nervous tend to fill silences with words just to stay calm, but that's a good way to stick your foot in your mouth. My "blithering disease" friend, in the midst of a nervous opening, asked if a photo on the wall was a father or grandfather. "No, it's Martin Luther King, Jr.," came the icy reply. Brrr!

2. Transition

If you've told your friends you'll only stay 45 minutes to an hour, make the transition to your presentation after 15 minutes. Don't wait until they bring it up. A former secretary of mine, who is extremely personable, was asked by her hosts, "Lisa, was there something you wanted to show us?" Good question, because they'd been happily chatting for two hours.

I usually say something like this: "As I mentioned on the phone, I want to show you an exciting seven-minute video (or ministry notebook) explaining my ministry. Perhaps we could take a look at that now?"

This usually signals the host to fire up the electronics. Even if you aren't showing a video, you should rearrange the seating so everyone can easily see your presentation notebook. I prefer sitting at a dining-room or kitchen table instead of being buried in a soft billowy sofa or chair across the room. Don't hesitate to take a minute or two to rearrange the seating—it will pay off as you go through your presentation.

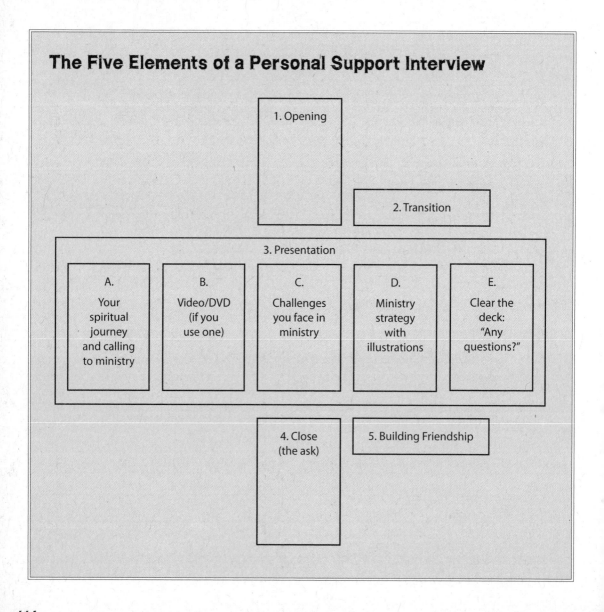

The Five Elements of a Personal Support Interview

1. Opening

2. Transition

3. Presentation

A.	B.	C.	D.	E.
Your spiritual journey and calling to ministry	Video/DVD (if you use one)	Challenges you face in ministry	Ministry strategy with illustrations	Clear the deck: "Any questions?"

4. Close (the ask)

5. Building Friendship

3. Presentation

Now you're ready to launch into your presentation, and it's broken into five sections.

Spiritual Journey and Calling

Briefly review your spiritual journey—how you came to Christ and how God called you to this ministry. I like to start like this: "My adventure with The Navigators began the day our neighbor, Emil Johnson, drove his 1949 Chevrolet pickup into my dad's barnyard. That's the day I prayed my first serious prayer." That's how my testimony begins.

Jeremiah 51:10 says, "Come and let us recount in Zion the work of the LORD our God!" Give your testimony of how you came to Christ. But keep it to three to five minutes. Then ask your hosts about their spiritual journey. Most believers are never asked, and it does them good to explain it as Jeremiah exhorts.

If they are hazy on their spiritual journey, your antennae are probably up, and you're ready to present the Gospel instead of your ministry. But hold on to that for now. You

Keep your presentations simple. They don't need to know your life's history, just compelling reasons to support your ministry.

will have ample opportunities later. They did not invite you to their home to be preached to. Use their interest as a springboard.

Then explain how God called you to this ministry. Use a Scripture verse, if possible. Take only a minute.

Video

Now it's time to show your video, if you have one. If you don't, just go ahead into the next section.

Here's how I segue into the video: "This video shows the underlying values that drive our ministry—not facts and figures. It features staff, lay leaders, and new believers from our 10 field-ministry divisions. It also includes background on how our ministries are funded. It moves fast, so hang on!"

After it's over, I like to give my hosts a chance to comment—"Well, that's our ministry. Any comments or questions?" Or "What impressions of our ministry stood out?" As you go through your presentation folder, ask questions that stimulate *dialogue*. Monologues work for Jay Leno, but they aren't appropriate in fundraising appeals.

You may wonder if a video is really necessary. No, but if you have one, why not let it work for you to convey the emotion and breadth of your ministry? Too many missionaries are not as persuasive as they think they are!

Challenges You Face in Ministry

As you present your ministry challenges, it's essential you use a handout with an outline your hosts can follow. Some missionaries honestly believe they are more effective if they are free to ramble as they describe their ministry. But you will be much more effective if you have an outline and stick to it. The better you know your stuff, the easier it is to be flexible.

Also, a presentation handout or two gives both you and the listener something to stare at besides one another. Constant eye contact is sometimes threatening.

Now what should a good presentation booklet look like? Your mission may have one, or you may have to develop it yourself. No matter; build upon this pillar—*state the problems* your mission hopes to solve. Before you tell what your ministry does, explain why it needs to be done. That is, don't give the answers before you examine the questions. For example, if you are trying to evangelize America, you might use statistics or quotes like the examples in the box above.

> ## Examples of the Problem of Secularization
>
> *"The percentage of people attending a Christian church each weekend decreased significantly from 1990 (20.4%) to 2005 (15.5%). If the present trends continue, the percentage of the population that attends church in 2050 will be almost half of what it was in 1990."*
> —David T. Olson, www.theamericanchurch.org
>
> *"I usually have about 40 other things I want to do on Sunday morning. If I can't do any of the other 39, then I'll come to church with you."*
> —Seattle friend
>
> Our spiritual heritage is forsaken:
>
> *"The fact that, compared to the inhabitants of Africa and Russia, we still live well, cannot ease the pain of feeling that we no longer live nobly."*
> —John Updike, novelist

People need to be reminded of the problem, not just hear the solution. Think of statistics, quotes, or charts that you can include to help your listeners emotionally connect with the problem. If you serve overseas, include statistics and quotes about the country or people. State the problem. Give a sobering picture of the issues your people face.

But don't merely read your statistics! Point to one and explain it, then add a personal story that highlights the issue. For example, I say: "I see secularization in my personal world too. Last Christmas I went into a popular music store with thousands of CDs, tapes, and videos, confident I would find a CD of 'Handel's Messiah.'

"Not finding it, I sought out the young clerk behind the cash register. He had multiple body piercings and an earring. I asked him if they had 'The Messiah,' thinking he would quickly point me to the right bin. Instead, he frowned and asked quizzically, 'Is that a new group?' "

Then I ask my listeners if they've seen any examples of secularization in their worlds. *Dialogue!*

Don't feel obligated to explain every quote or statistic. This page should take only five minutes. Simply answer the question: What problems in today's world does my ministry hope to solve?

Now, before you go to the next page, which is your ministry strategy, you'll need a clear transition. I say it something like this: "It is easy to feel overwhelmed with all these problems, but the answer is Jesus Christ. We rely on Him, not social programs or our own efforts. Here is our strategy to bring the message of Christ to America (or the college campus, or Japan, etc.)."

Then I turn the page to my mission statement and strategy.

Illustrating—rather than explaining—your ministry will keep your listener more interested.

Ministry Strategy with Illustrations

I read the ministry calling statement slowly. Rather than trying to exegete the entire statement missiologically, I say: "Let me highlight three (or two or four) key words."

Then I illustrate by describing an evangelism encounter in my ministry. Then a story. I explain my ministry through illustrations—telling stories. That's what people remember, not missiological explanations. And make sure your stories are current—not from 20 years ago!

A philosophical explanation or, worse yet, a defense of your ministry may excite you, but it bores the average listener!

Clear the Deck ("Any questions?")

Now give your listeners an opportunity to ask questions or to clarify what they've heard. Hopefully, they will have a question or two. I simply say: "Well, that's what I do in ministry. Does it make sense? Perhaps you have a question?"

I'm also ready at this point to share another ministry "war story" that once again reinforces my mission. The goal here is to get some dialogue going, because you ought not go to the close if your listeners have questions, misunderstandings, or, in extreme cases, latent hostility toward you or your agency.

If they have no questions, then it's time to transition into the close.

4. Close (the ask)

This is where you ask for a stewardship decision. For most missionaries, this is the most difficult part of the presentation. Here are a couple of suggestions:

- Build up to the ask, and make sure they know you are asking. I've watched some missionaries—perhaps out of nervousness—mix the appeal into their other comments so that the listeners don't even know they've been asked. This makes them feel sneaked up on. Instead, I say something like this: "Bob and Nancy, you've heard about our ministry tonight, and I've explained our financial challenge. Now it's time for me to ask you a very important question (pause). Will you pray about joining our team at $50 to $100 per month?" Stop!
- After you've made the appeal, look them in the eye and keep quiet. Once you've blurted out the question, there will be a few seconds of silence. It will seem awkward. You'll want to fill the silence with words. Any words. Your mind will race. *What are they thinking? I've offended them for sure. Why don't they say something? Anything. Oh, why did I even come? I should have sent a letter. Why is he looking at me like that? I've offended them for sure. Is this the right calling for me? Maybe I should have kept my job at the foundry. They're mad now. I've lost a friend for life. Somebody should say something. I'm sweating. It's pouring down my back. This is awful. Nancy looks unhappy. Now she's looking at Bob. They're going to tell me they hate me and never want to see me again. Wait, Bob's going to speak. No, he's not. They'll probably reject me. I don't blame them.*

Don't let self-doubt cause you to water down your appeal.

Actually, only three seconds have passed. Don't break the silence with an inane comment like, "Actually, we don't need support that bad." Or "Nice weather we've been having." No. Don't speak. It is their turn to speak. Don't water down your appeal.

- Be prepared for disclaimers—a seemingly logical reason why your listener may not be able to give. For example, "Our church just had a funding drive for a new fellowship hall." Or "We're not sure Bob will be able to keep his job much longer." Or "We get appeals all the time."

Rather than deflating like a four-day-old state fair balloon, I acknowledge the disclaimer and continue. "Yes, that must be wonderful to have a new building at your church. That's really important. I'm sure it meets a big need. Now in our situation, we are asking people to pray about . . ."

A disclaimer doesn't imply Bob and Nancy won't support you. They simply want you to know that they already give and can't support everything.

Similarly, how do we respond when a friend is seriously considering Christ but gives a disclaimer, such as, "What about all those who have never heard?" We would never say, "OK. That's a good point. I've never thought of that. I guess I'd better not tell you any more about Christ."

Ridiculous! Likewise, in raising support, genuinely acknowledge the disclaimer but realize it's not a reason to abandon your appeal.

- If they say yes, affirm them and review the pledge card.

If your hosts already support your mission and are familiar with monthly giving, simply explain how to fill out the pledge card. If they don't have experience in supporting a missionary, review the card in more detail. Remember, no pledge card, no money!

Some missionaries make the mistake of being flippant or downplaying the card. That's unwise. Even the way you physically handle the card and the importance you give to it will dictate the importance with which your friends will treat it.

Also, I try to avoid calling it a "pledge card." Some people have a negative reaction to those words. Sometimes I'll say "response slip."

- Close with 2 Corinthians 9:7, but avoid an apologetic attitude.

I make a nonapologetic appeal, but if my friends are not yet ready to decide, I say something like this: "Thank you for your willingness to bring this before the Lord. I've suggested you pray about a pledge of $50 to $100 monthly, but let me remind you of 2 Corinthians 9:7, which says we are not to give grudgingly or under compulsion, for God loves a cheerful giver. Whatever your decision, I trust it will be cheerful and as unto the Lord."

Face-to-face financial appeals are not sales calls. I do not want a person's gift if it is given under compulsion.

- If they say no, I thank them for the privilege of explaining my ministry and ask if I can keep sending my newsletter for prayer. I need that too. And sometimes, if they seem like they would like to give but are currently financially overstretched, I suggest that I'll keep them informed and will check back in a couple of years.

- If they haven't decided at the close, they'll usually say they would like to think about it for a few days. I encourage them that this is appropriate and wise. I'll say, "These kinds of decisions ought to be prayed over. Do you think you could send the card back to me by the 14th?"—seven days from today. Or "Could I phone you in a week to see how the Lord has led?"

Either response is OK, but I prefer the first. Of course, if I don't hear from them in seven days, I'll phone them anyway. But usually they send the card.

Either way, check back. Too many missionaries sit by the mailbox waiting for answers from prospective donors who are now busy painting the spare room and have forgotten about your pledge card languishing beneath a pile of papers.

5. Building Friendship

Now it's time to stop talking about yourself and money and switch the subject to their interests. I'll say something like, "Well, we've been talking about my work all evening. Tell me, how are things going with you?"

Ask about their careers, family, and church. It may also be appropriate to ask about their spiritual journey, particularly if you got a fuzzy response on their testimony earlier. I may say, "Tell me, what lessons are you learning in your walk with Christ these days?"

Rarely does anyone ask them that! Remember, you are in their home not only to gain a support partner but also to encourage them in their faith. As Paul reminded the Corinthians, "It is in the sight of God that we have been speaking in Christ; and all for your *upbuilding*, beloved" (2 Corinthians 12:19, italics added).

Here are some additional suggestions:

- Have a few materials to give away. I like to leave an appropriate booklet or CD with them at the end of the evening.
- Close with prayer at the door. Most of the time that will be appropriate and appreciated. But keep it brief. Break their stereotype of long-winded missionaries.
- If the visit was in their home, send a short thank-you note expressing gratefulness that they opened their home to you. You needn't say anything about money unless they already pledged.

Now you're ready to launch out on your first appeal to a potential major donor. Hang on!

Chapter Eleven
HOW TO APPEAL TO MAJOR DONORS

When I first heard the term "major donor" (also known as "anchor donor"), I thought, "I don't know any millionaires." But I've come to discover that you can recruit major donors to your support team without knowing "rich" people.

If your missions budget exceeds $2,500 a month, you will need to recruit major donors or you will not reach your goal. The career missionaries I know who are up to budget year after year always have a few major donors on their teams. It's not optional. Sorry.

But it's not impossible either.

First, let's define "major donor." Some organizations consider a major donor someone who could write out a check for $50,000. But individual missionaries need not think in such a large amount—at least not at first. Rather than being overwhelmed with such huge figures, think instead about asking people to give $2,000 to $5,000. That's not such a big jump.

So, where do you start?

I've found great encouragement from studying a man of God who was fearful as he appealed to a major donor candidate. I can identify with that! His story contains valuable tips for appealing to potential major donors.

Our study subject? Nehemiah (from Nehemiah 1:1–4).

Most missionaries need a few major donors to anchor their team and help them reach 100 percent of their budget.

1. Have passion for the cause.

During Nehemiah's day, the Jewish nation was exiled in Persia (present-day Iran/Iraq). Nehemiah was employed by Artaxerxes, the Persian king, as cupbearer—the one who sampled the king's drinks to make sure they were not poisoned. Not an enviable job!

In the month of Chislev (November 15 to December 15) in the year 445 B.C., an entourage from Jerusalem visited, and Nehemiah "asked them concerning the Jews who had escaped and had survived the captivity, and about Jerusalem" (1:2). They replied that the Jewish remnant who had not been carried captive to Persia were in great distress. The walls of Jerusalem were broken down, and the huge gates that once protected the city were burned.

This report from back home devastated Nehemiah, and in verse 4, we see him weeping and mourning "for days." But his mourning and weeping is not mere sentimental sadness. It drives him to prayer. Verses 5–11 capture Nehemiah's prayer of confession for himself and his nation. He also reminds God of the promise He made to Moses: that if Israel would obey Him, He would gather them from where they had been scattered and bring them back to "the place where I have chosen to cause My name to dwell."

Nehemiah had a deep-seated passion for his people that went beyond sentimentality or patriotism. It drove him to mourning and to prayer.

This is where we, too, must begin. If you do not have a passion for your cause, you will not raise much money—and your fancy presentation won't help!

For example, a friend of mine in Minneapolis was appealed to by an unenthusiastic college student heading for South America to play basketball and share Christ. The organization sponsoring the trip was sound and the young man was sincere, but he lacked passion as he described the trip. Finally, my friend David said, "You don't really want to take this trip, do you?"

"Yeah, I do," came the reply.

"Nah, I don't think you do!" David countered. "You just want to get away from your folks for a few weeks to have a little fun. Isn't that right?"

Blushing, the young basketball player gathered his courage and thundered, "I want to go on this missions trip to serve God!"

"Great!" David said. "Now finish your presentation like you really believe in it, and I'll gladly support you."

My Minneapolis friend did this young man a tremendous favor by helping him bring passion to his presentation. "Just wanted to see if he believed in his own project," David told me later with a wink.

How about you? How deeply do you believe in your calling to ministry? Does it drive you to prayer and mourning as it did Nehemiah? Is it strong enough to make you leave your comfort zone to appeal to a major donor?

Or have you drifted into ministry, or maybe you were exhorted to do it but feel no call of God? Maybe you need to do more homework to better understand your cause—that may produce the emotion you need. Or have you chosen the wrong cause?

To discover your true passion, ask yourself, "What makes me sad or mad?" When Nehemiah got the news about Jerusalem, he became sad and wept. He probably also became mad about the walls being down and Judah's enemies dominating his Jewish countrymen.

If the cause you now represent does not make you sad or mad, then can you discover an *aspect* of the cause that does? Maybe you need to tailor your job to a certain part of the cause that grabs you. Or maybe it's time to admit that you need to review your passions and dreams. This may signal a career change, but that's OK. Life is too short to feign passion for a cause that does not motivate you. Keep this adage in mind: "Few actions of consequence in the world have been accomplished without passion" (Jerold Panas, *Megagifts*).

2. Pray much.

In chapter 2, Nehemiah is before the king. It's now the month of Nisan (not the car), which is March 15 to April 15—four months after he heard the devastating news about Jerusalem. His mourning and praying for Jerusalem was not a quick once-or-twice appeal to God. Although he may have wanted to spring into action, he did nothing. Instead, he prayed for four months while performing his official duties at the palace.

I wish I were better at this kind of sustained prayer. I tend to mourn and pray primarily when I'm in a scrape and not much afterward—until another scrape occurs. But here's what helps me: I've written my life mission on the prayer page of my journal where I look at it every day. Also, to keep my passions before me, I have made it a habit to review my life goals every time I get on an airplane. As soon as I take my seat, I pull out my "life goals" folder and pray through it. What a joy!

Keep your passion before you, and pray about it every day.

And pray about it in the heat of opportunity. In chapter 2, verse 2, the king noticed Nehemiah's sad, fallen countenance. That was a "no-no" in the Persian court. The hired help was not supposed to show emotion or bring personal problems to the job. In fact, the proper way to exit the court was to leave slowly, never turning your back on the king. Also, you were to make sure you didn't breathe on the king. Remember the hassle Queen Esther endured to get a proper audience with the king? Her story took place in the same palace only 30 years earlier.

So, Artaxerxes discovered Nehemiah's sadness. But instead of panicking, Nehemiah prayed. "So I prayed to the God of heaven" (Nehemiah 2:4).

Long-term sustained praying as well as short, spur-of-the-moment praying typified Nehemiah's life. He backed his passion with his prayers, even to the point of risk.

3. Take a risk.

When King Artaxerxes confronted Nehemiah about his fallen countenance, Nehemiah could have laughed it off to save his skin. Instead, he took a risk. He said, "Why should my face not be sad when the city, the place of my fathers' tombs, lies desolate and its gates have been consumed by fire?" (2:3).

This was a courageous stand. Not only were cupbearers not supposed to bring their personal problems to the job, but this was just 17 years after Artaxerxes had denied the Jews permission to rebuild the city. And Nehemiah proposes building!

Although the comparison is inadequate, it would be similar to a renter asking for permission to build a fence on the rented property from a landlord who had forbidden her (in writing) to build such a fence 17 years earlier because of complaints from neighbors! And then the renter has the temerity to send the landlord the bill for the lumber!

We know it was a risk for Nehemiah because he says parenthetically in verse 2, "Then I was very much afraid." Similarly, you may be fearful to go to a major donor. That's OK. Take a risk like Nehemiah and tell "the king" what is on your heart—like my friend Glenn.

Glenn, a fellow missionary, made his first major donor appeal over lunch with a friend. He made the appeal with a calm countenance—smiling and confidently explaining the project.

As he finished his presentation, he heard a faint tinkling noise in the background that had been there during his entire talk. It was then he discovered he had "white-knuckled" his coffee cup out of terror and was rattling it against the saucer. He also noticed he had not eaten any of his meal while his would-be donor had finished his long ago.

Sure, Glenn was fearful, as we all can be. But he finished his appeal, and the donor gave, even asking, "Are you sure that's enough?"

Yes, it will take courage, but don't let stark-naked terror prevent you from sharing your dazzling vision with a major donor. Be like Nehemiah. Be like Glenn—only relax your grip!

4. Ask big—ask specifically.

When it comes time for the appeal, Nehemiah doesn't hold back. He tells King Artaxerxes exactly what he needs. He doesn't water it down. He doesn't go for only part of the goal. He doesn't compromise. He goes for all he needs.

His request is short and to the point: "Send me to Judah, to the city of my fathers' tombs, that I may rebuild it" (2:5). In addition to a building permit, he also is asking for time off from serving as cupbearer in the Susa palace. But he doesn't stop there. He also asks for official letters of passage to ensure his safety during the 800-mile trip through Artaxerxes' other provinces and for timber from the king's forest with which to build the gates of the wall. In effect, his request is in four parts, each one growing more bold.

What good would it be to secure a building permit without safe passage to Jerusalem? What good would it do to show up among the poor, beaten-down people of Jerusalem and expect them to rally around the call to build without having building materials?

Too often our appeals are vague and ill-defined. Or they are full of vision without giving any idea of how we are going to spend the money.

I like the cartoon with a fundraising thermometer set up in front of a church. It shows 30 percent of the goal is raised. Two people are standing in front of this supposedly motivating artifact of fundraising genius—one of them looking dour and the other exclaiming excitedly, "Oh, nothing in particular. I just thought we could use some extra funds!"

Explain to your major donor candidates exactly why you need the money—no filler, no fluff, no schmoozing. And don't hold back. Don't worry about the amount being too large or the vision being too preposterous. You should almost always suggest a specific range, and make it high!

A professional athlete was once asked for $5,000 by a missionary for an exciting ministry project. The total project need was $15,000, but the missionary, for some reason, couldn't bring himself to ask for that. After the gift was given some months later, the athlete confessed that he would have given the entire amount had he been asked. Don't be afraid to ask big.

5. Get to the point clearly.

Nehemiah didn't beat around the bush with lengthy introductions or preambles to his appeal. He states his need in one sentence: "Send me to Judah, to the city of my fathers' tombs, that I may rebuild it." Too often we try to schmooze our way through an appeal. I've seen too much of vague generalities and wordiness in funding appeals. Nehemiah just comes out and says what he needs.

Years ago my friend Don Kutz, who has received many missionary and charitable appeals, told me over breakfast: "Scott, tell the missionaries to just come out and ask! Don't let them beat around the bush!" Well said.

Furthermore, major donors are usually busy people who don't have time for us to hem and haw. If you've

Major donors are usually busy people. Don't waste their time by going into your presentation unorganized.

done a good job on the phone, they know why you are there—get on with it.

6. Build a credible relationship.

Note the phrase in verse 2:5, "If your servant has found favor before you. . . ."

This shows that Nehemiah had won the respect of Artaxerxes during his years of service. The king was therefore willing to hear Nehemiah's story.

It is possible to receive large gifts without a good relationship with your donors, and now and then you hear of a major gift on a "cold appeal." But not usually. The largest gifts are given by donors who have a good relationship with the asker and the organization he or she represents.

For example, Bill McConkey of McConkey and Johnson Consulting told the Christian Stewardship Association that of the donors who each gave $1 million or more to Campus Crusade's "Here's Life, World" campaign, their first gift to Crusade averaged $15. That shows they were cultivated in partnership and friendship over a period of years.

Sure, you can get a few gifts without a relationship, but you'll get more gifts and bigger gifts as you build genuine friendships. With small givers, we know that people give to people, and that is true for major donors also.

I'm not saying you must become best friends with every major donor prospect. As a major donor told a member of our department, "I appreciate your coming to my home. But I'm also grateful that you are sensitive to my limited time. I'm not looking for a new 'best friend.'"

7. Know how to answer questions.

In Nehemiah 2:6, the king questions the fund-raiser. "How long will your journey be, and when will you return?" asks the king. Good questions! The king wanted Nehemiah to return, revealing that Nehemiah was probably a dependable worker—but more than that, a loyal companion to the king.

Nehemiah gave the king a definite time. He answered the question satisfactorily.

How well are you prepared to answer a donor's questions? To answer questions well, you must know the entire project and not merely have pat PR answers. Nehemiah had thought through the entire project. He knew what to say.

It is worth your time to anticipate questions and be ready to give definite answers. If you don't know the answers, find out. It may mean you'll need to prod the ministry leaders to make up their minds on some issues. That's OK. You may even be accused of trying to run the project. That's OK too. To raise the money, you must have answers.

8. Avoid buzzwords.

Because Artaxerxes had turned down a building permit to these troublesome Jews 17 years earlier, Nehemiah had to be tactful. Although the text does not give us details, notice that Nehemiah never once used the "J-word"—Jerusalem. Perhaps it is only coincidental, but we must note that Nehemiah wisely did not use the one word that would trigger negative thoughts for Artaxerxes. Instead, Nehemiah refers to Jerusalem as "the city of my fathers' tombs."

Your role is to give people the opportunity to join your team. Let them decide how to respond.

What negative buzzwords does your prospective major donor have? For example, some donors do not like these terms: fund drive, pledge card, deputation, building project. Avoid those terms, but don't avoid asking your listeners to make a commitment to the project.

Now, before we look at the final tip from Nehemiah, it is time to list possible donors who could give $2,000 to $10,000 or more. Perhaps names already have come to mind. Rather than succumbing to the temptation to eliminate them, ask this question: "Would this person be willing to hear my story and pray about becoming an anchor to my donor team for $2,000 to $10,000?" Do not ask: "Will this person give?" Wrong question. That's between them and God. Your role is simply to invite them to pray about the project.

But how do you know if they can afford it? You don't! Remember, it is impossible to determine their giving potential merely by looking at external appearances. Whether they seem obviously wealthy or not, be prepared to ask for a $5,000 to $10,000 project. Another reason to do your homework! If both partners work or if the main breadwinner owns a company, $10,000 or more is not out of the question.

How do you ask? Adopt your own way of asking as you become comfortable with going to major donors. But to start, try this: "Bill, you've heard my vision of ministry for Russia (or the campus, this city's poor, etc.). I'll need a few partners to anchor my ministry support team. So I'd like to ask you this important question: *Will you pray about anchoring my team with a special gift in the $4,000 to $10,000 range?*"

Appearances can be deceiving. Many wealthy people don't look wealthy.

Then be still. Forget about how much money that may seem to you. If it seems like a lot of money, maybe you are stuck in a $25 paradigm. Furthermore, you are not asking for gifts of charity but rather for resources for the Kingdom.

9. Give glory to God.

Nehemiah was quick to give glory to God. In Nehemiah 2:8, he says, "And the king granted them to me because the good hand of my God was on me." That's an example we all can learn from. It is so tempting to take the credit ourselves because of our hard work, our great videos, or our do-everything software. True, you need to do your part just as Nehemiah did, but let's remember to give the credit where it is truly due.

You'll be wise to recruit at least a few major donors to your support team. Having these "anchors" on your team will significantly lighten your fundraising load. And be sure to introduce them to your agency. They likely will not give more than $5,000 to $10,000 toward your personal support, but they might top that with a $100,000 gift to your agency if the relationship is cultivated.

Chapter Twelve
APPEALING TO CHURCHES

This is a short chapter—not because church support is unimportant, but because most missionaries will be more successful in funding if they focus on individuals rather than churches.

In many missionaries' minds, deputation consists of traveling to 52 churches in 52 weeks making Sunday school presentations to strangers. Friendly, smiling strangers, but strangers nonetheless. That strategy may have worked years ago (though I question it), but it will not work today unless you are guaranteed funding by your denomination's churches and they want to meet you face-to-face. Yet the myth persists that church solicitation is effective, even though many missionary candidates spend up to five years doing deputation.

You will do better if you focus on only a few churches—especially your home church or an "anchor church"—instead of many. Then spend the majority of your time appealing to individuals.

The exception is those missionaries who have attractive overseas ministries. Churches show more interest in across-the-water projects than across-the-interstate projects. One missionary I know in Kazakhstan has seven supporting churches. Another who had a secret ministry in Eastern Europe before the fall of communism had 12. But if you're trying to reach college students in your own country or businesspeople downtown, you sit at the bottom of the missions committee's list—in baseball terminology, the "cellar-dweller."

Furthermore, churches are becoming more sophisticated in deciding which missionaries to support. Years ago, if you gave a good talk and your kids sang a special song at the Sunday service, you would get support. But today churches have priorities for the types of missionaries they sponsor and a checklist to determine how much to give.

I applaud that. The Kingdom is better served when churches give

Missions committees are bombarded with appeals from missionaries, and their guidelines for choosing which to support are becoming more sophisticated.

strategically. The old way often forced missions-committee members to play favorites, especially if the candidate was the Sunday school superintendent's cousin. Though it means jumping through more hoops, the new selection process is better.

Now that I've discouraged church appeals, here are a few suggestions to make them easier!

1. Focus on your home church or an "anchor church."

All missionaries, even if they serve with an interdenominational agency, need a church home. It provides a sense of belonging and an emotional home. But it's possible you grew up in a church that does not believe in missions. No "home" there! If that's your situation, develop an "anchor church" in which you feel warm ties with people. And urge your home or anchor church to support you significantly, at least 10 to 50 percent of your budget.

If you are looking for a home church, keep in mind you will have a tough time raising money if you move around from church to church. A pastor friend told me, "If future missionaries constantly church-hop during their formative years, don't count on much church support."

2. Develop an advocate.

For years, our church in Minneapolis supported Greg, a successful missionary who had grown up in the church. His father was a stalwart pillar! But Greg was the "cellar-dweller," receiving only token financial support. I was shocked because I knew of his huge, effective ministry in Latin America. As a new member on the missions committee, I decided to keep silent and see what happened.

As budget time rolled around, Greg's name again went to the bottom of the list. So I asked if anyone on the committee knew him. Silence. Someone volunteered that he had been ac-

Have an advocate on your team who will represent you to the church's decision-makers.

tive in the church years ago. No one knew about his huge ministry in Latin America. Despite my arguments, he stayed at the bottom of the list that year and soon after was dropped.

Why? He had no annual advocate on the missions committee! Many of the old-timers in the church appreciated him, but they did not get word to the committee.

Because missions committees change, because decision-makers in the church change, you must have an advocate who will represent you to the church's decision-makers. Without an advocate, it is only a matter of time until you'll be the cellar-dweller. People give to those they know.

3. Keep the church—particularly the decision-makers—informed.

Besides not having an advocate, Greg, in the previous example, did not keep the church adequately informed. Don't overlook sending the church your newsletters and other ministry news, and make sure it gets into the hands of the missions committee and the decision-makers.

One missionary found out his letters addressed to the church were not being delivered to the committee—for years!

Keeping the church informed also means attending the church's missions festivals, even though they are never held at a convenient time in your schedule. Of course, if you are overseas, you may not be able to come annually, but plan on coming back periodically.

4. Church appeals are a process—not an event.

It will take several encounters to be approved for support, and that's normal. Your first visit to the church might only enable you to find out who you should talk to about the application process. The second trip might get you officially entered into the process. And on the third visit, perhaps you will meet the missions pastor or the missions-committee chairman over lunch. On the fourth visit, you might actually make a presentation to the missions committee.

Don't give up. These decision-makers are handling other people's money, and they will want you to jump through the proper hoops.

Throughout the process, communicate well—newsletters, visits, CDs and DVDs, cards, and formal reports. It will take time. One missionary friend said it usually takes five visits to be accepted for support. Keep at it!

Regular communication and thorough paperwork will keep you in good standing with donor churches. This will require some administrative help.

5. Do the paperwork.

With individuals you know well, you may be tempted to downplay the importance of "paperwork." After all, it's just you! But with a church, the application form and résumé are essential. No responsible church will send you money unless it has done homework on you and your organization. How well you've done your paperwork indicates to the church how well you do your ministry.

6. Speak the church's language.

Before you make your official appeal, find out the church's missions interests. Otherwise, you may unknowingly present your ministry in an unattractive way. For example, if you know the committee is keen on church planting, explain how your ministry aids in church planting (if it does). Or if the church is interested in recruiting national leaders overseas, show how your mission does that.

Do your homework and slant your presentation, but do it honestly! If your mission does a ministry the church is not interested in, admit it. Maybe they will become interested after hearing your story.

7. Know what you're talking about.

A mission leader came home from overseas and visited his supporting churches. He was well received, but the churches told him they were disappointed that other missionaries from his organization did not know the facts about the mission. They knew only about their personal ministry—nothing about the agency in general, such as number of staff, ministry locations, doctrinal statement, or current policies. He was embarrassed.

Take time to find out what your sending agency is doing. Get the facts and figures. Have the doctrinal statement and other pertinent documents ready. Here are a few "organizational questions" you may be asked:

- How many countries are you in? How many staff?
- Does your agency plant churches?
- How does your mission view training national leaders?
- What percentage of gifts is taken out for overhead?
- What does your mission believe about the charismatic gifts?
- What does your mission believe about Christian liberties?
- Is your mission a member of the ECFA? IFMA? EFMA?
- We could support a national for one-fifth of your cost. How can you justify such a high budget?

8. Serve in the church.

Even if the church is not your home church, offer to pitch in and help as you are able. If you are good at teaching, offer to lead a Sunday school class. Or suggest meeting with the youth directors to do an analysis of the area schools. Or, if desperate, offer to watch the two-year-olds in the nursery. Church decision-makers see your willingness to help as significant. Don't underestimate it!

9. Exempt giving candidates one by one from no-ask policies.

Some churches say that if they support you through the missions budget, you are not allowed to appeal to individuals in the congregation. For some it is a policy, and for others, a suggestion. But it can cripple a missionary's funding strategy, particularly if most of your giving prospects are in the church. The purpose for such a policy is to protect the congregation from unscrupulous outsiders swooping through the congregation slurping up cash, leaving nothing for the church program.

Though unfair, such a position is understandable. If you or I were the pastor, we would probably endorse it. Here is how I dealt with it, and it has seemed to work for others too. I asked the missions-committee chairperson, with whom I had a good relationship, if the policy meant I could not appeal to Ted, who had been in my Yawn Patrol Bible study since its inception. "No, of course it doesn't mean that," she replied. Then I asked if it meant I could not appeal to Brian, whom I had met with several times to personally disciple. "No, of course not," she said. And so on down the list of 20 people I wanted to appeal to individually.

Identify those you want to appeal to and exempt them one by one. The policy—designed to protect the church—need not harm your funding.

10. Prepare a formal résumé.

If you apply for support, it is important to provide a formal résumé for the church. Below is a sample format you may find helpful. Have available as well: doctrinal statement, agency literature (don't overdo it), response card and envelope, and your annual budget.

This is simply an introduction—not your presentation for support. But they may ask for this ahead of time. Or you can use this as a leave-behind piece. By the way, I would not give a missions committee my budget without explaining it verbally. Committee members will compare your budget with other missionary budgets, but they're often comparing apples and oranges.

Résumé Outline for a Church

Page 1	Color photo (include family, if married)
Page 2	Your calling to ministry and your spiritual testimony
Page 3	Ministry experience, education, and training
Page 4	Description of ministry target and problems your ministry attempts to solve
Page 5	Your ministry strategy and outcomes
Page 6	Financial explanation/appeal

11. Ask for a significant amount.

We missionaries are used to asking for modest amounts from individuals ($50 to $100 per month), but we need to increase the amount significantly for churches. Remember, a church is a collection of many individuals. I'd suggest asking for 10 to 50 percent of your budget, depending on the size of the church and your relationship with it.

Years ago, I encouraged a young Wisconsin short-term missionary to ask her home church for $500 per month, about 20 percent of her budget. She thought it would be a stretch to even ask for $50 per month. "You don't understand," she said. "They never give more than $50 and never outside the denomination." I agreed with her that it looked daunting, but she was willing to give it a try because it was the church she grew up in.

Her interview was going fair—not great—and then it was time to ask.

Gathering up her courage, she blurted out the $500 ask. The missions committee was aghast. "Young lady," they said, "we don't even support people serving outside our denomination and never for an amount that large."

She didn't flinch. "Would you pray about $500 per month?" she repeated. Kathy eventually headed off to France with $500 in monthly support from her home church! Policies are not in concrete. Think bigger.

Every church will have its own rules and guidelines, but review this chapter before you make your appeal, and you will be better prepared.

Next, how to keep the donors you already have.

DONOR MINISTRY:
HOW TO KEEP YOUR GIVERS GIVING

Some call ministry to donors "donor maintenance," but this is an unfortunate term. "Maintenance" refers to things, not people. The county maintains rural roads. The sales rep maintains the copier. The data-entry clerk maintains files.

Those who support us are not ATM machines that need maintenance, but people with daily struggles over health, job security, and fungus in their lawns. They need appreciation, information, and encouragement. They need ministry—not maintenance.

Furthermore, we are not merely to "maintain" donors at their current levels of giving and prayer. We minister to them to enable them to grow—not only in their commitment to us but also in their relationship with the Lord and in their outreach to others.

This distinction is important, because it will dictate how we treat our donors. Here are seven important suggestions:

1. Accept donor ministry as part of your calling.

Missionaries often feel guilty when they take time for donors. They think they are "wasting" time on donors—time that could be given to evangelism or leading a Bible study. But they need to keep the money coming, so they reluctantly (and sometimes angrily) spend a few hours communicating with their constituency.

With an attitude like this, no amount of time spent writing thank-you letters will cover the disdain lying an inch below the surface.

If you've accepted fundraising as part of your ministry, go one step further and accept donor ministry as well. After all, it is much easier to keep donors than to win back those who become disenchanted because they rarely hear from you.

Donor ministry is not optional. Ignore them and you may lose them.

But obstacles loom in the path of donor ministry. Here are a few I've had to fight my way through:

- No time. When I consider adding donor ministry to my already packed schedule, my circuits overheat.
- No help. For years, I tried to correspond with donors by myself. Although I had accepted

donor ministry as part of the job, I still didn't have the administrative capacity to quickly get out personal letters or to keep our address file updated. So I postponed donor ministry until enough guilt piled up to goad me into catching up on six months of "stuff" in one frantic afternoon. I was always behind.

- No plan. Creating a newsletter or sending a Thanksgiving gift to our donor team was an exercise in last-minute arm flailing.

As in fundraising, we must start with our attitude. I find encouragement from Philippians 4:17. Paul says, "Not that I seek the gift itself, but I seek for the profit which increases to your account." Paul saw those who financially supported him as people with real needs—not support machines. He was interested in their spiritual "profit," not just their money. He affirmed their step of faith in sending him gifts; Philippians 4 is the first missionary thank-you letter. And Paul found time to do it!

Like fundraising, donor ministry is part of your calling. You need not feel guilty taking time to write donors, send thank-you gifts, or keep your mailing list up to date. It's just as important as the other ministry work you do. Plan it into your schedule and stop resenting it. If you have chosen to accept the gifts of others, then you also have chosen to accept responsibility to inform and encourage those who support you. If you believe your giving partners are people rather than robots with money, then you must say thank you.

2. Be attentive to your constituency.

In *How to Win Customers and Keep Them for Life,* Michael LeBoeuf researched why customers quit buying. Here are his findings:

1%	die
3%	move away
5%	develop other friendships
9%	leave for competitive reasons
14%	are dissatisfied with the product
68%	quit because of an attitude of indifference toward customers by an employee

True, these figures are for businesses and not missions organizations, but let's heed LeBoeuf's warning. This excerpt of a letter to a ministry vice president reinforces his findings:

"Dear Mr. Libby,

"I regret to inform you that I am writing to let you know that we will no longer be providing support for [a missionary family].

"I realize that a missionary family is busy, with the focus of their ministry going

to spreading the Gospel. To ask them to maintain regular personal contact with every family who provides support for them would improperly drain from them the time and effort that needs to be devoted to Christ's Kingdom.

"That being said, occasionally it would be nice if—instead of another generic form letter that attempts to pass on the 'lowest common denominator' of information to the support network—we could from time to time, as circumstances permit, receive a personal note or letter that lets us know that they do know we're here and that it means something to them and that they really do want our prayers and input."

Some of us don't have the administrative skills to communicate well with our donors. Find some help.

The writer goes on to say that he had written the missionary, asking a question about a sensitive personal issue. He looked forward to a response but heard nothing. Several months passed, but he received only a generic postcard asking for funds. He continues:

"I do not wish to impose ourselves on this family in a relationship that, for whatever reason, they are unable to maintain. Originally, I was just not going to make any further contributions to your organization. But upon further reflection with God, I feel that I at least owe someone the courtesy of explaining, right or wrong, the reasons for my actions. As far as doing this (stopping our support) puts a burden on this family's ministry, I am sorry. I guess we just reached a point that we felt like we were being taken for granted and were just being 'left out in the cold.'

"Please believe me that I do not write this in anger or resentment, but only in sadness."

What went wrong here? Assuming this donor's letter was not lost in the mail, the missionary should have responded with a thoughtful answer to his sensitive question. The donor was looking for more than generic newsletters and financial appeals.

Attentiveness is the issue. For whatever reason, the missionary did not communicate that he valued the individual. Attentiveness would have solved the problem.

This story from management consultant Tom Peters in the *Herald Times* says it well.

"I'm 52. I've been around. And I'm a service fanatic. (A demanding customer—i.e., a pain.) But, truth is, I could count on the fingers of one hand the number of times I've sent a meal back to a restaurant's kitchen.

"Well, I sent one back the other night at a place that normally serves fine food. (I had ordered the vegetarian plate, which turned out to be a lump of bland pasta with a glob of nondescript melted cheese on top—made Swanson's old macaroni and cheese TV dinners look like haute cuisine). And I learned something in the process.

"The owner, who was on hand (good!), quickly came by the table. The first words out of her mouth were . . . about money. To wit: She'd remove the meal from the tab.

"Well, fine. But . . .

"But I was left with a sour taste, and it wasn't just the food. The issue wasn't money. Truth is, $16 isn't going to significantly alter my bank balance (nor yours).

"Something was missing.

"That something spontaneously arrived when our waitress next stopped by the table. She said she'd worked for another restaurant that always toyed with its nightly vegetarian entree, and that triggered a five-minute conversation about vegetarian cooking and the like.

"What she provided was worth 100 times $16. She offered attentiveness. The most powerful force in the universe? Perhaps."

Too many of us use generic newsletters as our only method of communication with our constituencies. Newsletters put words in front of each donor, but they do not necessarily communicate meaningfully with each one. Personal attentiveness is needed. That leads to the next suggestion.

3. Segment your list.

It is impossible to give personal attentiveness to the people on your mailing list unless you segment. If your list contains more than 200 names (and it should), segmenting is a must. Your constituents do not have identical interest in you, nor the same attention span for reading your timeless prose.

The lonely donor in the earlier example needed more attention than other donors. And of course, longtime friends may have higher expectations than strangers. Some don't want to hear from you but once a quarter; others want to read your daily diary! Don't treat everyone the same.

The chart on the following page shows how I segment my list into three groups and how frequently I communicate with each.

I mail a general newsletter four times a year. Everyone gets that—donors, nondonors, family, nonbelievers, strangers I met on the airplane—everybody. You might ask, "My Christmas card list?" Right. Everyone. Of course, this letter has to be written so strangers and nonbelievers will understand. It can't be cluttered with Christian lingo.

This letter, 90 percent of the time, should be only one page long. It should have a picture with a caption. And I personally sign each letter in heavy blue ink 100 percent of the time.

	Jan.	Feb.	Mar.	Apr.	May	June	July	Aug.	Sept.	Oct.	Nov.	Dec.
General (4)	X				X			X		X	X	
Donor (4+4=8)	X		X		X		X	X		X	Cal.*	
Prayer Warriors (4+2+5=11)	X	+	X	+	X	+	X	X	+	X		+

* Each year at Thanksgiving, I send a gift calendar to each donor from the past 24 months.
X = Letter sent
+ = Informal, unsigned prayer-flash memo

As I write this letter, I visualize my Aunt Phyllis in northern Minnesota. Aunt Phyllis is a wonderful lady and a no-nonsense pragmatist. You need only watch her decapitate and clean a chicken from her chicken coop to understand she does not countenance pretentiousness. Nor will she put up with missiological "Christianese." After all, she's Methodist.

Writing with Aunt Phyllis in mind forces me to use plain words instead of Christian jargon and reminds me to make my points quickly. Aunt Phyllis has other chores to do besides wade through a tome from me.

Donors on my list receive four (at least) additional letters between the general newsletters. These letters are more intimate, shorter, and often on monarch-size stationery. I tell more about my personal challenges and give more intimate prayer requests. After all, donors generally want to know more.

The third group is my prayer warrior team. I don't keep this segment up and running all the time. But on occasion I write e-mail prayer memos to 25 or so friends who have agreed to pray earnestly for crucial requests. These notes go out unsigned, and I feel no obligation to write a personal message on any of them. This was previously agreed to when I invited the prayer warrior to be on my team. If I had to add a personal P.S. on each one, I would never find the time to write in the first place. I told each prayer warrior this would be a fast, unedited flash of prayer news, and they agreed that is what they wanted.

Furthermore, these prayer memos are not scheduled. I send them out whenever I sense a need for special prayer. This group could hear from me up to 12 times a year (four general, three donor, and five prayer flashes).

In addition, I send all donors from the past 24 months a calendar at Thanksgiving. I include a warm, short thank-you letter expressing my gratefulness for their partnership in the Gospel, even if they have given only one time. Though the letter is generic, I frequently write a personal note on many of them.

So far, this segmenting concept is fairly tidy, but there's one more element that is messy. It can't be organized. It's called "As I Think of You."

I keep a supply of thank-you cards handy in my desk drawer (and in my briefcase when I travel). I can easily send a note if I think of someone during the day (frequently in my prayer time). I'll simply say, "I was thinking of you today. You came to my mind, and I just want to let you know I appreciate you." Then I'll add another paragraph of news, and it's done.

Similarly, I respond to each letter I receive from a mailing-list friend (except for Christmas cards, unless they ask a question). I dictate these letters, have them typed up, and sign them personally.

This cannot be organized; just send a note when you think of someone. And don't try to do 14 at a time!

If you segment your list and follow a similar "As I Think of You" plan, your donors and friends will marvel at your attentiveness.

What about e-mail and other electronic communication? By all means, use it. Use e-mail to say thank you, provide ministry news, and send photos. Direct donors to your organization's website and your personal site too, if you have one. But heed this advice from Judith Martin, the nationally syndicated "Miss Manners":

> *"Many people mistakenly think a new technology cancels out an old one. People are charmed by handwritten letters precisely because they are rarer. You glance at an e-mail. You give more attention to a real letter."*

I agree. Just today I received a short handwritten thank-you card from a missionary. I'll give again!

4. Appreciate your donors. Say thank you.

If a donor comes to mind, send a note or an e-mail expressing appreciation.

I learned from my mother early in life the importance of saying thank you. A grateful spirit is woven deeply into her life, and she was quick to teach that to us kids. Mom taught us to be grateful for small as well as large things.

But a grateful spirit is contrary to the "demand-your-rights, they-owe-it-to-you" spirit of today. And this is true not just among the "worldly" but even among missionaries, who ought to be models of thankfulness.

Unfortunately, missionaries do not ooze with appreciation. We have noticed in our personal giving that we only receive thank-you notes about half the time from missionaries to whom we send unannounced, once-in-a-while gifts. Not that we demand to be thanked; after all, we are giving to the Lord. But it would be nice to hear if they got the gift. Who knows? We might do it again! Perhaps you've experienced that too.

Why don't we missionaries appreciate our donors more? Here are some possibilities:

- "They owe us" mentality. Some missionaries think support is owed to them because they have condescended to be part of Christian ministry. Such people do not understand Hebrews 12:28, which says, "Therefore, since we receive a kingdom which cannot be shaken, let us show gratitude, by which we may offer to God an acceptable service with reverence and awe." Gratitude is the only possible response to a God who has done so much for us.

- We fail to study donor reports. I wonder if some missionaries even look at their donor reports. I read my monthly donor report with a pen in hand, circling names of new donors, restarted donors, or donors who jumped from $55 to $70. They all need a thank you. What poverty of values would cause missionaries to browse through their donor reports carelessly?

- We're unable to handle the logistical work. If missionaries have no clerical help, they may be so overwhelmed with work they just can't get it done, even if they have good intentions.

I am continually amazed at the story of Jesus and the 10 lepers in Luke 17:14. He told them: " 'Go and show yourselves to the priests.' And it came about that as they were going, they were cleansed."

But one of them, when he saw he was cleansed, came back to Jesus to glorify God out of appreciation. Jesus accepted his gratefulness but asked, "Were there not ten cleansed? But the nine—where are they?" (Luke 17:17). It is obvious Jesus would have been pleased had all 10 come back to offer praise to God.

You can't fake appreciation. Either you appreciate your donors or you don't. If you don't, that can quickly be remedied by repentance. Is repentance too strong a word? I don't think so. Ingratitude is a serious sin.

Here are a couple of practical tips:

- Study your donor reports carefully. Notice if there are new givers or changes in givers' amounts. This exercise takes only a few minutes, but it is crucial if you hope to be an effective "thanker."

It's easier to be attentive to new donors, but don't take your regular supporters for granted.

- When you receive a donor's first gift, send a thank-you note or phone that person within 48 hours. I don't know about you, but when I see a new donor on our income report, I get excited! Stop the world! This is good news! I try to write (or phone) to welcome them to our team within 48 hours. I also include a small booklet that I sign on the inside cover, welcoming them as partners in our ministry. This goes to any first-time donor, whether monthly or annual. Here is what I say in my welcome letter:

> *"We just received our pay envelope, and your name was in it for $50. Thank you so much! And welcome to the Morton Team of Ropeholders! Your gift comes at a good time. Well done.*
>
> *"Enclosed is a small booklet on prayer that we pass on to all our giving partners. When I was a struggling young believer living at the TKE Fraternity House at Iowa State University, this little booklet helped me survive spiritually. I'd read a chapter from it each night before going to bed in the cold dorm. (Why fraternity guys think they have to sleep with the windows open year-round is beyond me!)*
>
> *"Though the language of the booklet is dated, the principles are not. I still reread it periodically. I hope it will encourage you in prayer as much as it has me.*
>
> *"As you think of us this week, here is an important prayer request . . ."*

Do you get the idea? This immediate affirmation endorses the good work the new donor has done. Affirm them immediately. Jesus did that when He saw faith in action. Paul did that when he received the Philippians' gift. We do that with our kids. Why not with our donors?

5. Keep accurate records. (Know the state of your flock.)

In expressing appreciation, one size does not fit all. When you single out an individual donor for a specific gift or for increasing a monthly gift, you communicate attentiveness. Study your donor reports well. Look for address changes, support increases, support stoppages!

You can learn much about your donors by studying their giving patterns. And don't merely look at the past month or two; you must study 12 to 48 previous months or risk drawing the wrong conclusions.

When I discover that a donor has not missed a month all year (12 for 12), I frequently send a note telling them I noticed their faithfulness.

Poor record keeping can be embarrassing, as I discovered driving across Wisconsin a few years ago. We were on our way back to Minneapolis after visiting donors, and of course, we were driving on the back roads as is my custom and Alma's accommodation. On a highway sign, I read the name of a town that sounded familiar, and I remembered we had a donor in that town we had overlooked when planning the trip. Though Alma believed they'd quit giving, we agreed to drive into town and invite them to lunch.

Because the town was small, we quickly found the donor working at his machine shop, and he was glad to see us. As I inwardly congratulated myself for boldly seizing an opportunity, he graciously invited us to his house for hot dogs because there wasn't a restaurant in town. I avoided giving a smug glance to Alma, who seemed impressed by how well things were going.

Donor Record/Prayer Page

Donor Name _____

Address _____

City _____ State _____ ZIP _____

Phone _____

E-mail _____

Personal History

_____

_____

_____

Testimony/Spiritual Background

_____

_____

His Job/Her Job

_____

_____

Notes

_____

_____

Prayer Record

_____

_____

_____

Financial Record

Year	Pledge	Jan.	Feb.	Mar.	Apr.	May	June	July	Aug.	Sept.	Oct.	Nov.	Dec.	Total

Communication Record

Visits _____

Gifts _____

Phone Calls _____

Other _____

At lunch in their small but comfortable home, we were having a wonderful time getting reacquainted. Then I announced, "One of the reasons we stopped was to thank you for your financial support." If I had quit right there, I would have been OK. But like a fool, I kept going. "In fact," I announced triumphantly, "you are becoming one of our most faithful donors!"

With a greasy hot dog still in my mouth, I beamed as I awaited our hosts' reply. It came like a fastball tailing inside. "Don't know how you can say that. We stopped giving two years ago," said our host, not even looking up from his plate.

I froze, daring not to look at Alma, who had tried to convince me the entire ride into town that they were not currently giving. Hours passed. Finally I said, "Well, how about starting again?" Out of the corner of my eye, I noticed Alma staring at me in disbelief. A flicker of an "I-told-you-so" smile crossed her face.

On the rest of the trip back to Minneapolis, we rode in silence. And we took the interstate.

As in your personal finances, "Know well the condition of your flocks, and pay attention to your herds" (Proverbs 27:23). Take the time to study your people, and stay off the back roads!

On the previous page is a sample **Donor Record/Prayer Page**. Photocopy it or adapt it for your own use. Better yet, make it electronic.

6. Write well.

Because most of the communication between you and your donors will be written rather than verbal, it is essential that you learn to write well. Sadly, many missionaries and church leaders act as if good writing were optional. Wrong. As missionaries, you live in the world of ideas, so you must learn to communicate well, especially in writing.

But take heart, you do not need to write like Ernest Hemingway! You will be amazed at how quickly you can improve your writing by following the simple suggestions in Chapter 14.

Let me leave you with one easy improvement now: Get rid of state-of-being verbs, such as "is," "was," "are," "am," and "be." State-of-being verbs do not move action along. They slow down and stifle your writing; use them as little as possible. Use action verbs instead.

For example, I could say, "There were 14 students at the Bible study last week, and they *were having* pizza and a discussion on dating guidelines." Note the state-of-being verbs. How about this instead: "Fourteen students *crowded* into the Bible study circle, *inhaling* six giant pepperoni pizzas as they *argued* about the Bible's view of dating relationships."

Note the verbs: crowded, inhaling, argued. Do you see the difference? The second sentence is easier to visualize and moves the action along.

That's one writing tip you can easily put into practice. Watch for verbs in your reading this week, then begin to *plug* (good verb!) action verbs into your writing.

7. Use tremendous trifles.

A "tremendous trifle" is a small, spontaneous act of love. You can't plan it—you just do it.

I recently noticed an article in the newspaper about a woman in Cincinnati who was arrested for plugging (Boy, I like that verb!) coins into expired parking meters just before the attendant wrote a ticket. She was protecting the unknowing car owner from a fine. It was her random act of kindness, I guess.

I cut the article out of the newspaper and sent it to a friend (and potential donor) in Cincinnati. I thought he might get a chuckle out of it. And I included a short note saying his town made the news 1,500 miles away. What does this communicate? It told my friend that I was thinking of him. It's an understated but effective demonstration of attentiveness.

One Sunday in church, I caught Ev as he was racing down the stairs to his class. "Ev, just wanted to thank you for fixing our front-door lock a month ago. Before you fixed that lock, I'd worry every time I left the house. Last night when I locked up and went to bed, I thought of you and the good job you did. Thanks."

Ev beamed, then turned to clamber down the stairs. It took five seconds. Even though I'd thanked Ev previously in writing when I sent his company a check, this little tremendous trifle was an encouragement to him that day.

You employ tremendous trifles in your other relationships, don't you? They are essential to marriage (a "Happy Friday" present lying on the counter just because it's Friday), parenting ("Hey, son! Look what I found for you at the garage sale!"), and on the job ("I picked up this notepad for you because I noticed you were out.").

Glenn Balsis, a missionary friend, has taught me to keep a supply of postcards and thank-you notes both at my desk and in my daily planner. I can easily send an encouraging word or say thank you when a friend's name comes to mind. He also taught me to keep a supply of postage stamps and the addresses of my donors with me at all times.

Glenn keeps records of his donors' birthdays and anniversaries and sometimes sends cards for those occasions, though he does not feel obligated to do it every time for every person.

You can't plan tremendous trifles. But neither will they happen if you're preoccupied with yourself. Perhaps you already do tremendous trifles in other areas of life—now apply them to your donors.

In summary, you owe your donors and mailing-list audience appreciation, information, and stimulation. That boils down to ministry. But you do not owe them a personal discipling relationship. Nor are you the chief mentor in their lives. There's also an additional, practical reason to minister to your donors—because you want to keep them giving.

A few years ago, Bruce Swezey, a friend of The Navigators from Wisconsin, told me of a study he was doing as part of his graduate degree. His study asked the question: "Why do donors stop supporting Navigator missionaries?" Here are his results:

Swezey found 19 percent of donors stop support because they did not receive enough news. That's one out of five! If you have 65 donors and don't communicate faithfully and meaningfully to them, 12 will stop during the next two or three years. Just sending meaningful ministry news could retain those 12. Is it worth it? You bet!

Why Donors Stop Giving

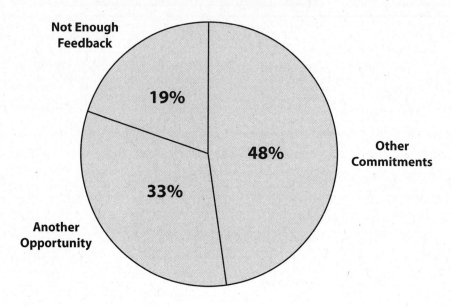

Not Enough Feedback

19%

48%

Other Commitments

33%

Another Opportunity

But look at the 33 percent segment. These donors were satisfied with the amount of information, but they dropped to support a different "opportunity." Can anything be done about that? I think so. Think about it—these donors are not committed enough to your ministry to say no to other giving opportunities. They are hanging on to you with a weak grasp! When a more attrac-

Life History of Donors

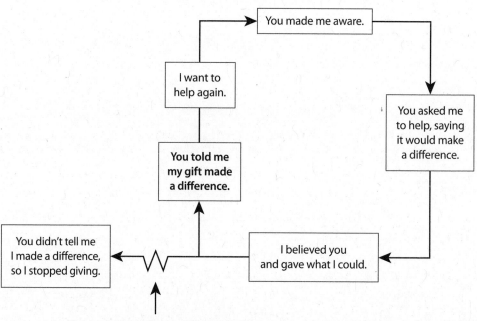

You made me aware.

I want to help again.

You asked me to help, saying it would make a difference.

You told me my gift made a difference.

I believed you and gave what I could.

You didn't tell me I made a difference, so I stopped giving.

This is where missionaries drop the ball.

tive giving opportunity comes along, they kiss you good-bye in a heartbeat.

True, some of your donors should support other appropriate giving opportunities, such as a family member attending seminary, or perhaps they've neglected their church giving in the past. But most of these people could be retained with better donor ministry.

I'm grateful to consultant Dwight Maltby for this helpful diagram (on page 146) on the life history of donors.

People must know that they are making a difference!

Maltby also says, "We have lost the ability to communicate stories of changed lives. Instead, we're giving statistical information about the number of people who have been fed through our soup kitchens."

Maybe today's donors are too fickle, too demanding. That may be, but lamenting will not change it. Instead, let's do better to inform, appreciate, and stimulate our giving partners. Help them see how impor-

Sometimes, regardless of how attentive and appreciative you are, you'll lose a donor. Don't lose heart. Donor attrition is natural.

tant their contribution is. It is easier to keep donors than to find new ones. It's time to get serious about donor ministry.

In the next chapter, we'll look at how we can do this through our newsletters.

Chapter Fourteen
HOW TO WRITE NEWSLETTERS PEOPLE ACTUALLY READ

Be honest—do you look forward to reading the missionary newsletters buried in a pile of mail on your kitchen counter? I confess I do not. Most missionary newsletters you and I receive are long; they meander from topic to topic like a black-and-yellow bumblebee floating lazily from flower to flower on a hot summer day. Often they contain a sermonette from the missionary's quiet time and a long list of strangers to pray for.

This is not to say that missionaries (stateside or overseas) lead dull lives. On the contrary, just recently Alma and I spent an enjoyable two and a half hours listening intently to a missionary we support in Belgium. Talking to him was fascinating, but somehow, when missionaries try to capture their interesting lives in letters, they fall flat. I truly believe that there is no such thing as a dull topic, but there *are* dull writers!

On a positive note, I've sensed that, over the years, missionary letters have improved as the writers realize their readers have little time to wade through meandering prose. Still, much work remains.

By following these 12 suggestions, you can improve your letters dramatically and cause your busy readers to look forward to your mail. And you needn't become an expert writer or an award-winning graphic artist to do it.

1. Limit your letter to one topic, one page.

Your readers will understand you and your ministry better if you develop one topic well rather than floating around seven topics of great interest only to you. "Oh, but I have so much to say," you argue. Maybe the problem is infrequency in writing. If you sent letters more often, you wouldn't have to gang seven topics together in one small-print, four-page tome.

Don't meander from visa problems to family news to the difficulties of buying food at the open-air market to getting on the Internet to the seminar you recently attended to challenges in

Your newsletters compete with a lot of other mail, not to mention the urgent demands of life. Writing well helps them get read.

language study to an encounter with a nonbeliever, then back to how the kids are doing in soccer. And then don't end your letter by listing half a dozen strangers for me to pray for when you haven't introduced me to them in an interesting way. You have not motivated me.

Sorry, even though I like you, I am not going to wade through a poorly written letter. I may skim it and ask my wife for her executive summary, but she feels the same. She has other things to do today.

What about family or personal news? Do it in a short paragraph or in the P.S. at the end. Or, once in awhile, dedicate one letter to personal or family news exclusively. To be sure, a few of your close-in readers want to know every detail about the kids' braces, Hector the cat, and Bubbles the fish. But most readers (especially your donors) prefer to know how your ministry is going. Sure, they care about your personal life, but they pray and give because of your calling to missions.

Note: The exception to the one-page rule is a cash-project letter, in which you make a direct, unapologetic financial appeal. See Chapter 15.

2. Include a photo.

Adding a photo to your letter means extra work. Usually, as we drive home from a great ministry event, we remember the camera. Too late! Plan ahead. Think about your readers. Even a simple photo will intrigue them, especially if you serve overseas. If a picture is worth a thousand words, then plan a photo in every letter! Keep in mind that many readers will not read your letter at all—but they will look at a picture and read the caption below it.

Captions! That's another "must." Write a well-thought-through, newsy caption below each photo. Be sure it's a complete sentence. That is the only story "browsers" will get.

How important are captions? Notice your own habits. When you read a newspaper or magazine, your eye goes to the headlines first and then to the pictures. And when you look at the pictures, you always read the captions under them, don't you! It's human nature. Capitalize on it.

Here's another tip on photos. In evaluating the suitability of photos or in determining how to take a photo, keep in mind two criteria.

- Does the picture tell a story? That is, can you look at the photo and see the story it tells without a caption?
- Are the blacks black and the whites white? If your photo has little contrast, it will reproduce poorly. Choose color photos with the greatest contrast. To test what your color print will look like in your black-and-white newsletter, photocopy it; what you see is what you'll get.

3. Use simple graphics and plenty of white space.

I see two common mistakes in the "look" of missionary newsletters. First, most are too crowded. They don't have enough white space, especially in the margins. A crowded newsletter shouts to the reader: "This is going to be hard to wade through. Better skim it!" In your attempt to squeeze in more news by filling the page to the edge, you lose readership. Less is more.

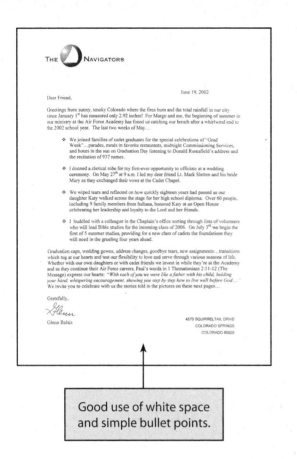

Good use of white space and simple bullet points.

Allow a margin of at least one inch to one and one-half inches on the sides of your letter—one inch is the bare minimum. If you must cut copy to preserve a one-inch margin, do it. Your readers will appreciate it. Note the "clean" look of the letter above on the left. Compare that letter with the one next to it. Although this letter contains interesting information, most readers will not have the persistence to finish it.

Second, missionaries are following the cultural trend of most computer owners—trying to become graphic artists. As a result, their newsletters are cluttered with 11 different fonts and three borders. If your letter has more than three fonts, stop!

You must use basic rules of design. Ask the unthinkable question: "Can this be easily read by someone who is not in love with my software?" And think of the time you'll save by keeping it simple! (By the way, consider having a talented volunteer or a friend prepare your newsletters for the printer. Why do you need to be an expert at graphics?)

Here are five simple rules of graphic design that are timeless (and will save you much time):

- Use white space generously.
- Limit yourself to two fonts (three at the most).
- Always use serif typeface for body copy. Readership studies consistently show that the human eye, reading English, can more easily read fonts with serifs (hooks) than sans-serif (no hooks). Don't violate this one. Your readers will tire and get lost in the copy and not

know why. (This is serif; this is sans-serif.)

- Clean and simple is better than cute and cluttered.
- Use a "ragged edge" for the right margin on body copy—not justified or "blocked." This is a letter—not a newspaper.

4. Find an interesting lead—a grabber opening.

The opening is where your newsletter is different from a letter to your mom. With mom, you can start off rambling about the weather, how your garden is doing, and the hassle with Billie Bob's fifth-grade teacher. Mom will hang onto every word. But a newsletter should start with an interesting story, a question, an illustration, or a conversation. Also, avoid the tendency to apologize in your opening with statements like, "It's sure been a long time since we've written." If you feel you need to apologize to your readers, figure out which ones specifically (a few names will come to mind!) and add a handwritten note to them.

In the box below, compare the effective opening in the third sample with the bland openings in the first two:

> *"Dear Friends,*
> *Much has transpired since our last letter. We continue to sense the caring and encouraging work of the Holy Spirit in our lives."*
>
> *"Dear Friends,*
> *Please excuse the impersonal nature of this letter, but I wanted to communicate my new address and phone number as soon as possible and give a brief update."*
>
> *" 'Now I knew I had a relationship with God!' These were the surprising words Dagmar spoke to me last Friday evening after our pizza Bible study in the dormitory. Let me tell you how it started."*

5. Tell ministry stories.

Most missionaries underestimate the power of storytelling. They explain, but they don't illustrate and so they miss their best opportunity for communicating effectively.

For example, can you remember the main points of last Sunday's sermon? Think for a moment. I've asked this question to dozens of churchgoers. They stammer. Then they smile, realizing that I'm not St. Peter and their eternal salvation is not at stake.

Next I ask, "Can you remember anything at all about last Sunday's sermon?" Then it starts to slowly dribble out. "Yes, a story the pastor told . . . something about a baseball player . . . a big crowd . . . yes, he ran to third, then to second, then to first!" Finally triumphant, they now pour forth more about the sermon and the pastor (what a marvelous speaker!) than I wanted to know.

The *story* was what they remembered, and they reconstructed the sermon from it. Your readers will not remember your pontifications on the strategic implications of your ministry, but they will remember your stories if you skillfully tell them. And without your having to explain your ministry, they will understand it.

Compare these two examples:

> *"God has shown Himself faithful to us in providing both physically and spiritually. He has been faithful in changing our character so that it is more Christlike. It's really been exciting to see the change in attitude."*

As you read that paragraph, did visual images come to mind? The reader longs to ask *how* God has been faithful. Give an *example. What* specifically brought about the changes in attitudes? Note the differences below:

> *"September 16 at 4 P.M. I accompanied our Wisconsin staff member to campus to visit a friend of his. We met him at the door to his dorm room; he was carrying two cans of Old Milwaukee and a package of bratwurst—Schweigert, I think.*
>
> *He welcomed us warmly, and we started talking as he poured the two beers into an electric frying pan. One of the beers exploded onto his books and clothes. 'Someone must have shook this one up,' he said. Then he dumped the Schweigert bratwursts into the beer (on simmer) and kept turning them while we talked.*
>
> *His roommate soon arrived carrying a can of Del Monte cream-style corn. He scraped it into an electric coffeepot already plugged into the wall. Naturally, the pot was too hot, and soon he was futilely trying to stir the burning corn at the bottom of the pot.*
>
> *'Nice balanced meal,' I said. 'Beats dorm food,' they replied. Will you join me in praying for Wisconsin students?"*

What visual images came to your mind in that story?

Remember, it is difficult to *explain* your ministry, but you can *illustrate* it!

6. Weed out unnecessary words.

A friend of mine, writer David McCasland, has authored a booklet for missionaries called *How to Write Effective Newsletters*. He says: "Good writing is concise. The Lord's Prayer has 56 words. Lincoln's Gettysburg Address has 266. The Ten Commandments has 297. The Declaration of

Independence has 300. A recent government order setting the price of cabbage has 26,911."

Most people underestimate the powerful difference that pruning words makes in effective communication. The speakers and writers we instinctively prefer are those who prune, prune, prune in both their writing and speaking. Note the difference in the examples in the box below.

By the way, start by pruning the words "very" and "really." I mean, really, what do they add to a sentence? Not very much. Professor Kunerth, my Iowa State journalism professor, used to say, "If you must use 'very' or 'really,' use 'damn' instead. If 'damn' doesn't help the copy, then you don't need 'very' or 'really.' "

I like Thomas Jefferson's comment: "The most valuable of all talents is that of never using two words when one will do."

George Orwell, in his famous essay *Politics and the English Language,* said, "If it is possible to cut a word out, always cut it out" (*Communications Briefings,* October 2005).

"During furlough it has been very refreshing for us to have a series of visits and contacts from those we've ministered to in the past." (25 words)

> *"During furlough we felt refreshed through visiting friends we ministered to in the past."* (14 words and no meaning lost)

"There were a great number of students crowded into the living room for our first rally, which takes place every Friday night." (22 words)

> *"Thirty-eight students crowded into our living room for the first of our Friday night studies."* (16 words)

"It was kind of like the line I just read in Tozer's book, Knowledge of the Holy, *where he said . . . "* (20 words)

> *"As Tozer said in* Knowledge of the Holy . . . " (8 words)

---

7. Use action verbs; avoid state-of-being verbs.

State-of-being verbs, such as "is," "was," "are," "am," and "be" are useful in their proper place, but they do not move the action forward. Instead, they tend to slow down your writing.

Check out the following examples, noting how the revised verbs develop more action.

- You can also <u>be</u> praying for our ministry thrust this summer. (Rewrite: *Please <u>pray</u> for our ministry thrust this summer.*)

- There <u>are</u> 19 students attending our Tuesday night Bible study on Ephesians this summer. (Rewrite: *Nineteen students <u>cram</u> into our apartment every Tuesday night to study Ephesians.*)

- I <u>will be</u> receiving my assignment next month. (Rewrite: *I <u>receive</u> my assignment next month.*)

- We <u>were able</u> to set up our first evangelistic dessert for business leaders last month. (Rewrite: *We <u>launched</u> an evangelistic dessert for business leaders last month.*)

Do you see the difference? In addition, when you use action verbs, you cut down the number of words and make your letter more readable. It's not that hard—you can do this!

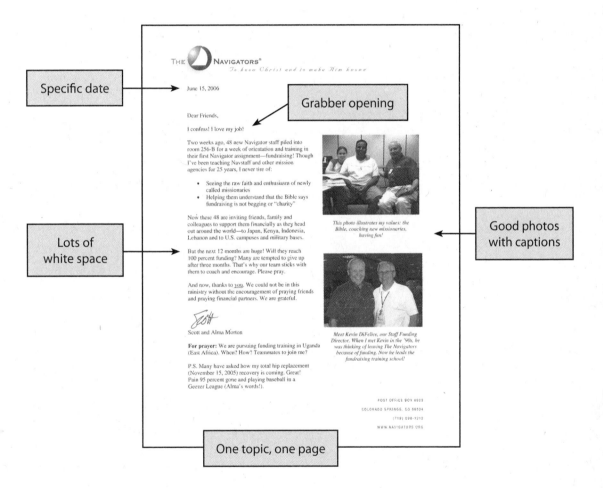

8. Avoid jargon and shop talk.

Again from David McCasland, how would you explain the following paragraph from an Australian magazine?

> *"Temperamental bowler, Rodney Hogg, smashed down his stumps after being given run out in Australia's first test against Pakistan at the MCG. Hogg was run out by Javed Miandad when he was out of his crease to pat down the wicket after a defensive no-ball play."*

If you understand (and who doesn't!) the curious game of cricket, then you found the paragraph sensible and perhaps even fascinating. And you probably have a picture in your mind of poor Rodney smashing down his stumps.

The American game of baseball is no better! What does this jargon mean? "He looped a Texas-leaguer into center." "Come on, big right-hander, paint the corners." "That ball just fell off the table." "Bend your back and give him a little chin music."

A few years ago, I went with a group of American ballplayers on a two-week adventure to teach Bulgarian athletes to play baseball. We hoped to prepare them for eventually having an Olympic baseball team. Never mind that it took America 100 years to develop the designated hitter; we were going to train these superb Bulgarian athletes in two weeks.

I was in the outfield when the third out was made; it was our turn to bat so I started running to the sidelines. But I noticed the Bulgarians were leisurely walking in. So I enthusiastically hollered, "Let's hustle! Let's hustle." And they dutifully began to jog to the sidelines after me. But as we ran, one Bulgarian friend, Victor, said, "Scott, to hustle? Does it mean to run?"

Check your newsletters to make sure they're "jargon-free." Even phrases such as "older Christians" may be confusing.

I overlooked the obvious. That is what we do when we use jargon.

Evangelical jargon might include:

- I asked about his "walk."
- We "fellowship" at Open Bible.
- He's really "down to business."
- I'm on "deputation" for "frontier" missions in the "10/40 Window."

What jargon do you use that your ministry associates understand but that your Aunt Gladys in Ohio would not?

9. Avoid generalities; use facts.

Generalities are the refuge of a lazy mind. Here are four examples of general phrases desperately in need of facts:

- *"Recently."* When exactly? Three days ago, last Tuesday, seven weeks ago, 1954? Find out!
- *"Much has happened."* What exactly happened?
- *"Few, many, several, some."* Exactly how many? Give me a number!
- *"Had a great time."* What made it great?

To make these generalities specific, the writer must painfully probe to discover the details. It means asking questions or making phone calls to discover the facts. It will take time and sometimes it's a pain. But most good writing is.

Be specific! More from Professor Kunerth: "How many? What kind? When exactly? For example!" I hated his questions then, and I hate them now, but he made me dive to the bottom of issues rather than float along on meaningless generalities.

10. Use a specific date.

Your newsletter is a letter—not a brochure or billboard or flyer. Give it a specific date, like September 15, 2007—not September 2007 or Autumn 2007.

The argument against using a specific date is obvious: What if I don't get the letter out by that date? "September" gives me 30 days of grace!

With that logic, why not say "Autumn 07"? That gives 90 days or so. Or how

Wordy letters confuse, overwhelm, and bore readers.

about just "2007"? Then you've got a whole year to get your letter out. Or how about, "The first decade of the 21st century" if you really want to give yourself enough time?

Sorry. The reason against using a specific date just doesn't hold up if you're writing a news*letter*. Use a specific date, and your letter will be more urgent.

11. Give news, not just sermonettes.

Too often a missionary can't think of what to say in a newsletter, so he resorts to sharing his quiet time instead. Don't do that. Although this may minister to your constituency once or twice, it is not effective if you do it constantly. Your readers don't want a sermon in every letter—they want interesting news.

On the other hand, if you are telling a story about someone in your ministry and God taught you an important lesson, go ahead and share it; use a verse of Scripture as well. It will not come across as a sermonette but as a part of your ministry.

If you have a burning message from God to share with your readers, why not include it as an extra page in your envelope? Say on the body of your letter something like this: "God is teaching me a huge lesson through the tough times of village evangelism and the book of Acts. I have enclosed an outline of chapters 4–9 with my key observations. Hope you enjoy it as much as I have."

A sermonette in the body of your letter is no substitute for hard news.

12. Don't mention money or hint about money.

Of course say thank you, but save your financial appeal for a focused, well thought-out cash-project appeal. More on that in the next chapter.

In conclusion, may I ask you this personal question? Do you believe the pain and effort that goes into good writing is worth it? Does it make any difference?

I believe it does. Though your readers may never compliment you for such skills as weeding out extraneous words, they will be grateful they don't have to pray for grace to endure your copy. As Mark Twain said, "If the writer doesn't sweat, the reader will" (*Communications Briefings,* May 2004).

But there is a more important reason to communicate well. God Himself is an excellent communicator. Jesus Christ during His time on earth was an excellent communicator. Sloppy communication does not reflect the God we represent. And that's all the reason we need.

You can find many more suggestions for writing effective newsletters, but these 12 will take you to the top 98th percentile. (For you who are interested in going deeper, I recommend a book by Sandy Weyeneth, *Writing Exceptional Missionary Newsletters,* available at WCLBooks.com.)

If you can make only one change right now, put your emphasis on your writing. A well-written letter—with good verbs and no extraneous words—is the place to start. Let the words lead and the graphics follow.

Chapter Fifteen

HOW TO WRITE DIRECT-MAIL APPEALS THAT GET RESULTS
(And Still Respect Yourself in the Morning)

It was Saturday. I had just finished my weekend errands and sat down at my desk to enjoy a letter from missionary friends, Fred and Wilma (not their real names). I brought the letter home from the office so I could leisurely browse through it. I expected a financial appeal because this experienced missionary couple was preparing to return overseas, and the envelope seemed "fat." But I was not prepared for what I found.

Though part of their letter was interesting, it violated some simple principles of effective appeals. Based on many cash-project letters I've studied, this appeal would not produce much money. Their departure would be delayed and they would declare, "The Lord's will be done," mistakenly thinking that was the best they could do.

Too many missionaries equate effective appeal letters with sweepstakes-type letters. They swallow their pride and produce slick, begging letters. But that's not what I'm talking about! Put those begging letters out of your mind and follow these 13 suggestions. (And remember, cash-project letters don't recruit much monthly support, but they work fine for one-time cash appeals.)

Avoid dropping haphazard "letter bombs" on your donors. Take the time to write effective appeal letters that will get results.

1. Do I have a response slip?

If you do not include a response slip with your appeal, you will significantly lower your response. This slip gives the donor a vehicle by which she can express her commitment. Even though she may want to give, the lack of a response device stalls her intent. She wonders what to do first. To you it's obvious, but unless you make it easy for readers to respond, they hesitate.

One missionary told me, "My donors are familiar with our mission's receipting system and know what to do." Sorry. I don't buy it. Don't mistake loyalty for knowledge. Donors may love you, but they still need simple instructions and a response device at hand. Sure, they could ransack their desks to find an envelope, find your agency's address, write out the check, and mail it in, carefully recording your account number in an extra note, but why make them do the extra work?

Instead, serve them by making it easy to respond. Don't make them do your work.

Response slips also serve another purpose. As your slip sits quietly on the donor's desk—amid papers, bills, and articles she intends to read but probably never will—it is your silent advocate, reminding her to make a stewardship decision. Last week when she read your letter, she intended to make a decision but set it aside. Now your letter is out of sight and out of mind. But your faithful response slip will remind her.

For best results, write your response slip *before* you write the letter.

Elements of a Good Response Slip

Write your vision statement at the top. It will focus your letter. Also, your response slip must be able to "stand alone" because your reader may throw away your letter.

Note that only money choices are given.

☐ **YES**, Al and Nancy, I want to help you reach your goal of $23,000 to continue evangelizing and discipling Italians. Here is my gift of:

_____ $100 _____ $200 _____ $500 _____ $1,000 _____ Other $_____

EMF#000011 (Italy project)

Name_____ Phone (_____) _____

Address _____

City _____ State _____ ZIP _____

Please return this card with your check payable to The Navigators by September 24 . . . that's the day we board a plane for Italy!

This card is not a legally binding contract nor a promise to give. We consider it a free-will expression of intent to give to The Navigators.

P.O. Box 6000, Colorado Springs, CO 80934

Tell how to give and a due date for when you need the money.

Most people don't take this suggestion seriously, but they should. Writing the response slip forces you to answer the question, "What action do I want the reader to take?" That is not an easy question. To read some appeal letters, you'd think the writer's goal is for the reader to feel sorry for him, or to pray, or to pass this information on to friends or to the missions committee. Maybe all three.

What exactly do you want the reader to do? In an appeal letter, there is only one answer: to stimulate the reader to prayerfully consider making a special gift to your ministry. If you have other goals, save them for a future letter. Multiple goals create fog and inhibit response.

The response slip also should restate the purpose of the letter, because sometimes the reader tosses the letter and keeps only the slip. That slip must remind her of what her gift will accomplish. It is the last thing she looks at before she writes her check.

Of course, you also must include a return envelope to make it easy for the donors to respond. It need not be postage-paid. The people on your mailing list know you, so they are not likely to say, "Gee, no postage on the return envelope—I'm not going to give!" That is where your letter differs from mass institutional direct mail.

Also, make sure your response slip offers only money choices. This is not the place to check a box for prayer support or literature requests. Water seeks its lowest level, and so do your readers.

2. Is my letter focused on my cash project?

Most missionaries want to kill two or three birds with one stone. But in an appeal letter, limit the number of topics to one—the appeal itself.

Mixing additional news diffuses the response. In a recent comparison of 11 Navigator cash-project letters, we found those that combined a newsletter with an appeal got only one-third the response of cash appeals only (3.5 percent versus 14 percent).

But won't readers be offended if you talk only about money? That depends. They certainly may be if you rarely write newsletters and the only time they hear from you is when you need money. But if you have discussed other topics in your past four newsletters, then only one letter in five is about money. That's not offensive. (Of course, I'm assuming you don't hint about money in your regular newsletters.)

If you have other topics you feel you must talk about, save them for future letters. Better yet, plan your communication strategy 12 or even 24 months ahead to ensure you will not over-communicate about money.

Most missionaries feel compelled to "sneak up" on the money topic, mixing it with other topics so the readers won't know they are being asked. But can't you spot that in the letters you receive? Why wouldn't your readers spot it too? I wonder if, deep down, missionaries are embarrassed to ask.

Alvera Mickelsen, in *How to Write Missionary Letters,* says, "Decide the thrust of your letter before you begin to write. A letter focused on one idea or incident is more forceful."

See from this example why it's important to focus on one topic:

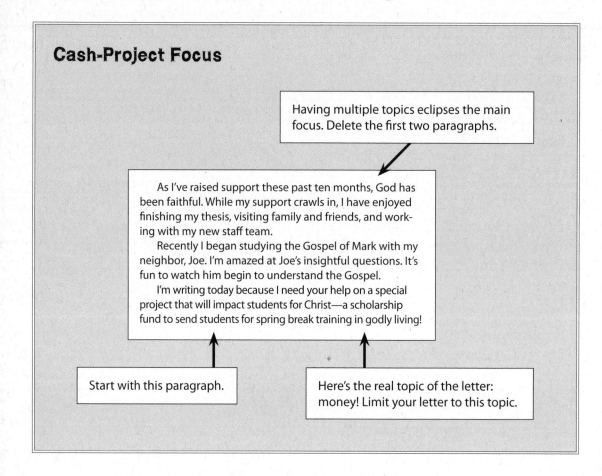

Cash-Project Focus

Having multiple topics eclipses the main focus. Delete the first two paragraphs.

As I've raised support these past ten months, God has been faithful. While my support crawls in, I have enjoyed finishing my thesis, visiting family and friends, and working with my new staff team.

Recently I began studying the Gospel of Mark with my neighbor, Joe. I'm amazed at Joe's insightful questions. It's fun to watch him begin to understand the Gospel.

I'm writing today because I need your help on a special project that will impact students for Christ—a scholarship fund to send students for spring break training in godly living!

Start with this paragraph.

Here's the real topic of the letter: money! Limit your letter to this topic.

3. Did I mention early in the letter why I'm writing?

An engineer from Illinois told me, "With all the mail I get, if I don't see the purpose of the letter in the first paragraph or two, I lay it aside."

A few years ago, I conducted a test on direct-mail appeals, comparing first-paragraph explanations for writing versus fourth-paragraph explanations. The results convincingly showed that when the reason for writing was mentioned in the first paragraph, the response was higher.

Avoid the temptation to "warm up" the readers; they are ready! Don't ease into your appeal the way you ease into the cold waters of the YMCA pool at 6 A.M. Tell them right away why you're writing.

Here is an example of a good first paragraph:

"Dear Friend, I'm writing today to invite you to become a partner in our second missionary journey to one of the most needy parts of the world, South America! On March 20 at 10 A.M., all four of us will board a flight to Peru for a four-week special assignment."

Notice that this first paragraph doesn't ask for a gift; it simply announces the purpose of the letter. Don't waste readers' time with a long preamble. They know you'll be making an appeal—the pledge card falling out of the envelope gives it away immediately. So much for sneaking up on them!

4. Did I clearly state the financial need?

People appreciate knowing how much you need, when you need it, and why you need it. Being vague about the amount frustrates your readers and lowers your response.

Tell the readers the exact amount of your financial goal—even if it seems huge to you. Then explain how it will help accomplish your ministry.

You have only a few seconds to engage your readers. Tell them in the first paragraph why you're writing.

5. Did I offer the readers a range for giving?

Baby boomers say it this way: "Tell me what you want me to do. I can't read your mind. I don't know whether to pray about giving $50, $500, or $5,000." Most donors like to know what they could do for you that would really help.

But here is a caution: Don't go overboard telling people how much to give. They must retain the honor of deciding for themselves. By being too insistent on the exact amount, you rob them of the dignity of giving voluntarily and joyfully. Instead, say something like this:

> *"As you consider a special gift toward our $8,700 challenge, would you pray about a gift in the $75 to $150 range? Of course, the amount is up to you according to 2 Corinthians 9:7, 'God loves a cheerful giver.' Thank you in advance for whatever the Lord leads you to do."*

If I think the donor would consider a larger amount, I'll write:

> *"To achieve our challenge of $8,700, we will need gifts of $500, $1,000, or more to anchor the project. May I ask you to pray about one of these amounts, say $500 or $1,000? Of course the amount is up to you. Gifts of all sizes will be cheerfully accepted as they are cheerfully given—'God loves a cheerful giver' (2 Corinthians 9:7). Thank you in advance for whatever the Lord leads you to do."*

Be sure you don't set your range too low. People tend to give what you suggest. In national direct-mail appeals for The Navigators' devotional guide, *Daily Walk,* the average gift on 20,000-piece mailings consistently averages within a dollar of the lowest suggested gift. One year we suggested $18, and we got a little more than $18. The next year we suggested $20. From thousands of donors, the gift average was $21. You'll get what you ask for!

Are you scared or embarrassed to mention money in your cash-project letter? Don't be! Well-written cash appeals can serve donors' interests.

In suggesting an amount, you will do better if you have a logical reason for the gift size you suggest. In the *Daily Walk* example, we told readers it costs $20 to supply one person with the magazine for a year.

In another example, a veteran missionary asked his readers to consider picking up one or two days of his ministry trip to Africa—$163.89 for one day or $327.78 for two. Many of his gifts were for exactly those amounts.

6. Did I communicate urgency?

To communicate urgency, simply answer these questions:

- Why do I need the money?
- Why do I need it now?

If you do not have good answers to these questions, I am skeptical about your need for the money. "To pay my bills" is not a good answer. People do not give simply so you can pay your bills. They support you because they believe you can make a difference in the world. Here's a better answer: "So we can launch a new evangelism thrust starting August 26—that's the day students return to class. We want to be there ready to tell them about Christ."

Do you see the urgency?

These two questions will require you to think and pray. The result will be a letter that is much more credible—not to mention more honoring to the Lord.

Your readers best understand urgency by the due date—the deadline by which the money needs to be received. Is that too pushy? No. Most people are like the famous "theologian," bandleader Duke Ellington, who said, "If it weren't for deadlines, baby, I wouldn't do nothing!"

Set the deadline six to eight weeks from the time the readers receive your letter. One missionary wanted to send his letter in December for a project coming due the following June. But to the readers, that's too far away. They will set your letter aside and forget about it.

7. Did I tell the readers how to make a gift?

Don't assume your readers know how to give a gift, even though the response slip and return envelope fall out into their laps. You still need to tell them how to respond. I like to explain it in the P.S., because a P.S. usually will be read. I say something like this:

> "P.S.: *To give, please fill out the enclosed response card and return it with your check, payable to The Navigators, by June 10. Thanks in advance.*"

Do not overlook telling readers how to respond. To you it's obvious. But while you were immersed in your letter writing, your readers have been immersed in *Seinfeld* reruns, mowing their lawns, and explaining to two-year-olds that they shouldn't play with Elmer's glue and the dog at the same time.

8. Did I illustrate my ministry?

I remember reading a missionary letter that had a wonderful thought about living for Christ, but it was devoid of illustrations. Twenty minutes after reading it, I couldn't remember the writer's main point. I tried. I searched my mind frantically, but nothing came.

And why? Because I had no hooks upon which to hang the writer's excellent material.

Think back to your pastor's sermon last Sunday. Can you remember the title or the theme? Chances are you can remember an illustration, and from there you may be able to work back to his main point.

Appeal letters without interesting ministry "war stories" usually produce an anemic response. Help the readers to "be there" with you as you describe a late-night Bible study in a dormitory lounge with pizza boxes strewn around. Or describe your first encounter at the village market trying to speak Urdu amid various types of dead fowl hanging from vendors' stalls. Or tell about a young skeptic in a three-piece suit who listens intently to the Gospel at your Friday-morning Bible discussion.

Illustrations help readers know how their money will benefit the Kingdom. It is not enough to *explain* your dire financial need. People don't give to bail you out; they give to help you reach those students late at night or that young Friday-morning skeptic.

Compare the two examples on the next page, one of which *explains* ministry while the other *illustrates* it.

How did Jesus communicate? He told stories! Matthew 13 in *The Message* summarizes the motive behind Jesus' parables: "That's why I tell stories: to create readiness, to nudge the people toward receptive insight."

9. Did I personally hand-sign each letter?

Personally hand-sign each letter! And that goes for your regular newsletters as well as financial appeals. I'm kidding, right? No!

Explaining vs. Illustrating a Ministry

An important and exciting ministry, but the reader gets an explanation instead of an illustration.

I lead two Bible studies at Dixon Paper Company. I'm committed to reaching women in the marketplace. I'm excited that these professional women will be effective in multiplying their lives as they reach out to others.

I want to continually be effective in reaching women in the workplace. That's why I can't wait to go to the "Reaching Today's Businesswoman" seminar next month.

The same ministry activity as the example on the left, but illustrated. This engages the reader and helps him or her visualize what you do.

It's 11:30 A.M., Tuesday. I finish packing my turkey sandwich and bundle up to drive 20 minutes to Dixon Paper Company. As I enter the office, I can hear five phones ringing and one angry customer cussing out the sales rep for delivering cases of gray 25 lb. instead of ivory. Four tired-but-smiling professional women enter the corner lunch room, and we chit-chat for 10 minutes.

"We're on page 10," I remind them. Eyes dart down or away when I ask, "So, what do you think it means here when Jesus says, 'I am the truth'?"

Silence. Then Tricia broke the quiet, "How can you know that He is right? I mean, my husband thinks you should follow your instincts. That works just fine for me."

In order to keep reaching out to women like Tricia, I need to continually learn. That's why I can't wait to go to the "Reaching Today's Businesswoman" seminar next month.

In an age of technology, a personal signature shows attentiveness, that you value your readers. Hand-sign each one, and use something other than black ink so it will be more obvious to your readers—they'll notice! It is worth your time.

If you use a mailing service from overseas, of course this isn't possible. But perhaps your mailing-service representative could hand-sign them on your behalf with a note of explanation. Don't underestimate the power of a personal signature. After all, you notice it, don't you?

By the way, you do not need to write a personal note on every letter. It's impractical—you'll never get the letters out! One dear missionary friend still had half of her December Christmas letters sitting on her desk because she felt obligated to include a personal note on every one. And that was the following November!

Personally, I write a note on 30 to 40 each time. It takes one or two hours. And it's a different 30 to 40 each mailing, selected somewhat randomly, but close relatives are always included.

10. Did I use a first-class postage stamp?

First-class postage is worth the price. Furthermore, don't use a postage meter or a precanceled indicia printed on the letter. Studies show that the best results come from letters with regular stamps affixed. A first-class stamp signals to your readers that they are of value to you.

Can't afford it? How about asking a donor to make an extra gift to cover the postage? Explain how his gift to purchase 518 postage stamps will multiply as you receive many times that much from your appeal.

11. Did I apologize?

Don't start your letter with an apology. God has called you to something exciting, and your friends want to know! Never say this: "We've been so busy in the

Personally sign each letter, but don't feel obligated to write an individual note on each one.

ministry that we simply don't have time to write each one of you personally. Please forgive us as we have sent this appeal letter to all of you on our list."

Also, don't start like this: "I know you are probably inundated with financial appeals . . ."

12. Did I pad the envelope with extra handouts or brochures that are irrelevant to the project?

Unless it's a sweepstakes mailing, extra literature cuts down your response rate. Giving decisions are not based on volumes of information but on emotions and will.

13. Did I whine?

How do you like those "Woe is me!" letters? Emphasize your vision, not the sad state of your financial affairs.

How often should you send a cash-appeal letter? Once a year for sure, especially to nondonors. Obviously, following these guidelines will not guarantee perfect results every time. Kingdom ministry is not done by following formulas. I've seen poorly written letters get excellent results, and I've seen wonderful letters barely pay for themselves. But more often than not, following these tips will make your letter more understandable and more motivating to the readers. That will help. Of course, your project still has to have God's fingerprints on it. That is between you and Him.

Chapter Sixteen
ESPECIALLY FOR MINISTRY LEADERS

I may lose some friends in this chapter, but this has to be said and said loudly: One of the biggest problems in missionary funding is poor leadership.

Whether you are the CEO, a mid-level field manager, or the supervisor of only one staff, you harm your staff in funding when you inadvertently "lead" in one of the following ways. Do any of these leadership blindspots apply to you?

1. Silence About Money

It happened again yesterday. I was having supper with a field missionary who was lamenting his poor funding (with his wife in full agreement). After an hour I asked, "What does your supervisor think about your dilemma? What advice does he give?"

The reaction was predictable. John rolled his eyes. His wife suddenly got up to clear the dishes.

Silence.

Finally John said sadly, "He doesn't care. We talk about everything else, but never money."

Trying to be encouraging, I volunteered, "Perhaps he does care but doesn't know what to say."

John continued, "Maybe, but it *feels* like he doesn't care. He's not well funded either, and I don't think he feels confident talking to us about funding."

Dozens of missionaries have told me a similar story. It's a sad

As you help your staff with fundraising, your job is to provide hope, encouragement, accountability, and creative alternatives.

commentary on our leadership at every level. As leaders, we must understand that our staff live daily with the fears of not being able to pay the monthly bills or start saving for their kids' college. And they're embarrassed to bring up the subject of money lest they come across as unspiritual. It's like a big stinky elephant in the room, and they wonder why you, the spiritual shepherd, haven't noticed it.

To lead, you must address the elephant, even if you don't have insightful advice. Just ask a couple questions and listen. You don't have to have right answers but you do have to have the right questions.

Furthermore, bring up the subject of money frequently—on home visits, at staff meetings, in new-member orientation, in communiqués. If you talk about money frequently—and I don't mean whine about money!—and not just in a crisis, your staff will come to respect you more, and you will become known as a leader who deals in felt-need issues.

2. Failure to Model Good Fundraising

If you are not fully funded in your own support, you have a weak platform from which to advise your staff. Not wanting to be hypocritical, you say nothing. Although I commend you for not wanting to be a hypocrite, that doesn't bail you out. Your staff will copy you in their funding and donor ministry.

Of course, this is easily corrected—quietly do your own fundraising. Get yourself to 100 percent using reproducible tactics, and you'll minister to your staff at every level. No big announcements. No exhortations. Your use of time for fundraising will be noticed, and you will win the right to be listened to by your team.

3. Not Knowing How to Advise

Some leaders do ask their staff about money, but once the staff explain their dilemmas, the supervisors don't know what to say. Sometimes they do nothing, and sometimes they overreact and talk, talk, talk because they want to be a good leader!

Try this. Here are five questions to ask your staff (If you lead ethnic-minority staff, see Chapter 21):

- How is your funding going? What are your pressure points regarding money?
- What fundraising activities have you done in the past three months?
- How many face-to-face funding appointments have you had in the past three months? Tell me about a couple of them—how did they go?
- What do you think you are doing right in fundraising? What needs improvement?
- Of your past 10 face-to-face appeals, how many said yes? No? Still undecided? Did you make callbacks? Why not?

Asking these questions without offering correction will give you new insight into your staff. And even if you're not a great fundraiser yourself, you can still spot obvious errors in your staff's thinking or in their tactics. For sure you'll be able to see whether or not they are actively fundraising.

Note: If the staff you are talking to is male and married, have this "five questions" discussion with his wife present and fully free to participate. Otherwise, you might get "spin." Husbands don't intend to spin, but they will. His wife is the key to getting accurate answers and understanding their pain level.

4. Exhortation Only

As a supervisor, you are probably gifted at motivating and exhorting. But if all you do in response to your staff members' financial pain is exhort them to try harder, you will lose credibility.

If you can't help them, point them to another staff member who can. Or steer them to your mission's training department—whoever is responsible to help your staff in funding.

5. Failure to Give Your Staff Members Time and Money to Do Fundraising

If you tell them to take time for fundraising but fail to help them organize their schedules to find the time, you have failed them. Usually, supervisors affirm their staff members in funding as long as it's added on top of every-thing else they are doing. Leaders don't do this maliciously, but the effect is the same. For example: Be sure to make 20 funding appeals. And don't forget to recruit your team for the summer-training program! Be sure to meet with that new group from Oskaloosa! Hope you still plan to take that two-week vacation!

Conscientious missionaries try to do it all, and they usually fail. Help them succeed by meeting privately with each team member to review his or her priorities for

Help your staff organize their schedules to find time for fundraising.

the next 90 days, calendar in hand. Agree together on what to eliminate to ensure funding plans will be carried out. Then offer to pay for their fundraising costs from your special "leadership" account. You will not believe the morale boost these two simple leadership activities will give. It costs money and time to raise money. Free up your staff! (No leadership account? Raise it your-self or ask your supervisor. Push the system. Your staff are worth it!)

6. Settling for Less Than 100 Percent Funding

Most leaders think they are doing their staff members a favor when they relax the standards on full funding. But this is carbon monoxide to their ministry. When your married staff members limp along on 80 percent, wives notice it first. That puts pressure on the family. Then (married or single) they notice they are not saving for the future. This makes them feel they have no flexibility in their spending or their schedule. They start making decisions that are not in the best interest of the mission just to be around moneyed people. They will do goofy things just to stay afloat.

Help your staff see the dangers of living below their budgets.

Then, poor talk will start dominating their thoughts and conversations. Now morale is affected.

When you signed on for leadership, maybe no one told you that you needed to shepherd your team economically. But I'm telling you now! And do you see how leaders can be a bigger fundraising liability than a help?

You can learn to do this and do it well. Let's start a new day in missions to honor our staff by bringing the "m-word" into our leading. Pick out one or two of these six issues and start leading your staff in a new way today! Determine that you will work to build the skills and values necessary to deal with the stinky elephant in the room. Start today by bringing up the subject and then really listening.

Chapter Seventeen
ESPECIALLY FOR PASTORS AND MISSIONS COMMITTEES

You've seen it before. A bright young couple who grew up in your church burst into your office to explain how God has called them to the mission field. They've signed on with a reputable missions organization. Their friends in the congregation are excited that one of their own is going overseas; a few already have committed support. Missions-committee members hint that the church may provide 25 percent funding for a daunting budget approaching six figures per year. These young people are breathless with enthusiasm despite huge financial obstacles. Nothing can stop them.

But after a year of trying to sell a house, negotiating with their employers for more flexible hours, storing household goods, making whirlwind trips to the missions headquarters, and a frustrating experience in part-time "deputation," they again appear in your office. But this time they are worn out and doubtful. Only half their support is raised. They don't know where else to go for money. They are supposed to start language school overseas in 12 weeks. Disenchanted, they ask for your advice. What will you say?

This is a tough scenario for a pastor or missions committee. The advice you give

Frustrated missionaries may come to you seeking a light at the end of the tunnel. Be prepared to give them wise counsel and helpful tools, not just your opinion.

will have a significant impact on the Great Commission and on the lives of two dedicated people you love. Unfortunately, bad advice is frequently given by well-meaning church leaders. Let's review what *not* to say.

What *Not* to Say

1. "Just trust the Lord."
Yes, this young couple should trust the Lord, but what does that mean in fundraising? In my experience, money comes in after the missionaries have done their part in appropriately making the need known.

Avoid platitudes like "If you're called, the money will come in" and "God's will done in God's way never lacks God's supply." This young couple doesn't need a sermon so much as practical instruction on what to do next by faith. Resist the temptation to sermonize.

2. "Visit more churches."

Unless the couple is 100 percent funded by the denomination (and if they are, they probably are not in your office looking for help), it is unwise to build a funding strategy around church support. What is the point of going to unknown churches weekend after weekend to drum up support from strangers?

Better to base one's funding on personal appeals to individuals than on trying to impress congregations with a 10-minute speech, followed by lunch in the missions-committee chairman's home.

Furthermore, during home assignment in years to come, will the missionaries be asked to visit 52 churches in 52 weeks to keep their support? Also, because most of the supporting churches will not make sizable pledges to a stranger, the couple will likely be cellar-dwellers on the church's support list.

3. "Have a dessert!"

I'm not sure how this concept became so popular, because it produces little ongoing monthly support. Still, well-meaning friends frequently suggest this to missionaries.

The Navigators found from an 18-month study of fundraising desserts, only 9 percent of those attending pledged monthly support. Lest you be tempted to think that is a good result, the same study found that 46 percent pledge when seen face-to-face!

4. "God will bring in the rest once you get overseas."

Some missionaries have tried this, and I can't think of one who didn't regret it. There is a fine line between faith and presumption. Be careful not to overspiritualize funding.

5. "Try foundations."

We occasionally hear of a foundation providing massive support for a specific missions project, but foundation support is tough to get unless you personally know the foundation's decision-makers. And it takes a long time and much work—with no guarantees—to go through the application process. Remember, less than 5 percent of all money Americans give to charity comes from foundations. Another 5 percent comes from corporations, but 90 percent comes from individuals.

Now that we've identified the bad advice, let me suggest a different strategy to help your missionaries. But be warned, it will not sound "normal." When the next breathless young couple comes to you with their missions calling, affirm them (if you think God is in it), then steer them in this direction.

What to Say and Do

1. Ask them if they have ever done a Bible study on fundraising.

After hemming and hawing about a book they've read on family finances or a mutual-funds seminar they have attended, their answer will likely be no.

You can respond like this:

> *"Bob and Jill, we are excited that God is leading you to full-time ministry. It is the policy of our church that everyone considering missions go through this funding course and review it with our missions-committee funding representative.*
>
> *"As your sponsoring church, we have a Bible study to help you succeed at the toughest challenge you'll face before you get to the field. The study is called* Raising Personal Support,[1] *and it is our gift to you to help you get started on your calling."*

Too often we suggest activities to help candidates get money. Instead, we must first help them understand funding from a biblical perspective. No one automatically brings a biblical perspective on fundraising from their personal background.

Of course, this means that pastors, missions-committee members, and other leaders will need to be familiar with the study first. Then assign a motivated representative to debrief the candidates on the results of their personal study. It will be a great time of sharing and discovery.

Funding sponsors and missionaries need to work together closely and communicate regularly.

By the way, tell the candidates to put in 8 to 10 hours in preparation. If they don't, send them back to start again. We must break the mold that funding is a minor activity that they're already equipped for. They are not.

2. Assign a funding coach to work with them week by week.

Ideally, this would be the same person who reviewed their Bible study with them. The funding coach helps the candidates develop their strategy, monitors their funding progress, and serves as their advocate within the congregation.

---

1 I don't mean to sound self-serving, but there is not much else available on the biblical attitudes of fundraising. See the last page of this book for more information.

The coach's job is to check with the sending agency to coordinate schedules, funding progress, and departure dates. The coach also monitors the candidates in their presentation skills and their use of time.

The coach becomes a sponsor, prayer warrior, critic, and chief encourager. It is a key role and must be taken seriously. Having an effective coach will take the pressure off the pastor or the missions committee because you know someone is watching for problems before they occur.

3. Have the coach help the missionaries develop a first draft of their funding strategy, including a mailing list.

If the candidates can think of only 95 friends to put on a newsletter mailing list, you should reconsider their suitability. Here is what to look for in a good strategy:

- Large mailing list of potential donors, prayer supporters, and acquaintances (at least 200 for a single, 400 for couples).
- Significant support from "home" church.
- Focus on face-to-face appeals rather than relying on group meetings, church visits, letters, or phone calls. (For 6- to 12-month short-term missions trips, a cash-project letter is appropriate.)
- Realistic schedule. Two appointments per day of face-to-face appeals is minimal, but diligently do the follow-up.
- Effective presentation materials. Materials alone are not the key, but they are necessary. The candidate should be able to make his or her presentation in half an hour, including showing a video. That allows the listeners to ask questions before they tire of the presentation.
- A simple reporting/monitoring/accountability sheet. Reporting results or the lack of them is essential for making sure all things are done "decently and in order." They also keep the candidates encouraged.

4. Help them find training in fundraising.

After the Bible study, insist the candidates learn how to make presentations—both formal and informal. Your church should have the *Raising Personal Support* video study series (see the last page of this book for more information) or a few books such as this one to be given or loaned to candidates.

Also, find out what kind of training the sending agency offers. But be careful here. Some agencies do a fine job. Others simply show candidates how to set up meetings or do church presentations but offer little by way of training their missionaries in attitude or a biblical basis for fundraising. That's inadequate, and you will need to step in.

Now, what is the church's responsibility in funding? Should the church or church members feel obligated to meet 100 percent of the financial need? If you are sending them strictly as missionaries from your church and no other agency is involved, then probably yes. And some large churches are doing that.

But if your church is not the sending agency, you need not feel 100 percent of the burden. Be wary if your candidates have no acquaintances or funding contacts outside your church. That signals a difficult fundraising experience lies ahead, and you may be setting them up to fail. Expect the candidates to come up with names and funding potential outside the congregation.

These four steps are not a magic formula to get your candidates fully funded and on the field in record time. But by doing them, you have the assurance that you, as a home church, have done your part in helping your missionaries with the biggest task they will face before they arrive on the field. Help the candidates see that their missionary work begins the hour they tap into that Bible study you assign them. The calling begins here—in fundraising—not when they get off the plane in Kathmandu!

Chapter Eighteen
ESPECIALLY FOR OVERSEAS MISSIONARIES

Over the years, I've observed five mistakes that overseas missionaries make in funding, particularly when they return on home assignment. These mistakes are not impossible to remedy, but to correct them, you will have to change your thinking. Let's look at each one.

1. Leaving fundraising until the last few weeks of home assignment.

Home assignment, or "furlough" as some still call it (though that is an unfortunate term implying "rest"), also could be named "trying to accomplish too much in too short a time." Shorter, more frequent home assignments, rather than the traditional 12 months in four years, may solve language-school scheduling problems, but it doesn't decrease funding pressure.

Typically, with only five weeks of home assignment left, panic sets in. Though half a dozen friends mentioned supporting your ministry, you still haven't raised your monthly goal of $1,575 nor the $18,670 cash you need to return to the field. You haven't been lazy—just busy "resting": visiting family, getting acquainted with supporting churches, going to donors' kids' Little League games, taking a seminary graduate course, recruiting short-term helpers to return to the field with you, writing an important paper for your organization, attending missions conferences, handling an ugly personnel matter assigned by the country leader. And resting! One missionary told me he couldn't wait to get back to his third-world country so he could regain his sanity!

Having a solid plan in place before you return home will help you navigate the treacherous waters of fundraising on home assignment.

This issue is difficult to resolve but not impossible. Try these ideas:

- Write your fundraising plan *before* you return home. Once you arrive on home soil, you must spend generous time with your parents and relatives. If your fundraising plan is not written down with a detailed travel schedule, other important family activities will push it aside until five weeks before you leave, creating panic.

Although you'll have to contact some people by mail, remember that fundraising letters are easy to ignore and toss. Make as many face-to-face appeals as possible during your time at home.

Instead, arrive at home with your plan written down—with the names, addresses, and phone numbers of 35 to 50 people to ask for new monthly support, the names of your top 10 current major donors to thank in person, the three churches you will visit, and your pictures ready to show.

For example, if you are in Atlanta visiting your mission headquarters, schedule extra days to see two top donors and make three face-to-face appeals.

Do the hard work of planning your fundraising (and therefore your calendar) before you get on the airplane to come home.

- Find a sponsor who will hold you accountable to carry out your funding strategy—someone who will pitch in and work, not just give advice. Can he or she provide you with administrative help, find a phone number, set up meetings, or provide a vehicle, in addition to offering encouragement and accountability?

- Work with your mission to make sure your home-assignment objectives are realistic. What seems doable when you talk with your supervisor overseas is more difficult once you arrive in your home country. Before you commit to any plans, confer with your spouse and other veteran staff.

- In general, focus on your monthly support early in your home assignment. Next, work on major donors who will anchor the bulk of your outgoing expense. Third, about 10 weeks before you return, write your cash-project letter asking for outgoing cash. Don't rely on this letter to bring in monthly support—it won't happen. And of course, visit key donors throughout the home assignment.

2. Forgetting to switch back to your home country's communication preferences.

I was working with a furloughing missionary who was discouraged about the meager response to his appeals for monthly support. Bob had done a lot of things right. He started making appeals for monthly support early in his home assignment. He was seeing people in person and not relying on letters. He had adequate time set aside for fundraising, and he had a sharp presentation booklet describing his ministry in Asia. Yet he was disillusioned, having received only one or two "yeses" from 15 face-to-face appeals. I didn't know what to say.

Finally, on a hunch, I asked him why he spoke to me so softly. I could barely hear him even though we were sitting side by side. I also noticed he was reticent in demeanor, not looking me in the eye but quickly glancing away.

"That's the way I have to do it in Asia," he said. "The typical loud, brash American way of communicating is not well received."

"True," I said, "but is it possible Americans are mistaking your Asian cultural sensitivity for tentativeness or lack of confidence? They may wonder if God's hand is on you."

When Bob went back to speaking louder and looking American donors solidly in the eye, his results improved. But he had to remember to change back when he returned to Asia!

Do you see what I mean? Your home country's culture is different from your overseas culture. You must be able to switch. Don't change your personality—just make sure that you communicate well according to the listeners' standards. The apostle Paul said it this way, "I have become all things to all people" (1 Corinthians 9:12).

3. Assuming your donors' interest in your ministry is greater than their interest in their lawn or reality television.

Missionaries come home bursting with wonderful stories about ministry, lessons they've learned about God, and deep things to share about cross-cultural living. They can't wait for their donors to ask about it.

But after a few minutes, their donors lose interest and switch the subject to their kids, their lawn, their dog, their church, their personal problems, and their favorite TV shows. Even though you have traveled three hours to see them, they prefer to talk about themselves despite your exciting stories from the front.

A missionary friend who had just returned from an exciting ministry in Australia told me the attention span of his donors was 20 minutes—"no more." So he lowered his expectations, communicated the important things in 20 minutes, and then listened to his friends and tried to meet their needs for the rest of the evening. His donors think he is wonderful, and they continue supporting him.

Of course, a few donors have an insatiable capacity to hear your mission adventures hour after hour. And perhaps a short attention span is true only of Americans, but keep it in mind. Bale your communications hay tight—20 minutes worth!

4. Failing to add names to your mailing list.

When you serve overseas, you do not meet many new potential donors or prayer supporters. On home assignment, you must add names to your mailing list so you will never run out of potential donors.

After 10 years overseas, multiterm missionaries know the language and the culture. They have painstakingly built trust relationships. They are primed for great ministry. But though they were well funded by 245 people their first two terms, they are now drying up financially. Their budget has risen dramatically in 10 years, and some donors have stopped giving. And now, as they prepare to enter their most productive years of service, they also face the most financial pressure.

The tendency at this point is to lean on current donors to give more. "Can everyone increase?" the missionaries plead. Upgrading your donors should be a part of your strategy, but you quickly reach the point at which you simply need more cultivated people to appeal to.

While on home assignment, add names to your list. Try these ideas:

- Daily ask the Lord to grant you divine appointments with new people who will have a heart for you.
- Develop visibility in your home church.
- Teach a Sunday school class for young married couples. (Graciously decline invitations to teach kids' Sunday school classes; ask for the adults.)
- Attend the various social functions of the church.
- Meet the friends of your donors.
- When you speak at conferences or seminars, offer a sign-up list for guests to receive your newsletter. Don't ask for general prayer for the mission. Instead, tell the story of one needy person in your ministry and ask for prayer for just that person.
- Speak to service groups, such as the Kiwanis or Oddfellows. (Someone in the congregation of your home church is a member or knows someone who is.)

Remember, the goal is not to ask these new people for money. Just add them to your mailing list. After they have been receiving your newsletter for a year or two or four, they are aware of what you do and will gladly have you into their home when you call for a meeting.

Short on contacts? Ask friends and donors for referrals—but don't say, "Any referrals?"

You don't have to be pushy. I say something like this: "I've so enjoyed talking with you today, Burt. I didn't know we had so much in common. I wonder if I could add your name to our mailing list for our ministry overseas. We send a newsletter about once a quarter, and this will enable us to keep in touch."

I try to keep it light, but I also tell my friend that I am serious about the need for prayer. I've added dozens of names that way, and many of these "names" are now friends or donors.

5. Assuming your donors are just as committed to you while you're at home as they are when you're overseas.

I've heard it a hundred times: "Our support drops when we are on home assignment." Be sure to tell your donors that a lengthy home assignment does not lessen your need for support and that you are not on "vacation"!

For some missionaries, it is more expensive to live at home than overseas. Donors, however, may assume that their support is not as necessary when you're home. Take the time to educate them so attrition can be kept to a minimum.

I recommend a special letter to each individual donor, listing his or her support amount and explaining that you still need it on home assignment. Then explain the purpose of the home assignment and how it fits into the overall scheme of your ministry. Try something like this:

> *"I'm writing today not only to thank you for your generous support but also to urge you to continue it during our home assignment the next 12 months. Unfortunately, some giving friends assume that our expenses are somehow covered during our home assignments or that our ministry in Asia stops. Nothing could be further from the truth. On home assignment, we still are required to raise our support from our giving team—the home office does not subsidize us during this time. And although the ministry here is different from what we do overseas, it is crucial to our success there.*
>
> *"For example, here are some of the things we must accomplish between now and next January . . ."*

Then call a few strategic donors to make sure they understand.

Remember, a little planning and sticking to it will enable you to overcome these typical missionary problems in funding.

Chapter Nineteen
ESPECIALLY FOR BEGINNERS

If you are just starting out in missions as a career or on a short-term assignment, this chapter is for you. I commend you for your exuberance in launching a new phase of your life. Excited rookies often feel their fundraising challenge is unique, and they sometimes have exotic ideas about raising support.

Fine, but don't ignore what many start-up missionaries have already learned. It is easier to do it right the first time than to come back later (when you're discouraged) and correct your misfires. I can't guarantee you will be immune from difficulty—but even when you are driven to your knees in despair, God will be faithful to perfect your character. Hard times may come even if you follow these guidelines. But don't suffer for silly mistakes.

Here are some tips as you begin your adventure.

1. Are you "called" for special service?

If the Lord is not the "unseen caller" behind your dreams for missions, what is the point of trying to raise money? (The scary part is that you may actually raise some!)

This matter of calling is a mystery. The Scriptures give clues about calling to ministry but offer no set formula. In the Appendix of this book is a short Bible study that may help you de-

termine your calling. I'm not talking about the calling we all have to come to God—that's "general calling." The study considers special calling for special service. If you are questioning your future or having second thoughts, take time to do that study. Better to struggle with your calling now than in the middle of a frustrating day at language school.

Be assured it is OK to question your calling, especially at first. Rare is the missionary who never doubts what he or she is supposed to do.

Here are two crucial questions about your calling. First, are you run-

If you're just starting out, reaching 100 percent of budget may seem impossible! But if God has called you, ask Him for courage to do your part.

ning to the mission field to escape something? Some missionaries or pastors have felt "called" mainly because they were petrified by a career in the secular world. Missions or seminary became an escape from something they dreaded.

It is easy to feel "peace" about the mission field if you are trying to escape any difficult responsibility, such as family, career, or relationship problems. I've found I always have "peace" when I can delay or avoid a confrontation with a fearful circumstance. But it is not God's peace. As Jonah discovered, you can run, but God will find you!

Second, are you going into ministry because someone (such as a parent, pastor, or leader) says you should? Be sure your call is from God, not people!

2. Have you studied the Scriptures on fundraising?

You'll also find a Bible study on fundraising in the Appendix of this book. Many missionary candidates are tempted to skip or merely browse through this Bible study because they "know it already" or claim to be experienced. They think they need only a few key skills or catchy phrases to use with donors.

Watch out for that attitude! Biblical fundraising is more about attitudes and values than skills. Missionaries who simply tack hastily learned skills onto their personalities will come across like the slick charlatans they despise. Revisit Chapters 3 and 4.

You need to learn skills, but if your attitude about funding comes strictly from your own background, your skills are merely window dressing. Invest 10 to 15 hours in your career by doing a thorough study of what the Scriptures say about funding.

3. How many are on your mailing list?

If you're under budget, resist the temptation to trim your mailing list to save money. Don't remove anyone unless they ask to be removed.

If you cannot come up with 200 people as a single or 400 people as a married couple for your newsletter list, reconsider your calling. I've seen too many missionaries with only 45 or 110 people to hold the ropes for them, and that is not enough. I'm not talking about 200 or 400 donors—just friends, acquaintances, or contacts who would say yes to receiving your mailings. Remember, your newsletter list is not for donors only or even potential donors only. Your letter can be a ministry whether people give or not. And many of them will pray for you!

4. Do you have the backing of a "home church"?

More than financial help, a home church provides an emotional haven where you can find encouragement and a place for fellowship on home assignment.

Your home church may not be the church in which you grew up. Find a church warm to you and your mission. You might even be able to help them develop a greater interest in missions.

5. Do you have a fundraising sponsor?

Who will help you carry out your funding strategy? Ask God to give you someone who has the courage to hold your feet to the fire. Someone who will ask you, "Exactly how many calls did you make last week?" and follow up with, "How many is a 'bunch'?" Look for a sponsor *without* the gift of mercy!

Your sponsor need not be an accountant or banker. More important than being skilled in financial statements is your sponsor's understanding of your fundraising plan and his or her willingness to commit the time to hold you accountable, pray with you, and encourage you.

6. Which "anchor donors" will underwrite your start-up fundraising costs?

It takes money to raise money. Ask God for someone (maybe it's your home church) who will cover your travel and living expenses while you raise support. Explain thoroughly your fundraising plan to them so they know what they are getting into.

In conclusion, resist the temptation to take a "poor talk" view of fundraising that is so common today. Even your home church or faithful donors may unwittingly feed the poor-missionary, "woe is me" mentality. If God has called you, He will fund you as long as you're willing to do your part. Your exciting task is to find out who your ropeholders are!

Though it may seem burdensome for now, take the time to do the Bible study and walk through the ideas outlined in Chapters 3 and 4. You'll be glad you did it right the first time.

Chapter Twenty
ESPECIALLY FOR
SINGLE WOMEN MISSIONARIES

I'm the first to admit that I've goofed up when advising women missionaries about fundraising. Perhaps my most fabulous goof-up happened in Minneapolis.

A single woman who was new with The Navigators called me from downstate Wisconsin to report on her fundraising. During the first 45 seconds of our phone call she was talkative, but that soon gave way to prolonged silences. Then I noticed a quiver in her usually confident voice. She wanted to stop fundraising *now*—$1,000 short of her minimum monthly goal. "Can't I just get by on less?" she pleaded.

"Just get back out there!" I remonstrated enthusiastically, waving my arms wildly from the comfort of my Minneapolis office. "Keep going. You're doing fine. Not everyone will give, but you're getting appointments, right? And some are pledging, right?"

"Yes," she whimpered, "a few have given, but the amounts are smaller than you said. And most are cash, not monthly."

Missions organizations need to recognize that single women face unique challenges in fundraising.

"Keep asking big!" I blurted. "Suggest $50 to $200 per month. You can do this! Go for it! Are you giving them a pledge card? God has called you, hasn't He?"

I was on a roll. She was quiet.

I waited with the cheesy grin still on my face and my arm still in the air, expecting her to thank me for such an inspiring pep talk. Slowly I relaxed the peppy grin. Was that muffled sobbing I heard?

"OK," she said, trying to be strong, "I'll keep going." I reassured her I'd pray for her and told her to call me again in a few days for more "encouragement." But I hung up the phone feeling like a fool. I'd served her poorly. Something was wrong, but I didn't know what to do. Truthfully, I wasn't even sure I wanted to dive in to figure it out. It was easier to stick with tried-and-true formulas.

Today, I still don't have all the answers, but after observing dozens of single women in the fundraising process, I have come to accept and deal with the following trends:

1. American evangelicals have a bias against single women missionaries.

Evangelicals generally prefer giving to couples over single women. As soon as I began to suspect this, it was confirmed by Bonnie, a single woman on our staff. Bonnie made a funding appeal to a friendly, mature, nonweird evangelical couple from her church who seemed to appreciate her ministry. Perfect prospects! The appointment was going well. They were extremely polite. But then came the close. Bonnie asked if they would pray about monthly support. Hesitating, they told her to "come back and see us when you're married." And they gave nothing.

Bonnie looked pleadingly to me for answers, but I had none. In my heart, I wanted to throw a case of rotten eggs at their evangelical home. Though few donors verbalize it so bluntly, other single women have picked up on this hidden message.

2. Single women missionaries get smaller pledges.

They also receive one-time gifts rather than monthly commitments or generous annual commitments. Furthermore, much of their support comes from other single women because that is where they have built relationships and receive a warm welcome. Yet in America, in general, single women do not earn as much as couples, so their commitments are smaller.

Things can get even worse when a female donor marries. She may write her single missionary friend saying she is cutting back or stopping support because she feels she should defer to her husband's giving interests. "Sorry. I'll still pray for you."

These two trends require single women to spend more time and energy just to raise the same amount of money as a missionary couple. Supervisors must understand this, or they will lead poorly and give inane advice like, "Just get back out there!"

3. Single women face unique challenges in one-to-one fundraising.

To reach full funding, women must often set appointments with people they don't know. It can be risky. Although I know of one missionary who met her future husband on a fundraising appointment, it's more likely awkward and uncomfortable to meet with strange men. If you're meeting someone for the first time, take a friend or your sponsor with you.

Women missionaries are not asking for sympathy, but they need understanding—especially from their supervisors. What can be done?

First, don't fundraise alone. Find a partner to go with you and pray for you. Navigator women have told us that "doing fundraising alone" is by far their biggest de-motivator. Let's face it—setting appointments on the phone is lonely work for anyone. Just knowing a friend is across the room—or across town—praying for you can be a big help.

We've seen measurable results from forming funding teams—both formally and informally.

For example, some staff gather at one location to eat supper, pray, and get on their cell phones for 90 minutes of fundraising calls.

We've also seen success in setting up formal 90-day campaigns for 6 to 10 women at a time. They meet for three days of training and to set up their strategies. When women know that other women across the country are together in the same campaign, it helps them feel supported and not so alone. During a weekly conference call, they compare notes and pray for one another. It works.

Second, supervisors can be more helpful by thinking differently about women staff and individualized fundraising. When a single woman joins your staff, work out a funding strategy with her *before* she launches out. And make sure that you do your part by:

- Partially funding her yourself with your local ministry funds and even joining her support team from your personal giving.
- Making sure she has adequate fundraising training and materials.
- Ensuring she has qualified prospective donors to see.
- Introducing her to some of your donors.
- Going with her on at least five funding appointments. Nothing communicates you are "for her" as much as giving your time.
- Making sure her budget is generous—not just a "get-by" salary. Is there money allotted for creating a warm, inviting home?

STAYSKAL

Single women don't need to be afraid of fundraising. With the right support, they can be just as successful as men and couples.

- Giving her specific time to raise support. Just saying, "Take all the time you need" is not good leadership. Help her clear her schedule from other responsibilities because women (like many men) are prone to drop fundraising when a bleating sheep calls in need of counseling.
- Stepping up to the plate and providing her shortfall if she has worked hard at funding and the money is still not there. If you want her on your team, don't leave her to figure out her fundraising on her own.
- Not letting her start ministry until she is fully funded. That may seem harsh, and she may want a lower salary just to be done with fundraising. But don't succumb. Make sure the budget is realistic, and help her keep going or fund the rest of her budget yourself.

After I'd shared this last point at a training seminar, a new female staff came up immediately with tears in her eyes and thanked me for our "no-ministry-until-fully-funded" policy. She confided, "My supervisor thinks he is being kind by leaving it up to me to decide when I stop fundraising, but all it gives me is pressure and guilt."

Third, be who God made you to be. Missionary women tell me they feel we are training them to "do it like men." In funding training we emphasize, rightly so I think, the importance of being bold at the close of an appointment because that's when missionaries are prone to waffle or chicken out. But women feel they are expected to be "masculinely bold," and it feels unnatural to them.

I think they are right. As trainers, we inadvertently overlook how our teaching will be received and applied by women, especially conscientious young women wanting desperately to do it right. So let me correct that. Please don't fundraise like a "Type A" businessman if that's not who you are. Be clear and earnest, of course, and do it within the wonderful personality God has given you.

According to the Women & Philanthropy website (womenphil.org), today in America, 70 percent of professional fundraisers are women! They are using their uniquely feminine bent toward relationships, communication skills, and passion for the cause to move their missions forward. We can encourage and celebrate these skills in our women staff too!

My friend, Becky Brodin, however, has reminded me that sometimes we must be all things to all men to advance the Gospel (1 Corinthians 9:22). When you are with a "Type A" business leader, don't be afraid to "cut to the chase" or "tell it like it is." We adapt our communication style to our audience in evangelism, don't we? We can do it in fundraising too. Be yourself, but be flexible in how you communicate.

Obviously there's much more that can be said about women raising support, but I will end with this final thought: Without women missionaries, where would the advancement of the Gospel be? Through the centuries, women have carried the Gospel around the world, often with meager funding, and they have not wavered. To paraphrase Jesus, "You are worthy of full support."

Chapter Twenty-One
ESPECIALLY FOR ETHNIC-MINORITY MISSIONARIES

I have a confession. I used to believe that ethnic-minority missionaries could reach full funding just like anyone else if they simply made a gazillion funding appointments. When they struggled I'd say, "Try harder! Visit more people!" Some did try harder, but they rarely got as many appointments as they needed. Furthermore, their gifts were frequently one-time or pledges that lasted only a month or two.

My conclusion: They didn't stick with it long enough.

As the years went by, I noticed minority missionaries were leaving our staff. Funding difficulties were usually mentioned as a reason, but so were other issues. I persisted in my view that anyone could raise support if they made enough appointments.

As I continued to listen to my minority brothers and sisters describe their pain in fundraising, it occurred to me that I might be wrong. It finally became clear through a 90-day program called Dollar Match Initiative. The results on the following page are from five of our African-American staff appealing to African Americans and Anglos and from five of our Asian-American staff appealing to Asian Americans and Anglos. Ten staff, 90 days, four kinds of appeals. Take a look at the results:

Though not a huge sampling, these numbers are large enough to reveal interesting trends.[1] First, the African-American-to-African-American results:

- The face-to-face "yes" rate was an excellent 64%. That nearly equals the 60% response rate among Anglos to Anglos from a study made a few years ago (see page 68). But note that only 28% of the African Americans pledged monthly compared with 46% in the Anglo study. That spells a huge drop in long-term dollars received.
- The phone/letter results (1%) and letter-only results (less than 1%) are much lower than the Anglo study, 27% and 14% respectively (see page 68).
- The group-meeting monthly "yes" rate of 3% is lower than the Anglo rate of 9%. But note the encouraging 27% "yes" rate for one-time cash.

Now the Asian-American-to-Asian-American results:

- The face-to-face "yes" rate is an astounding 81%, with 56% agreeing to give monthly! This far surpasses the Anglo study, but notice that the five staff made only 27 appointments over the 90 days—five appointments each. This was supposed to be their priority task during these 90 days. Why so few appointments?
- The "yes" rates for monthly support on the phone/letter combination (27%) is encouraging, but only 22 such appeals were made. Note that 142 were made to Anglos.

---

1 Because these figures represent a dollar match initiative, amounts may be higher than normal in all giving categories. The Anglo study on page 68 did not involve a match.

Results from Ethnic Fundraising Appeals

	Face-to-Face Appeals	Yes Monthly/Amt	Yes Cash/Amt	% Who Gave
AfAm to AfAm	86	28% / $60	36% / $309	64%
AfAm to Anglo	82	39% / $54	29% / $1080	68%
AsAm to AsAm	27	56% / $226	26% / $246	82%
AsAm to Anglo	90	43% / $44	27% / $301	70%

	Phone/Letter	Yes Monthly/Amt	Yes Cash/Amt	% Who Gave
AfAm to AfAm	214	1% / $67	11% / $243	12%
AfAm to Anglo	171	4% / $61	18% / $288	22%
AsAm to AsAm	22	27% / $34	18% / $428	45%
AsAm to Anglo	142	11% / $57	11% / $297	22%

	Letter Only	Yes Monthly/Amt	Yes Cash/Amt	% Who Gave
AfAm to AfAm	264	0% / $0	5% / $50	5%
AfAm to Anglo	318	1% / $15	7% / $181	8%
AsAm to AsAm	19	5% / $50	53% / $143	58%
AsAm to Anglo	116	4% / $17	4% / $913	8%

	Group Meeting	Yes Monthly/Amt	Yes Cash/Amt	% Who Gave
AfAm to AfAm	37	3% / $500	27% / $257	30%
AfAm to Anglo	134	<1% / $0	41% / $158	41%
AsAm to AsAm	14	79% / $26	85% / $378	164%*
AsAm to Anglo	16	25% / $44	100% / $437	125%*

*Note: Most gave both monthly and cash.

What can we learn from this data? In trying to interpret these findings, my ethnic-minority brothers and sisters have told me the following:

- Nonwhite Americans know little about most evangelical parachurch organizations. Sending hard-earned money to an unknown organization in Colorado Springs for a Midwest campus ministry doesn't add up. On top of that, ethnic urban-dwellers understandably hesitate to send money to Colorado Springs when there are so many needs in their own neighborhoods. Could that be why "cash only" was frequently given? Shouldn't we take time to inform minority believers about our mission before we ask them to give?
- Monthly support is a strange concept for many, as is giving outside the local church. According to the *Ethnic Philanthropy Report* by the University of San Francisco (1994), the

local church is the focal point of giving among African Americans and Asian Americans, while giving informally to family is the highest charitable priority among Hispanics.

- Some minority missionaries hesitate to appeal to Anglos—even when Anglos are receptive. My friend Val, an African American from inner-city Chicago, taught me this. He had agreed to meet one of my donors and me out in the suburbs to present his downtown ministry. I was then prepared to invite my donor to support Val. When he arrived, he said, "Sorry I'm late. I feel safer downtown. It's scary out here in the 'burbs!" The donor gladly pledged after hearing Val's story. Your Anglo staff can help a lot by championing your ethnic staff. Val never would have come to the suburbs to fundraise without my being there. This kind of partnership should be part of your mission's strategy.

- Family pressure plays a big role in different cultures. Asian Americans are strongly encouraged by their parents to get an education and seek a professional career. The idea of their son or daughter becoming a missionary with an organization they haven't heard of is scary. Then add the strange practice of sending monthly support to a faraway corporate headquarters, and you've got the makings of serious tension in the family.

- Face-to-face appeals are received differently from culture to culture. The fact that five Asian-American staff made only 27 face-to-face appointments with other Asians is revealing. My Asian friends tell me that face-to-face asks are too confrontational for many (but not all!) Asian-background believers. My experience in Korea and Japan taught me that many Asians give answers you want to hear rather than saying no so that no one loses face. Making effective appeals while honoring the culture can be tricky.

Of course, these statistics offer promising news too. Look at the 100 percent response among Asian Americans at group meetings! That's something we can learn from and build on.

Two Extreme Solutions

In the midst of some discouraging findings, mission leaders might be tempted to have minority staff give up on raising personal support altogether. Maybe the best they can do is subsidize these staff from the general fund. Although this may seem magnanimous and even attractive to the missionaries, it hints at conclusions none of us likes. Does it imply that minority cultures don't have much money? That they aren't generous? That they don't care about the Great Commission?

Of course, none of that is true! Hispanics sacrificially send money back home to aging parents. African Americans give sacrificially to their extended family, local churches, and street missions that help the neighborhood. Asian parents sacrificially support family and their local churches. Generosity runs deep in these cultures.

At the other extreme, mission leaders can ignore these trends and tell their minority staff they'll succeed if they get a gazillion appointments. A few might succeed—survival of the fittest!

I don't have all the answers, but let's start by agreeing to avoid the extremes:

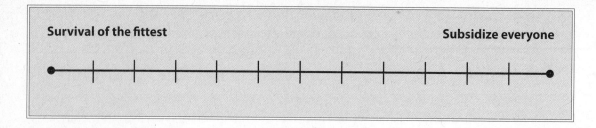

Chapter Twenty-One

Middle Ground

Somewhere between the two extremes is the logical, biblical solution of working together to face this challenge. Before I offer some suggestions, let's lay one bedrock assumption: Every culture must learn to give biblically, and every culture must learn to appeal biblically. Note that this does not require uniform methods within every culture. Keep in mind the missionary motto, "Not wrong, just different." If every culture has received the Great Commission, then every culture has the privilege of supporting the Great Commission. So no more nonsense about some cultures not being able to give or not being able to raise support. That's dishonoring to those people and to God.

Some ethnic minorities may not be familiar with the idea of raising personal support for ministry. Be prepared to counter the "begging" image they may have.

My first suggestion is to make sure both mission agency and missionary educate potential minority donors.

A new African-American missionary recently made her first phone call to set up an appointment with her grandmother. With excitement, she told her about the new assignment, and her grandmother was supportive. Then she asked her grandmother for an "appointment" to talk about monthly financial support. Silence.

"You mean they're not paying you!" the grandmother asked. "You come home right now!" Her granddaughter was crushed.

We might argue that this unfortunate incident could have been prevented with better preparation. But that begs the question: Who is informing this loving grandmother about how the agency is supported?

When people from a particular culture hesitate to give monthly support, it's usually related to education rather than an unwillingness to give. After all, it has taken evangelical Anglos 50 years to feel comfortable sending money to Colorado Springs, Wheaton, and Orlando!

To tackle the issue of sending monthly support outside the local church, you first must lavishly inform your potential minority donors. They need to know all about your mission, how it will make a difference in the world (and maybe their neighborhood), and how the funding mechanism works. That requires more than a brochure. The supervising staff may need to show up in person and explain why they need "your granddaughter" on staff and champion a "new" way of giving to support her.

But be ready for questions like:

- Is your organization white? This brochure looks awfully white!
- Why are there so few people of color on your national board?
- What are you doing for the poor and disenfranchised?
- Why aren't you doing this through local churches?
- Why don't you pay a salary like everybody else?
- Why haven't I heard of your mission agency before?
- What are you doing for my neighborhood? My church?

Second, offer creative incentives and partnering. What about giving strategic incentives that help minority staff both in the short and long term?

Instead of paying a guaranteed subsidy each month, offer $100 per face-to-face appointment and $500 for each group meeting at which appeals are made. Or credit the missionary's account with $10 for each person they recruit to an informational meeting. Incentives like these give minority missionaries short-term cash so they don't have to go back to a job to earn grocery money each month. It also gives them long-term income as they recruit monthly or annual donors.

Another experiment we tried in The Navigators matched money raised by ethnic-minority staff over a 90-day period. Monthly gifts were matched for 12 months. Both the staff and their minority donors liked the idea that a primarily Anglo ministry was proactive in funding minorities. Funding increased significantly the first year, and the program was a success. We're continuing it.

One popular incentive is to give new staff a decreasing amount each month until they get their support up. For example, they get $4,000 the first month, $3,800 the second, $3,600 the third, and so on until the subsidy stops at the 20th month. As ideal as this concept sounds, I've never heard of its broad success. A few years ago, we tried this with new Anglo staff and found that they left our ministry after the 20th month. Coaching staff and holding them accountable to build their donor base during the 20 months is the hard part. You'll also need to be sure the staff are appealing to qualified giving candidates.

InterVarsity Christian Fellowship (IV) has made great strides in ethnic-minority ministry by charging all IV staff one percent of donor income to help minority staff. Donna Wilson, field-training director of IV, says there have been no complaints from staff because of the historical commitment of IV toward developing multiethnic ministry. Some have even said, "Why can't we do more?"

But does this inadvertently feel like a "welfare system" to either the Anglo staff or the minority staff? Donna said no. Once the guidelines showing who gets the money are publicly articulated with input from supervisors, the welfare mentality disappears.

Should other agencies follow InterVarsity's lead? An IV ministry director answers this way: "Our multiethnic ministry would be decades behind if we didn't have the one-percent charge. It's a huge part of our numerical growth of staff of color."

Donna emphasized, "Decision-making and distribution of funds needs to rest with the multiethnic leaders and not be controlled by Anglo leadership. This takes trust!"

My final suggestion is to make sure staff members have prospective giving partners. One of the most frequently quoted clichés for ministry among the poor is the adage: "Give a man a fish and he eats for a day. Teach him how to fish and he eats for a lifetime." For years I've recognized wisdom in this little statement, but it seemed like something was missing. Oversimplified, maybe. I didn't know how to improve it until last January when I heard John Perkins, the legendary civil-rights leader from Mendenhall, Mississippi, scoff at the cliché. He thundered out a third line: "Give him access to the river!"

Just because we train our staff how to fundraise and show them how to tell compelling stories, we have not done enough if they have no one to go to! It reminds me of the Nature Channel where you see fishermen crammed together side by side fishing for salmon. Even the best-trained fisherman in Alaska with the most compelling bait would be out of luck if he couldn't get to the river.

The most obvious way to find prospective giving partners is asking for referrals or networking. Your agency should help here. Ask them to work with you in searching for appropriate leads from their donor base, possibly major donors who may have a heart for ethnic minorities.

Finally, one caution. Thomas Sowell, the African-American economist and syndicated columnist asked this question: "Who said, 'If the Negro cannot stand on his own two legs, let him fall'?"

I was repelled by his bold question and assumed it came from some narrow-minded racist. But no, it was Frederick Douglass, the 19th-century African-American crusader for justice. Sowell pointed out that sometimes we try to "help too much" and that inhibits excellence. As a teacher, Sowell found that "black students would meet higher standards if you refused to lower the standards for them."

Sowell offers us a good balance. My original view that anyone can be fully funded with a gazillion appointments was a survival-of-the-fittest notion. It's wrong. But neither should we dishonor our ethnic-minority friends by "helping too much."

Personal fundraising has many positives, but the great negative is the "every-person-for-himself" mentality. Why not employ the body concept of the New Testament? Instead of telling an ethnic-minority staff, "It's up to *you!*" why not say, "It's up to us! We as a team are going to help you get fully funded. You do your part, and we'll do ours."

No organization I know of has completely solved this issue. Let's continue to learn together.

The Role of the African-American Church in Fundraising

The following insight comes from Rich Berry, director of The Navigators' African-American ministry.

I am an African American. I have raised money for more than 35 years. I have learned that the individualized approach of going to businessmen has very limited effectiveness among African Americans. There is a better way.

I believe the Black church is an opportunity for raising money that is right before us. I find it unthinkable that in the 21st century, anyone trying to raise money in the Black community would not engage urban pastors. Having pastored an African-American church for 12 years, I know that the pastor is consulted for most of the congregation's life decisions. As a result, the church is the strongest, oldest, most revered, and most economically stable institution in the community. With this in mind, it would follow then that the Black church should become a vital part of a fundraising strategy. It makes practical sense. The church is a cultural reality that necessitates engagement if we are to make lasting impact in the African-American culture.

When I am raising monthly money from African Americans, I am frequently asked to talk to the person's pastor about my need. The average mission group is ill-equipped to address the Black pastor. Their brochures and videos are irrelevant at best and insensitive at worst. The staff candidate is then left to raise funds outside his or her culture with people whom he or she does not know. This is a challenge most young recruits cannot handle. They get discouraged and quit.

The sensitive organization may provide the ethnic recruit with subsidies to help in the early stages of raising support. This is helpful but could rob the recruits of their dignity and create contempt from some Anglos who themselves are having difficulty in fundraising.

My appeal to faith mission leaders is to do the homework that all effective missionaries do. Employ the principle that missiologists apply to ministry in foreign fields: Shape fundraising strategies to reflect the needs and values of the people being reached. Only when this principle is applied will there be a long-range solution to the problem of ethnic funding.

Chapter Twenty-Two
FINAL THOUGHTS

Whether you've read sequentially through this book or studied only selected chapters, congratulations! I commend you for having the farsightedness to understand that raising personal support is more than sending a big mailing or visiting a few Sunday school classes.

But the question remains: Will the principles, values, and techniques I've presented work *for you?* Can *you* be fully funded for a career in missions?

You will not succeed if you view what I've said as an automatic formula to guarantee results. Nor will it work if you rely merely on human energy. But if God has called you to your mission career (whether short term or longer) and if you trust Him step by step, then you can be confident that you have done your part. At the risk of shameless self-promotion, let me leave you with a quote from a missionary who was ready to leave the ministry until he applied these guidelines:

"I joined the mission thinking, 'Eighty percent of budget is OK. The ministry is far more important than fundraising.'

"Then one year our regional director brought in the Raising Personal Support *seminar. I was skeptical. I was used to our mission giving lip service to fundraising but not following through.*

"Nevertheless, I put in many hours doing the required homework and realized that this was the most work I'd ever done on fundraising. Then I developed a plan different from the halfhearted, hit-or-miss approach I had been using.

"With my wife's support and God's help, we diligently worked out our plan. I prayed a lot as well, and God came through in amazing ways.

"Remarkably, we raised $1,400 per month in just three weeks! We now had a strategy and biblical convic-

Becoming fully funded can be a long haul, but if you are called by God and if you do your part, you can be confident He will do His part as well.

tions, and I was actually doing fundraising instead of just worrying about it. My wife rejoiced. Next, we set our sights at 100 percent of budget, which we have achieved for the past few years. In fact, this year we finished at 102 percent, and I now spend part of my time helping other missionaries raise their finances. If I hadn't applied these guidelines, I'm not sure I would be in missions today. I now have hope, skills, and accountability that I didn't have before."

And from a Canadian missionary:

> *"The biblical study on how God funds His work has been the most important ingre-dient of my fundraising training. Through Bible study, reflection, and wrestling in dialogue with other missionaries, my convictions began to form. I believe it is crucial for missionaries to have their convictions grounded in the Scriptures if they are to raise personal support for the long haul.*
>
> *"One of the astonishing things I discovered is that the Bible has few examples of the 'tell-nobody-but-God' method of funding. I respect those who hold to this method, but I don't see this as the norm in Scripture.*
>
> *"I've come to realize that it is a tremendous privilege to be fully supported by friends, family, and churches for the work God has called my wife and me to.*
>
> *"The results speak for themselves. We have been fully funded for five years. We have savings, we have no debt, and we know that the key to fundraising for us is face-to-face appointments. We also know our fears and how to trust God with them. And we don't ques-tion our calling as we used to when we were below budget. The past five years have been some of the fullest and richest times in ministry. Also, since we know we can be fully funded, we can believe God for fellow missionaries to be fully funded as well. I feel like I've gotten to know God better, and I truly feel like I have been caring better for my wife and children."*

God has wonderfully worked in the lives of those who have used these materials. My prayer is that you, too, will experience a deeper walk with God as you do your part in raising support and that He will bless you with His faithfulness beyond all you could ask or think.

And now a final word—persistence:

- After Fred Astaire's first screen test, a 1933 memo from the MGM testing director said: "Can't act. Slightly bald. Can dance a little." Astaire kept that memo over the fireplace in his Beverly Hills home.
- An expert said of famous football coach Vince Lombardi: "He possesses minimal football knowledge. Lacks motivation."
- Louisa May Alcott, the author of *Little Women,* was advised by her family to find work as a servant or seamstress.
- Beethoven handled the violin awkwardly and preferred playing his own compositions instead of improving his technique. His teacher called him hopeless as a composer.
- Walt Disney was fired by a newspaper for lacking ideas. He also went bankrupt several times before he built Disneyland.
- Eighteen publishers turned down Richard Bach's 10,000-word story about a soaring seagull before Macmillan finally published it in 1970. By 1975, *Jonathan Livingston Seagull* had sold more than seven million copies in the United States alone.[1]

---

1 Jack Canfield and Mark V. Hansen, *Chicken Soup for the Soul: 101 Stories to Open the Heart and Rekindle the Spirit* (Deerfield Beach, FL: Health Communications, 1992).

If Fred Astaire, Vince Lombardi, Louisa May Alcott, and Walt Disney didn't give up, neither should you. Talk this over with the One who has called you to mission service. At His throne, you'll find "grace to help in time of need." God bless you!

INTRODUCTION TO APPENDIX

In addition to the Bible study I've mentioned at least 283 times, included in this Appendix are worksheets, study tools, and report forms to assist you in your funding strategy. Some of these resources are briefly mentioned in the text; others are explained thoroughly. Some I didn't discuss at all because you will grasp them without explanation.

This book is copyrighted, but feel free to photocopy Appendix pages for your personal use as you need to.

Funding the Work of God

One of the major obstacles new missionaries face is funding. Accusations have been made that churches, preachers, missionaries, and Christian ministries are, at best, inept in money matters and, at worst, downright scoundrels. On the other hand, missionaries have an extraordinary opportunity to model biblical finances to a watching world.

The Scriptures listed with each question are not meant to give a final answer but simply to get you started in your search.

If you are uncomfortable with this fill-in-the-blanks format, use the "List of Scriptures" page at the back of this section, then come back to answer the questions.

Before you begin, jot down any fears or concerns you have about raising financial support:

_____

_____

_____

_____

_____

Funding Examples

1. Funding examples in Scripture: Fill in the funding examples chart on the following pages. In light of these scriptural examples, what is your opinion of the George Mueller practice of "telling no one but God"?

_____

_____

_____

_____

_____

Note: George Mueller was a 19th-century pastor who ran an orphanage. He had been financially irresponsible before coming to Christ. After his conversion, he vowed not to make public appeals for needs and "to tell no one but God."

> *"Blessed are the money raisers, for in heaven they shall stand at the right hand of the martyrs."*
>
> —J. R. Mott

How God Funded Ministry in the Bible

Example	References	Provider/Receiver	Relationship of Provider/Receiver	Need Made Known?	Appeal? Suggested Amount?
Levitical	2 Chron. 31:4				
	Num. 18:21–24				
	Deut. 14:22–29				
Self-Support	Acts 18:1–5				
	1 Thess. 2:9				
	Neh. 13:10				
	2 Thess. 3:8–9				
Hospitality	Matt. 10:5–15				
Ministry Group	Luke 8:1–3				
	Gal. 6:6				
Quail-Manna	Exod. 16:13–17				
	Josh. 5:12				

How God Funded Ministry in the Bible

Example	References	Provider/Receiver	Relationship of Provider/Receiver	Need Made Known?	Appeal? Suggested Amount?
Personal Appeal	Rom. 15:20–24				
	2 Cor. 1:16				
	1 Cor. 16:6				
Third Party	Philemon				
	Titus 3:14				
	2 Cor. 8–9				
	1 Cor. 16:1–5				
	3 John 5–8				
	Rom. 15:25–29				
	Neh. 13:10–13				
	Acts 11:27–30				
Church Sponsor	Phil. 4:10–20				
Raven	1 Kings 17:1–7				

How God Funded Ministry in the Bible

Example	References	Provider/Receiver	Relationship of Provider/Receiver	Need Made Known?	Appeal? Suggested Amount?
Widow	1 Kings 17:8–16				
Angel	1 Kings 19:1–8				
Tabernacle	Exod. 25–31				
	Exod. 35–40				
Temple	1 Chron. 29				
	2 Chron. 2				
Community	Acts 4:32–5:11				
	Acts 2:44–45				
Joash Temple	2 Chron. 4:4–14				
Cyrus Temple	Ezra 1				
Nehemiah	Neh. 2:1–8				
Samuel	1 Sam. 9:7–8				
Synagogue	Luke 21:1–4				

Questions of Conscience

2. Missionaries sometimes feel guilty or like they're on "welfare." Is it biblical to be supported by others to do the work of God? Would it be better if missionaries were self-supporting "tentmakers"?

Numbers 18:21–24 _____

Numbers 8:14 _____

Luke 8:1–3 _____

1 Corinthians 9:1–18 _____

Philippians 4:10–20 _____

Acts 18:1–5 _____

1 Thessalonians 2:9 _____

Acts 20:33–35 _____

2 Thessalonians 3:6–12 _____

Other _____

Other _____

3. "I enjoy raising support for others but not for myself." Is it biblical for missionaries to make financial appeals for their own ministry?

Romans 15:20–24 _____

2 Corinthians 1:16 _____

1 Corinthians 16:5–6 _____

1 Kings 17:1–16 _____

Other _____

Other _____

4. Is it biblical to raise financial support from strangers—or from people you do not know well? Should support come primarily from those to whom you've ministered?

Galatians 6:6 _____

Romans 15:20–24 _____

3 John 5–8 _____

2 Corinthians 12:13 _____

Matthew 10:5–15 _____

Romans 15:27 _____

Other _____

Other _____

5. What about making financial appeals to nonbelievers? How about to family members?

Acts 10:2–4 _____

3 John 5–7 _____

Nehemiah 2:1–8 _____

Other _____

Other _____

6. What about financial appeals to those who are not as well off as you? Or who are already giving heavily?

2 Corinthians 9:7 _____

Philippians 4:17 _____

Deuteronomy 16:17 _____

2 Corinthians 8:2–3 _____

Luke 21:1–4 _____

Other _____

Other _____

Accountability

7. Should missionaries be required to raise their full support before starting an assignment?

_____

_____

_____

8. Do you agree with the statement, "God's will done in God's way never lacks God's supply"?

_____

_____

_____

Tentmaking

9. Under what circumstances (if any) should a missionary develop funding through "tentmaking"? How does "calling" relate to this issue?

Acts 18:1–5 _____

Nehemiah 13:10 _____

2 Thessalonians 3:6–12 _____

Other _____

Other _____

10. How does a missionary's outside job or business affect his or her donors?

_____

_____

_____

11. Should ministry friends be developed as customers for a missionary's personal business venture? What are the pros and cons? Are there any types of businesses a missionary ought to avoid?

_____

_____

_____

Personal Financial Management

12. According to Proverbs, list the guidelines for:

Becoming Wealthy:

3:16 _____

10:4 _____

11:24–26 _____

12:11 _____

14:23 _____

28:19 _____

28:27 _____

_____

Becoming Poor:

10:4 _____

13:18 _____

14:23 _____

20:4 _____

21:5 _____

21:17 _____

22:16 _____

23:21 _____

_____	28:19 _____
_____	28:22 _____
_____	28:27 _____

Observations/Comments on guidelines from Proverbs:

_____

_____

13. Do you agree with the statement, "Fundraising is just as valid as evangelism"? How about this one: "People are more important than money"?

Luke 16:10–12 _____

1 Timothy 5:8 _____

Other _____

Other _____

14. Better to have _____ than wealth.

Proverbs 10:22 _____

Proverbs 22:1 _____

Proverbs 16:16 _____

Proverbs 28:6 _____

Proverbs 17:1 _____

Proverbs 31:10 _____

Proverbs 20:15 _____

15. If a missionary's income is low, credit cards are often used to make up the difference. What do you consider to be the proper versus improper use of credit cards?

Proverbs 22:7 _____

Psalm 37:21 _____

Romans 13:8 _____

Proverbs 3:27–28 _____

Other _____

Other _____

16. Should missionaries dip into personal savings or personal investments to fund themselves—especially to get started?

_____

_____

_____

17. Should personal loans from friends or family be accepted for major purchases such as a home? What are the pros and cons?

Proverbs 11:15 _____

Proverbs 24:27 _____

Other _____

Other _____

18. At what standard should missionaries set their lifestyles?

Matthew 11:18–19 _____

Proverbs 30:9 _____

1 Corinthians 8:7–13 _____

1 Timothy 5:17–18 _____

Other _____

Other _____

19. If a missionary can get by in life and ministry at 80 percent of budget, should he or she try to reach 100 percent?

Proverbs 6:6–11 _____

Proverbs 13:22 _____

Proverbs 21:20 _____

Proverbs 30:24–25 _____

Other _____

Other _____

Summary

List five conclusions/observations as a result of your study:

1. _____

_____

2. _____

_____

3. _____

_____

4. _____

_____

5. _____

_____

Your "best verses" on financial matters:

1. _____

2. _____

Memory verse:

_____

_____

_____

Applications:

_____

_____

_____

Further Study Suggestions: Read through Proverbs, noting every verse that deals with finances. Meditate on them and catalog them topically.

List any unanswered questions or continuing concerns as a result of your study:

1. _____

_____

2. _____

_____

3. _____

_____

4. _____

_____

5. _____

_____

6. _____

_____

7. _____

_____

8. _____

_____

9. _____

_____

10. _____

_____

List of Scriptures

Selected Giving and Receiving Passages:

Exodus 16:13–17	Matthew 11:18–19	Romans 15:20–24
Exodus 25–31, 35–40	Luke 8:1–3	1 Corinthians 16:1–6, 11
Numbers 8:14	Luke 10:1–7	2 Corinthians 1:16
Numbers 18:21–24	Luke 16:10–12	2 Corinthians 8–9
Deuteronomy 14:27	Luke 21:1–4	2 Corinthians 12:13–18
Deuteronomy 16:17	Luke 22:35–38	Galatians 6:6
1 Samuel 9:7–8	John 12:3–8	Philippians 4:10–20
1 Kings 17:1–16	Acts 4:32–5:11	Colossians 4:10
2 Chronicles 31:3–19	Acts 10:1–4	1 Thessalonians 2:9
Nehemiah 2:1–8	Acts 11:27–30	2 Thessalonians 3:7–9
Nehemiah 13:10–14	Acts 18:1–5	1 Timothy 5:17–18
Proverbs 3:9–10	Acts 20:33–35	Titus 3:13
Matthew 10:5–15	Romans 15:25–28	3 John 5–8

Selected Financial Management Passages:

Deuteronomy 8:17–18	Proverbs 15:6	Proverbs 30:24–25
1 Chronicles 29:12–17	Proverbs 15:16–17	Ecclesiastes 5:10–11
Psalm 24:1	Proverbs 16:16	Jeremiah 8:10
Psalm 37:21	Proverbs 19:6	Haggai 2:8
Proverbs 1:13–15	Proverbs 19:17	Matthew 22:17–21
Proverbs 3:27–28	Proverbs 19:22	Matthew 25:14–30
Proverbs 6:1–5	Proverbs 21:5	Luke 12:15
Proverbs 6:6–11	Proverbs 21:17	Luke 16:1–13
Proverbs 10:2, 4	Proverbs 21:20	Luke 16:14
Proverbs 11:4	Proverbs 22:7	Romans 13:8
Proverbs 11:15	Proverbs 23:4–5	1 Thessalonians 4:11–12
Proverbs 11:24–25	Proverbs 23:10	1 Timothy 5:8
Proverbs 11:28	Proverbs 23:20–21	1 Timothy 6:6–19
Proverbs 12:11–12	Proverbs 24:27	2 Timothy 4:10
Proverbs 13:4, 7	Proverbs 27:23–27	Hebrews 13:5
Proverbs 13:11, 18	Proverbs 28:19–20, 22	James 5:1–6
Proverbs 13:22	Proverbs 28:27	
Proverbs 14:23	Proverbs 30:8–9	

Bibliography

Master Your Money, Ron Blue, Nelson Publishing

Debt-Free Living, Larry Burkett, Christian Financial Concepts

Friend Raising, Betty Barnett, YWAM Publishing

Getting Sent, Pete Sommer, InterVarsity Press

The Support-Raising Handbook, Brian Rust and Barry McLeish, InterVarsity Press

Mega Gifts: 2nd Edition, Revised and Updated, Jerold Panas, Emerson & Church, Publishers

Writing Exceptional Missionary Newsletters, Sandy Weyeneth, William Carey Library (WCLBooks.com)

Financial Stress Test for Missionaries

Answer the following questions honestly. If married, compare your answers with your spouse.*

		Yes, or Frequently				No, or Never	
A.	Mind occupied with finances: "Where's the money coming from?"	5	4	3	2	1	0
B.	Skip giving commitments or give less than pledged	5	4	3	2	1	0
C.	Difficulty paying credit card balances in full each month	5	4	3	2	1	0
D.	Receive past-due notices on bills several times a year	5	4	3	2	1	0
E.	Forego saving most months	5	4	3	2	1	0
F.	Charge items because "I'm short" in cash or checking account	5	4	3	2	1	0
G.	Net worth decreasing annually	5	4	3	2	1	0
H.	Housing payment exceeds 35% of gross monthly income	5	4	3	2	1	0
I.	Invade savings to meet current expenses	5	4	3	2	1	0
J.	Feel resentment toward creditors, government, headquarters	5	4	3	2	1	0
K.	Compare yourself materially with other missionaries, donors, siblings	5	4	3	2	1	0
L.	Use spending as emotional therapy (self-esteem)	5	4	3	2	1	0
M.	Ignore or exceed budget limits on clothing	5	4	3	2	1	0
N.	Wonder when you'll start saving for kids' college or for retirement	5	4	3	2	1	0
O.	"Emergency Only" savings less than two months' living expenses	5	4	3	2	1	0
P.	Less than 200 on mailing list	5	4	3	2	1	0
Q.	Current credit card balance is greater than $500	5	4	3	2	1	0
R.	Borrowed to buy current car	5	4	3	2	1	0

0-18	Excellent	
19-36	Good	Total for each column
37-54	Danger	
55-90	Financial Bondage	Total

What are your top two frustrations regarding your personal finances?

1. _____

2. _____

If you could do one thing to improve your financial situation, what would it be?

_____

_____

_____

* (If married) My spouse has filled out this page, and we have discussed our answers.

Spouse's initials: _____

Monthly Personal and Ministry Budgets

Note: Do not include ministry expenses such as ministry phone, ministry travel, entertainment on personal side.

Monthly Personal Budget

	What I'm Doing Currently	When I'm at Full Budget
Giving	$_____	$_____
Debt Repayment	$_____	$_____
Savings _____ purpose	$_____	$_____
Savings _____ purpose	$_____	$_____
Housing		
Mortgage (or rent), tax, ins.	$_____	$_____
Repair and Maintenance	$_____	$_____
Utilities	$_____	$_____
Personal Phone	$_____	$_____
Groceries/Paper Goods	$_____	$_____
Children		
Allowances	$_____	$_____
Private School	$_____	$_____
Lessons/Supplies	$_____	$_____
Clothes	$_____	$_____
Entertainment/Recreation	$_____	$_____
Babysitters	$_____	$_____
Subscriptions	$_____	$_____
Clubs/Memberships	$_____	$_____
Hobbies	$_____	$_____
Personal Health Insurance (your share)	$_____	$_____
Doctor (not covered by insurance)	$_____	$_____
Dentist (not covered by insurance)	$_____	$_____
Medicine (not covered by insurance)	$_____	$_____
Personal Life Insurance	$_____	$_____
Automobile (Personal)		
Insurance	$_____	$_____
Fuel/Oil	$_____	$_____
Repairs/Registration	$_____	$_____
Pet Care	$_____	$_____
Beauty/Barber	$_____	$_____
Household Furnishings	$_____	$_____
Lawn/Garden	$_____	$_____
Gifts (birthday, Christmas)	$_____	$_____
Miscellaneous	$_____	$_____
Other:_____	$_____	$_____
Other:_____	$_____	$_____
Total Personal Expenses	**$_____**	**$_____**
Add Fed. Inc. Tax (15–25%)	$_____	$_____
Add State/Local Tax (2–4%)	$_____	$_____
Add FICA (7.65%)	$_____	$_____
Total Salary Needed	**$_____**	**$_____**

Monthly Ministry Budget

	What I'm Doing Currently	When I'm at Full Budget
Mission		
Agency Fees	$_____	$_____
Service Charge	$_____	$_____
Health Insurance	$_____	$_____
Other	$_____	$_____
Tolls/Parking	$_____	$_____
Ministry Mileage Reimb. (personal car only)	$_____	$_____
Local Entertainment (restaurant and home)	$_____	$_____
Ministry Conferences	$_____	$_____
Overnight Ministry Travel (food, lodging, airfare)	$_____	$_____
Professional Development		
Conferences	$_____	$_____
Books/Tapes	$_____	$_____
Courses	$_____	$_____
Materials	$_____	$_____
Printing/Copying	$_____	$_____
Postage	$_____	$_____
Office Supplies	$_____	$_____
Phone (ministry)	$_____	$_____
Computer/Printer		
Internet Fees		
Miscellaneous	$_____	$_____
Other: _____	$_____	$_____
Other: _____	$_____	$_____
Total Ministry Expenses	**$_____**	**$_____**

(If married) Discussed in detail with spouse:
____ Yes ____ No

Discover Potential Donors
(for Veteran Missionaries Only)

1. Mailing List:

    How many are on your total general mailing list?
        Subtract current regular donors   _____
        Subtract other missionaries   _____
        Subtract unbelievers   _____
        Subtract family members   _____
        Remaining Total   _____
                         (This is your number of prospective donors.)

2. Which lapsed donors could you ask to rejoin your team?

_____   _____

_____   _____

_____   _____

3. Identify donors who have not increased support for three years. Which ones will you ask to increase now?

_____   _____

_____   _____

_____   _____

4. What churches can you approach for support?

_____   _____

_____   _____

_____   _____

5. List the names of donors who gave occasionally last year who could be approached to become regular donors.

_____   _____

_____   _____

_____   _____

6. List the names of annual donors from last year you can approach for a renewed commitment.

_____   _____

_____   _____

_____   _____

7. Who are "By Prayer Alone"?

_____   _____

_____   _____

_____   _____

8. Do you need to increase your mailing list? How will you do it? _____

_____

_____

Financial Appeal Worksheet (5 Ws)
(Photocopy extra sheets for personal use as needed.)

List below the names of people who you think would be willing to hear about your ministry and vision. You don't know if they will give or not—that is between them and the Lord—but you would like to give them an opportunity. Thinking in sets of 10 makes it a little more "bite-sized." Under "Appeal," limit your answer to the five possibilities listed.

	Preparation					Appeal		Results		
	Whom Shall I Invite?	Where Do They Live?	What Is Their Phone Number?	When Will I Appeal?	What Will I Ask?	Type of Appeal*/Date Made	Results (Monthly, Annual, Cash Gift, Undecided, No)	Sent Thank You	Money Received	Comment
	Jim Shoe	Los Angeles	210/520-0000	5/1–7/07	$50/month	F/May 5	$50/month	5/22	6/8	Moving to WA
1										
2										
3										
4										
5										
6										
7										
8										
9										
10										
11										
12										
13										
14										
15										

*F=Face-to-Face, L=Personal Letter, T=Telephone, G=Group Appeal, O=Other

Brainstorming for Partners

Don't ask, "Who will support me?" Only God knows that. Ask instead, "Who ought to hear about my ministry?"

If you have difficulty coming up with 200 to 400 names for your mailing list, use these brainstorming pages to help. Categories of friends and acquaintances are listed on the following pages to stimulate your thinking and to help you organize your names. Many of your acquaintances might fall under several categories. However, list each one only once. Don't feel that you need to fill every line in every category. Remember, it is easier to remove names from your list than to add names.

Note: Even if you don't have the address, put the name down anyway. You can get others to help track down an address. That person you can't get ahold of may be one whom God has appointed to support your ministry.

Acquaintances from church

1. _____
2. _____
3. _____
4. _____
5. _____
6. _____
7. _____
8. _____
9. _____
10. _____
11. _____
12. _____
13. _____
14. _____
15. _____
16. _____
17. _____
18. _____
19. _____
20. _____
21. _____

Acquaintances from your Sunday school class

1. _____
2. _____
3. _____
4. _____
5. _____
6. _____
7. _____
8. _____
9. _____
10. _____
11. _____
12. _____
13. _____
14. _____
15. _____

Acquaintances from other churches in your area and beyond

1. _____
2. _____
3. _____
4. _____
5. _____
6. _____
7. _____
8. _____
9. _____
10. _____
11. _____
12. _____
13. _____
14. _____
15. _____

Coworkers/Business associates

1. _____ 7. _____ 13. _____
2. _____ 8. _____ 14. _____
3. _____ 9. _____ 15. _____
4. _____ 10. _____ 16. _____
5. _____ 11. _____ 17. _____
6. _____ 12. _____ 18. _____

Neighbors

1. _____ 7. _____ 13. _____
2. _____ 8. _____ 14. _____
3. _____ 9. _____ 15. _____
4. _____ 10. _____ 16. _____
5. _____ 11. _____ 17. _____
6. _____ 12. _____ 18. _____

Friends from former residences, churches, or jobs

1. _____ 8. _____ 15. _____
2. _____ 9. _____ 16. _____
3. _____ 10. _____ 17. _____
4. _____ 11. _____ 18. _____
5. _____ 12. _____ 19. _____
6. _____ 13. _____ 20. _____
7. _____ 14. _____ 21. _____

Friends from college or military days

1. _____ 7. _____ 13. _____
2. _____ 8. _____ 14. _____
3. _____ 9. _____ 15. _____
4. _____ 10. _____ 16. _____
5. _____ 11. _____ 17. _____
6. _____ 12. _____ 18. _____

Friends from other cities

1. _____
2. _____
3. _____
4. _____
5. _____
6. _____
7. _____
8. _____
9. _____
10. _____
11. _____
12. _____
13. _____
14. _____
15. _____
16. _____
17. _____
18. _____

Relatives and family friends

1. _____
2. _____
3. _____
4. _____
5. _____
6. _____
7. _____
8. _____
9. _____
10. _____
11. _____
12. _____
13. _____
14. _____
15. _____

Friends from "back home" (where you grew up)

1. _____
2. _____
3. _____
4. _____
5. _____
6. _____
7. _____
8. _____
9. _____

Friends from athletic/social/service organizations

1. _____
2. _____
3. _____
4. _____
5. _____
6. _____
7. _____
8. _____
9. _____
10. _____
11. _____
12. _____
13. _____
14. _____
15. _____

People you've ministered to (Bible studies, etc.)

1. _____
2. _____
3. _____
4. _____
5. _____
6. _____
7. _____
8. _____
9. _____
10. _____
11. _____
12. _____
13. _____
14. _____
15. _____

You may also want to think of friends you have in the following career fields:

Accountants

Athletes

Auto industry

Bankers

Chiropractors

Contractors

Dentists

Doctors

Electricians

Engineers

Entrepreneurs

Executives

Farmers

Government

High Tech

Insurance

Landscaping

Large Companies

Lawyers

Nurses

Optometrists

Pastors

Pharmacists

Pilots

Printers

Real Estate

Retailers

Service Industries

Small Businesses

Teachers

Others

Donor Base Analysis (Veteran missionaries only)

Previous 12 Months

Month	Total Donor Income*	Number of Donors	Average Gift Size	Church/ Amount	Average Gift Without Church	$100 or More	$50–$99	$25–$49	$25 or Less
	$		$	$	$				
	$		$	$	$				
	$		$	$	$				
	$		$	$	$				
	$		$	$	$				
	$		$	$	$				
	$		$	$	$				
	$		$	$	$				
	$		$	$	$				
	$		$	$	$				
	$		$	$	$				
	$		$	$	$				
Total	$		$	$	$				
Averages									

Donor Base

* Do not include income from other sources such as boarder's rent or material sales. List donor income only.

Donor Base Analysis

A. What is the size of your total general (all included) mailing list? _____

B. In the past 12 months, how many regular monthly donors have skipped three or more months

without resuming? _____ (Check month-by-month donor summary.)

What will you do to restart them? _____

_____

C. How many financial appeals did you make during this time period? _____

Face-to-face _____ Telephone _____ Letter _____ Group _____

D. How many newsletters did you send during this time period? _____

E. Cash-project income/special income

Amount received $_____

Total number of donors _____

Number of first-time donors _____

Which of these first-time donors could be approached for regular monthly support?

_____

F. Other observations/comments _____

_____

_____

Financial Appeal Action Plan
(Be specific!)

Amount Needed to Raise $ _____ Monthly Due By: _____

Phase 1: To Raise $ _____ Monthly by _____ (date)

Phase 2: To Raise $ _____ Monthly by _____ (date)

Phase 3: To Raise $ _____ Monthly by _____ (date)

1. **Number on Mailing List:** _____ **Increase by** _____ **by** _____ **(date)**

   I will increase my mailing list through these actions:

   _____

   _____

2. **I will appeal to the following for major gifts (at least $200–$1,000 monthly or $2,500–$15,000 annually):**

Name	Amount	By (Date)	Name	Amount	By (Date)
_____	_____	_____	_____	_____	_____
_____	_____	_____	_____	_____	_____
_____	_____	_____	_____	_____	_____
_____	_____	_____	_____	_____	_____
_____	_____	_____	_____	_____	_____

3. **I will make _____ face-to-face appeals (names listed on attached 5 Ws).**

4. **I will make _____ letter/phone appeals (impossible to visit in person—names listed on attached 5 Ws).**

5. **I will invite _____ current donors to increase support (listed on attached 5 Ws).**

6. **I will network with _____, _____, _____, to appeal by referrals (if needed).**

7. **Other** _____

   _____

8. **I will trust the following to start giving through "prayer alone."**

   _____ _____ _____ _____

   I will e-mail a weekly report to my fundraising sponsor, who is

   _____ , e-mail address _____

Signed _____ **Today's Date** _____

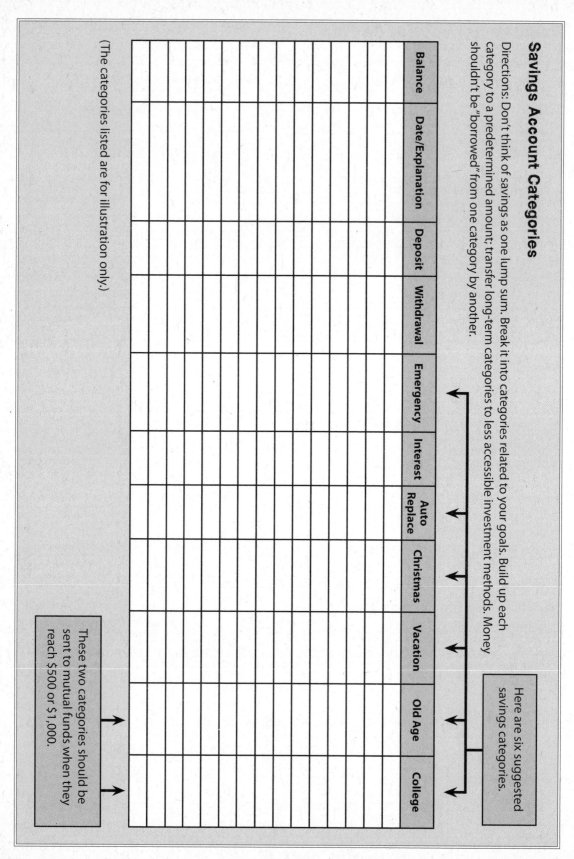

Savings Account Categories

Directions: Don't think of savings as one lump sum. Break it into categories related to your goals. Build up each category to a predetermined amount; transfer long-term categories to less accessible investment methods. Money shouldn't be "borrowed" from one category by another.

Here are six suggested savings categories.

Balance	Date/Explanation	Deposit	Withdrawal	Emergency	Interest	Auto Replace	Christmas	Vacation	Old Age	College

These two categories should be sent to mutual funds when they reach $500 or $1,000.

(The categories listed are for illustration only.)

The Mystery of "Calling"

What the Bible Says About Your Calling to Service

One of the glass ceilings missionaries face in reaching full funding is "calling." During times of disappointment, we especially question our calling. We struggle to explain it to ourselves, let alone to our potential giving partners. We sometimes communicate tentatively, timidly, or unclearly.

To help you explain your ministry . . . vision . . . calling . . . dreams . . . strategy (don't get hung up on semantics!), please prayerfully complete these questions and worksheet.

This worksheet is not designed to give you prefab answers for a church missions committee, but rather to help you answer these issues deeply *for yourself first.* Then you'll be better able to stimulate others to become passionate about your ministry.

And it all starts with the heart! Have fun!

Personal Motivation for Your Ministry

1. At times, we experience disappointment and heartache in ministry. What keeps you going day after day in your ministry?

2. What wears you down or dampens your enthusiasm for your mission?

> *"I long to accomplish a great and noble task, but it is my chief duty to accomplish small tasks as if they were great and noble."*
>
> —Helen Keller, to a five-year-old

3. Have you ever considered leaving missions? What was attractive about leaving? What kept you from leaving? Be specific.

4. What Scriptures do you find yourself going back to over and over that give you a reason or motivation for your ministry? They might be promises, motivating verses, or guiding verses. (Have you thoroughly studied them?)

Passage   Direction or guidance for me

5. How has God "called" His servants? (study guide)

Now it's time to spend 60 to 90 minutes enjoying meditating on 14 calling examples in the Scriptures. Perhaps as you review how others have been specially called by God, you'll receive new insight and confidence in your own calling. Compare the 14 with your own calling.

Fill out the **Calling Worksheet,** which begins on page 235, and record your observations and conclusions.

Do this study before going on to Question 6.

6. Describe your personal call to the ministry. How did it happen? When did you first sense a "call"?

7. Suppose one of your giving partners were to ask, *"Why are you in missions? Couldn't you serve equally well as a layperson? Or on a church staff? Or with another mission agency?"* What would you say?

8. You're with a friend discussing your local ministry. Finally she turns to you and asks, *"So tell me in two sentences what you're really trying to do in your ministry."* What would you say? Write your two sentences here.

9. Then your friend asks, *"And how are you doing that? What's your ministry strategy?"* Write your response.

> *"Nothing happens unless first a dream."*
> —Carl Sandburg

How Has God Called His Servants?

Note: This study does not deal with general or "salvation calling" (1 Thess. 2:12), but rather with 14 examples of how God "called" individuals for specific ministry (plus you!). What can you learn from these examples?

"Callee"	Called to Do What?	Was Call Temporary or Lifelong?	Expected to Change Career or Location?	Response of Callee/ Comments
Mary Luke 1:26–35				
Peter John 21:15–23				
Seven Servers Acts 6:1–6				
Barnabas and Saul Acts 13:1–5				
Timothy Acts 16:1–5				
Paul's Team Acts 16:6–10				
Paul Acts 26:12–18 (Also 22:12–21)				

"Callee"	Called to Do What?	Was Call Temporary or Lifelong?	Expected to Change Career or Location?	Response of Callee/ Comments
Moses Exodus 3:1–15 Exodus 4:1–18				
Bezalel and Oholiab Exodus 31:1–11				
Levites Numbers 3:5–9				
Elijah 1 Kings 19:9–18				
Isaiah Isaiah 6:1–10				
Jeremiah Jeremiah 1:4–10				
Jonah Jonah 1:1–3; 3:1–5				
Me!				

Observations:

_____

_____

_____

_____

Conclusions:

_____

_____

_____

_____

Courage

Missionaries frequently struggle with courage, especially as it relates to raising support. Let's face it, we've all "chickened out" on a finance call or on the telephone. Sometimes we don't even make it to the phone!

But courage is also needed in evangelism, launching a ministry to a street gang, offering to lead a Bible study in the marketplace, and just plain speaking out in the name of Christ.

Take 60 to 90 minutes to meditate on these 27 classic passages on courage, fear, and faith. Then honestly answer the questions. Enjoy!

> *"He does not fear bad news, nor live in dread of what may happen. For he is settled in his mind that Jehovah will take care of him."*
>
> —Psalm 112:7, *The Living Bible*

Developing Courage

Passage	Observations
Joshua 1:5–9	
1 Chronicles 28:10	
2 Chronicles 15:7	
2 Chronicles 32:7–8	
Ezra 10:4	
Psalm 27:14	
Haggai 2:4–5	
Matthew 14:22–27	

Overcoming Fear

Passage	Observations
Deuteronomy 20:8	
Psalm 23:4	
Psalm 34:4	
Psalm 46:1–3	
Psalm 55:4–8	

Psalm 56:3–4 _____

Psalm 94:19 _____

Proverbs 10:24_____

Proverbs 28:1_____

Proverbs 29:25 _____

Isaiah 41:10, 13–14 _____

Matthew 8:26* _____

Matthew 10:29–33 _____

Matthew 25:25–26 _____

John 14:27* _____

1 Corinthians 2:3_____

2 Corinthians 7:5_____

2 Timothy 1:7*_____

Hebrews 13:6_____

* The word for afraid is *deilia*. "The word denotes cowardice and is never used in a good sense." (Vine)

Issues and Conclusions

Based on your study . . .

1. A believer walking with Christ has no fears. Agree? Disagree?

2. A friend asks you how she can develop more courage. What suggestions would you give?

3. How does faith relate to fear?

4. What is the relationship between courage and calling?

5. What kinds of things do missionaries tend to fear?

Application and Lessons

6. What are typical (but ineffective) ways missionaries cope with fear?

7. Have you identified your fears? Be specific.

At times I am fearful of . . .

8. Name individuals of whom you are sometimes fearful (initials only).

9. What are your normal ways of coping with your fears?

10. Is raising support fearful for you? What aspects?

11. What specific steps can you take to handle fear more biblically?

12. I would be more courageous if I . . .

13. My personal application to this study is to . . .

14. My best verse on courage, fear, or faith is . . .

Lessons from Ancient Fundraising History

You may question the relevance of fundraising history to your personal funding strategy. But especially for experienced fundraisers, these history lessons give us unique perspective, warnings, and encouragement. The old maxim about history is true in fundraising also: Those who don't study it are doomed to repeat it.

We should also study funding history because money is where the church is most vulnerable. Money grabbing in religion is nothing new!

Finally, funding history gives us greater perspective and makes us wiser counselors. For example, passing the offering plate on Sunday morning has only been used in the West for the past 100 years. Curiously, just realizing that is helpful.

Most of the information in this section comes from the late Luther Powell, a Presbyterian minister, who wrote *Money and the Church*. I stumbled across it in the Denver Seminary library in 1989. Finding it was out of print, I finally tracked down Powell's widow who graciously sent me a few of "Luther's old books in the basement." Though Powell only scratches the surface, his is the only book I've found summarizing this topic in both Catholic and Protestant traditions.

Don't worry, what follows is not an exhaustive chronological history, but rather six observations followed by four suggested applications for today. But first a warning: Some of what you're about to read may contradict your stewardship convictions. You may not like it! But thanks for telling us the truth, Luther Powell!

Observation 1. Tithing was not emphasized in the early church.

I was surprised to see that the early church did not emphasize tithing. Why not? Let's start at the beginning.

The apostle Paul taught giving and generosity, but the word "tithing" never made it into his letters. Look at Paul's exhortations in 2 Corinthians 8 and 9, the classic chapters on Christian giving. He commends:

- generous and sacrificial giving
- finishing a giving commitment from a year prior
- sowing bountifully and reaping bountifully
- giving hilariously (cheerfully)
- deciding in your heart what to give

This would have been the ideal place to teach tithing to untutored new believers, but Paul doesn't do it. Couldn't this good Jewish rabbi have said *something* about tithing?

No. To be consistent with his teaching on grace, Paul could not transport an Old Testament law onto the backs of New Testament believers. At the Jerusalem Council, Paul opposed the teaching that said, "Unless you are circumcised according to the custom of Moses, you cannot be saved" (Acts 15:1). And the Council agreed that the new way of Jesus was not to be encumbered with Jewish laws and traditions. That includes tithing!

For 300 years after Jesus, the church fathers did not advocate tithing. Listen to Irenaeus (A.D. 120–202):

> "... and instead of the law enjoining the giving of tithes, [He told us] to share all our possessions with the poor; and not to love our neighbors only, but even our enemies" (page 21).

This lack of teaching about the tithe in the first 300 years after Christ is important because it sharply contrasts with many who strongly emphasize tithing today, 2,000 years later. Hmmm.

Observation 2. Tithing migrated into religious and civil law.

As the growing church became more popular, more money was needed. Powell summarizes, "As we proceed beyond the 4th century we find a growing emphasis on tithing until it becomes, first, a law of the church, and, finally, a law of the civil courts" (page 26). Ambrose of Milan (A.D. 340–397) starts down this slippery slope:

> "God has reserved the tenth part to Himself, and therefore it is not lawful for a man to retain what God has reserved for Himself. To Thee He has given nine parts, for Himself He has reserved the tenth part, and if thou shalt not give to God the tenth part, God will take from thee the nine parts" (page 27).

Do you see the subtle movement from a Jewish cultural law to a law for the church? And do you notice the implied threat for not giving the tithe? Even the beloved Augustine (A.D. 354–430) said the tithes "are due as a debt" (page 28).

In A.D. 585, the second Council of Mascon went still further:

> "Wherefore we do appoint and decree, that the ancient custom be revived among the faithful, and that all the people bring in their Tithes to those who attend the Divine offices of the Church. If any one shall be contumacious [rebellious] to these our most wholesome orders, let him be forever separated from the communion of the Church" (page 30, italics added).

In just 585 years after Christ, believers now must tithe or face excommunication!

Fast-forward 1,100 years to England. The Protestants did no better. Tithing laws became exceedingly complicated. For example, a farmer was not required to tithe on food he or his family consumed, but if it was used to feed livestock, a tithe must be paid.

> "If a Man gather green pease to spend in his house ... no Tithes shall be paid for the same; but if he gather them to sell or to feed Hogs, there Tithes shall be paid for them" (page 69).

Parishioners were annoyed, then angered by these petty rules. A farmer who caught fish from a lake in a different parish from his home had to pay tithes to both parishes. Frustrated dairymaids brought their pail of tithe-milk to the church. Not finding the parson, they poured it on the floor in front of the altar. Farmers purposely bound their sheaves of grain so badly that they fell apart when the parsons came to collect. Church servants sent to collect the tithe were assaulted or their horses stolen so they could not take the produce to the church.

Many believers were fined or imprisoned due to their insufficient tithing. William Francis Luton of Bedfordshire was imprisoned 19 months for failing to tithe a four-pence silver piece. Some were even martyred for suggesting compulsory tithing was contrary to God's will. The Anabaptists and the Mennonites were among those who claimed tithing was against New Testament teaching.

So exasperated were the parishioners that they made up new lyrics to the tune of the beloved hymn, "Old Hundred" ("Praise God from Whom All Blessings Flow"):

> "God save us from these raiding priests,
> Who seize our crops and steal our beasts,
> Who pray, 'Give us our daily bread,'
> And take it for themselves instead."

Ahhh-men! Powell writes that many clergymen quit the church rather than collect the tithes.

And what about America? My grade-school history books said many colonists came "for religious reasons." But they didn't mention that many of the religious reasons were because they couldn't stomach the invasive tithing laws in Europe.

Did the American colonists make a fresh start making tithing voluntary? No, because the perplexing issue of how to support the churches still had to be decided. The colonists thought "church rates" (tithing laws) were OK but that it had been abused in Europe. Though the "voluntary principle" was affirmed, the colonists soon reverted to taxation similar to what they had left. As early as August 23, 1630, the state of Massachusetts decreed that ministers should be maintained "at the public charge." And ". . . if a man did not pay his assessment 'voluntarily,' he would be compelled to pay it" (page 105).

Sadly, compulsory tithing had merely moved across the Atlantic. Even patriot Patrick Henry proposed in the Virginia House of Burgesses in 1784 that a law be passed "for the support of the Christian religion." James Madison led the charge against it (page 118).

Observation 3. Under pressure to fund a growing movement, Christian leaders violated their integrity.

Today it's easy to identify errors of 1,000 years ago, but we must understand the tremendous financial pressure these leaders were under. And many were sincerely dedicated believers seeking to do the right thing. Here are a few examples of integrity lapses:

- Visitation expenses but no visitation. Church leaders in the Middle Ages traveled with great entourages to visit parishes in faraway lands. Local bishops were glad for such visits and showed lavish hospitality. But sometimes the visiting leader canceled his travel plans saying, "Since I didn't come to visit you, please send an amount equal to whatever you would have spent on me and my entourage."

- The pallium. Originally a robe of honor, the pallium was purchased at high prices by newly appointed priests. As years went by, the robes became smaller, but the purchase price stayed high. It finally became a patch of cloth with an insignia.

- Appealing to fear. Instead of emphasizing voluntary freewill giving, fear of losing salvation and guilt over others suffering in hell became the motivation. Listen to successful fund-raiser John Tetzel raising money in Germany:

  "Indulgences are the most precious and the most noble of God's gifts. Come and I will give you letters, all properly sealed, by which even the sins that you intend to commit may be pardoned. I would not change my privileges for those of St. Peter in Heaven; for I have saved more souls by my indulgences than the Apostle by his sermons" (page 59).

- Appealing to guilt. Tetzel knew the importance of emotion in fundraising:

  "Priest! Noble! Merchant! Wife! Youth! Maiden! Do you not hear your parents and your other friends who are dead, and who cry from the bottom of the abyss: We are suffering horrible torments! A trifling alms would deliver us; you can give it, and you will not!" (page 59).

Tetzel's manipulative fundraising drove Martin Luther to post his 95 theses on the door of the Wittenberg Church October 31, 1517. But in later years, even Martin Luther succumbed to railing against his own parishioners. Listen to this guilt-inducing diatribe:

  "I understand that this is the week for the church collection, and many of you do not want to give a thing. You ungrateful people should be ashamed of yourselves. You Wittenbergers have been relieved of schools and hospitals, which have been taken over by the common chest, and now you want to know why you are asked to give four pennies."[1]

- Subscription lists. These lists showed the amounts parishioners had pledged to give, but they were not kept secret. Pastors circulated the lists, provoking guilt and a "keep-up-with-the-Joneses" mentality.

Observation 4. Pew rent replaced tithing laws.

From the days of George Washington until the early 1900s, renting or selling pews funded Protestant churches. Church committees agonized over setting pew prices; the more expensive ones

---

1 Bainton, Roland, *Here I Stand: A Life of Martin Luther* (Nashville, TN: Abingdon Press, 1950), 351–352.

were near the front, with a freebie or two in the back for walk-ins or the poor. Families sat in "their pew" for years, sometimes with a plaque announcing the owner.

The February 8, 1919, edition of *The Literary Digest* magazine headlined a story that "free pews" had been adopted by Trinity Church in New York as an expression to Almighty God for the victory [World War 1]. The "sittings" would be free to all, first come, first served.

The article told the story of naval war hero Bob Evans, who went to a prominent New York church and sat in a pew at random.

> *"The rich pew owner arrived not long after with his numerous family and cast disapproving looks on the intruder. Evans however, was serene even after he had received a slip of paper on which the indignant church member had scribbled: 'I pay $4000 for this pew.' Quick with his pencil, Evans scrawled, 'You pay too d--- much!' "*[2]

Pew rent died slowly!

Observation 5: Poor pay for preachers proved counter productive.

We can learn much from the Methodists. Francis Asbury, the leader of Methodism on the American frontier, was heard to pray, "Lord, keep our preachers poor." One of Asbury's cohorts commented humorously, "Such a prayer was quite unnecessary!" (page 101).

Asbury thought low pay produced more dedicated preachers. He didn't want them to "locate"—settle in one town—but to continue itinerant preaching across the frontier. Asbury opined, "Lovers of earthly riches will not long remain traveling preachers" (page 102).

Asbury's preachers provide us today with a wonderful example of enduring hardship (and low pay) for the sake of the Gospel. But many of his preachers did "locate," especially after a few years on the frontier.

Did they quit because of low pay? There may have been several reasons, but we would be naïve to think funding wasn't one of them.

Observation 6. Focusing on small givers is not enough.

Again, Francis Asbury. Asbury loved "mite-giving," in memory of the generous woman in Luke 21:1–4 who gave her two "mites" (King James Version) to the temple. Asbury's great heart for the poor made him appreciate those who sacrificially gave small amounts to the Methodist cause. He himself was a tireless fundraiser, going door-to-door begging for widow's-mite gifts (valued at about one dollar) for his poor preachers. One of his last requests "was for Mr. Bond to read the 'mite subscription' list as he lay dying" (page 102).

Despite his success in procuring mite-gifts, his traveling preachers received less than the minimum salaries recommended by the Methodist boards. Small gifts weren't enough.

---

2 *The Literary Digest*, February 8, 1919, Vol. LX, No. 6 (New York, NY: Funk and Wagnalls Company), 354–360.

Applications for Today

OK, there you have it—six observations from fundraising history. Now, what can we learn?

First of all, tithing. Today many Christian leaders aggressively teach tithing as the standard for giving. But the church fathers had it right—the tithe is *not* the New Testament standard.

Challenging people to give 10 percent is justified by many pastors because most believers don't give nearly that amount. But should we burden New Testament people with a standard intended for Israel?

Some say that giving 10 percent is symbolic of our 100 percent commitment to the Lord. Something about the "one out of ten" idea is special. Maybe, but it's a stretch.

What about Malachi 3:10? "Bring the whole tithe into the storehouse, so that there may be food in My house, and test Me now in this," says the Lord of hosts, "if I will not open for you the windows of heaven, and pour out for you a blessing until there is no more need."

From Malachi chapter one, we see that the Jews were taking shortcuts. They brought lame lambs to the altar rather than their best as the law commanded. "Give them to your civil governor," Malachi chided, "see if he accepts them!" The point of the book of Malachi is not: "Tithe!" He is warning the Israelites, "Don't try to get by with giving as little as you can to the Lord." That is an important message for today too. Giving should be a joy, not a religious obligation in which you hold back the best for yourself.

Though the storehouse in Malachi's day was literally a "storage building," some Christian leaders think that today's "storehouse" is the "church-house." Your 10 percent should go to your local church. If you want to give to other ministries, you'll have to give above and beyond the tithe. Your gift to the American Bible Society to distribute Bibles in India must not come out of the local church's 10 percent.

Don't these applications stretch hermeneutical boundaries? Do we really want to equate the church with the nation of Israel? Malachi has a wonderful message for today, but his intent was not to mandate a certain percentage that must be given or dictate to whom it must be given.

Should tithing be a goal to shoot for? Possibly, but don't leave it there. Shouldn't a believer with a $300,000 annual income give more than 10 percent? Being forced to eke out a living on $270,000 is not in the spirit of New Testament teaching.

What is the standard for Christian giving if it is not 10 percent? To discover Jesus' view on "how much is enough," check out Luke 21:1–4.

Ask yourself: Why is tithing emphasized so much today if it was not emphasized by Paul or Jesus or by the patriarchs for 300 years? Did they understand something we don't?

Here is a second lesson: Fundraising history teaches us that for 2,000 years, clergy have been suspicious that laypeople will not give enough. Out of a genuine desire (most of the time) to see the Kingdom expanded, we have "coaxed" God's people to be generous by enacting tithing laws, threatening the faithful with hell, imposing guilt on them, renting them pews for the privilege of attending services, and "leaning" on them to keep up with the Christian Joneses.

For 2,000 years, Christian leaders thought that if the parishioners were left to their own devices with grace alone as their guide, they would not give nearly enough to support the work of God. So they came up with schemes and "doctrine" to help the faithful decide how much is enough. Are we also guilty?

Consider some of these questionable but well-used appeals:

- If you really want to be blessed, tithe!
- Give a seed gift so God can bless you.
- Don't let these children die from an unnecessary disease. You can help them for the cost of what you feed your dog each week.

Third, the early Methodists: We can learn much from Francis Asbury. Certainly he was right that "lovers of earthly riches" are in danger. First Timothy 6:10 warns us that "the love of money is a root of all sorts of evil." But does being up to budget imply we love riches? It could. Some Christian workers are undoubtedly lovers of riches and their aggressive fundraising efforts disguise their materialistic heart. To a lover of riches, even a book like this will be construed as license to go after money.

But leaving motives aside, let's ask: Are we ministers and missionaries more effective when we are poor?

In my first assignment, Alma and I saw many conversions and changed lives—and we were severely underfunded! Did staying poor keep us productive? I don't think so. How long could we have held out with low funding? Not as long as Asbury's preachers!

Interestingly, during those "poverty years," I also started taking steps of faith to invite others to join our financial team. The exercise of fundraising faith was just as heartfelt and stretching as my evangelism and discipling faith.

Though I commend Asbury for his tireless work both at preaching and fundraising, wouldn't he have been more effective if he had gone after larger gifts for his "poor preachers"? Was he working hard? Yes. Was he working smart? You decide. With the size of today's missionary budgets, you will not reach full funding with only "mite" gifts. Add to them some major-donor gifts or you will not make your goal.

Furthermore, missionaries who scrape by on low funding year after year also experience pressure that erodes their confidence—and sometimes their marriages. Never having enough is emotionally and physically draining!

In my experience, many poor people are consumed mentally and emotionally with where the next meal is coming from. And so are underfunded missionaries. Oh, it's exciting for a few weeks, but soon they are worn out.

Here's the fourth application: As money becomes more necessary, spiritual leaders justify goofy tactics for the sake of ministry progress. Remember the prayer sock I mentioned in Chapter 3? Here are a few other examples:

- One evangelist sent a letter containing two vials filled with dirt taken from the very ground upon which the evangelist knelt when he prayed for you last weekend. Send one back with your gift.

- What about the common "please-pray-for-our-finances" note on the bottom of missionary newsletters? I read one just a few hours ago. Usually it is a disguised appeal for funds.

As ministries grow, financial demands grow. And with these demands, jaded men and women who have devotions every day do goofy or unethical things in the name of ministry.

Are we guilty of suggesting that if our constituents do not give generously the Lord will be unhappy with them? A poem appeared in England years ago that warns us today against the danger of coercion: "For lambe, pig and calf, and other the like, Tithe so as thy cattle the Lord do not strike."[3]

Is it possible that since A.D. 300 we have been fearful of giving people total freedom to decide how much to give?

The lesson is to avoid demandingness. OK, that's not a word, but you get the idea. And also, we must avoid judging someone because they are not giving as generously as we think they could. As fundraisers, we must not make the mistake of putting rules on our giving partners. Biblical giving is voluntary; coercing believers toward generosity demeans them.

I encourage you to be careful of falling into the traps that have plagued full-time workers and ministers for the past 2,000 years. What will a 21st-century Luther Powell write about us?

---

3 George-Pitt Rivers, *The Revolt Against Tithes, The Nineteenth Century* (1934).